DATE DUE

100M—3-65—58395—Ark.P.&L.Co.

FIRST PERSON SINGULAR

Books by Herbert Gold

NOVELS

THE BIRTH OF A HERO

THE PROSPECT BEFORE US

THE MAN WHO WAS NOT WITH IT

THE OPTIMIST

THEREFORE BE BOLD

SALT

SHORT STORIES

LOVE AND LIKE

FICTION OF THE FIFTIES *(Editor)*

ESSAYS

THE AGE OF HAPPY PROBLEMS

FIRST PERSON SINGULAR:
Essays for the Sixties (Editor)

FIRST PERSON SINGULAR

ESSAYS FOR THE SIXTIES

EDITED AND
WITH AN INTRODUCTION BY
HERBERT GOLD

THE DIAL PRESS, NEW YORK, 1963

Library of Congress Catalog Card Number: 63-10557

DESIGNED BY ALAN M. HEICKLEN
MANUFACTURED IN THE UNITED STATES OF AMERICA
BY THE HADDON CRAFTSMEN, SCRANTON, PA.

Acknowledgments

Algren, Nelson: "Down With All Hands" copyright © 1961 by Nelson Algren. Reprinted from the *Atlantic Monthly*, November 1961.

Baldwin, James: "Fifth Avenue Uptown: A Letter from Harlem" and "East River Downtown: Postscript to A Letter from Harlem" reprinted from NOBODY KNOWS MY NAME copyright © 1961, 1960 by James Balwin and used with the permission of the publishers, The Dial Press.

Bellow, Saul: "Literary Notes on Khrushchev" copyright © 1961 by Esquire Inc. First published in *Esquire*. Used by permission of the author.

Blau, Herbert: "The Public Art of Crisis in the Suburbs of Hell" first appeared in THE NOBLE SAVAGE 5, a Meridian Periodical, published by The World Publishing Company. Copyright © 1962 by The World Publishing Company. By permission of the author and The World Publishing Company.

Elliott, George P.: "Why Are They Driving Me Crazy?" used with the permission of the author.

Gold, Herbert: "Death in Miami Beach" reprinted from THE AGE OF HAPPY PROBLEMS copyright © 1962, 1961 by Herbert Gold and used with the permission of the publishers, The Dial Press.

Goodman, Paul: "The Devolution of Democracy" from DRAWING THE LINE by Paul Goodman. Copyright © 1962 by Paul Goodman. Reprinted by permission of Random House, Inc.

Hardwick, Elizabeth: "The Life and Death of Caryl Chessman" reprinted from A VIEW OF MY OWN by Elizabeth Hardwick by permission of Farrar, Straus & Cudahy, Inc. Copyright © 1960, 1962 by Elizabeth Hardwick.

Krim, Seymour: "The Insanity Bit" reprinted from VIEWS OF A NEARSIGHTED CANNONEER copyright © 1961 by Seymour Krim. By permission of the author.

McCarthy, Mary: "America the Beautiful: The Humanist in the Bathtub" reprinted from ON THE CONTRARY by permission of the author. Copyright © 1961 by Mary McCarthy.

Miller, Arthur: "The Bored and the Violent" reprinted from *Harper's Magazine,* November 1962. Copyright © 1962 by Arthur Miller.

Miller, Warren: "Poor Columbus" copyright © 1961 by Warren Miller. Reprinted from THE NOBLE SAVAGE 3.

Saroyan, William: "The Debt" and "The Time" reprinted from HERE COMES THERE GOES YOU KNOW WHO by William Saroyan. Copyright © 1961 by William Saroyan and used with the permission of Trident Press.

Styron, William: "Mrs. Aadland's Little Girl, Beverly" reprinted by permission of the author. The essay first appeared in *Esquire.*

Swados, Harvey: "The Pilot as Precursor" reprinted from A RADICAL'S AMERICA. Copyright © 1961 by Harvey Swados. Used with the permission of Little, Brown and Co.—Atlantic Monthly Press.

Vidal, Gore: "Barry Goldwater: A Chat" reprinted from ROCKING THE BOAT by Gore Vidal. Copyright © 1961 by Gore Vidal. Used with the permission of Little, Brown and Co.

Table of Contents

INTRODUCTION

How Else Can a Novelist Say It?

It is not quite a revolutionary turn in behavior for the novelist to take pen in hand and heart in mouth in order to issue a direct communiqué from the battlefield of his life, without the intermediaries of invented character and story. The novelist, in the grand and nonspecialized tradition, has often been as much *writer* as novelist. Dostoevsky filled a newspaper column with his tics, fulminations, speculations, passions; Balzac, Stendhal, and Dickens sometimes preached their sermons directly to audiences; Tolstoy, who is a better model of the literary saint than Flaubert, consecrated a large part of his life to analysis and comment, the point of which might be summarized with the title of one of his books, *What Can a Man Do?* In fact, the limiting of the novelist's attack to the cautious secreting of masterpieces—like the silkworm in its cocoon—is a phenomenon of special times and schools. There were specific causes for this rule. There are compelling reasons for breaking it now.

In recent times there has been a revival of the direct and personal essay, attempting to name a truth about the world, by writers whose "normal" mask is that of story-teller. An audience willing to listen to them, wanting to find some truths, has also appeared out of the somewhere of America. James Baldwin on middle-class housing in Harlem, Saul Bellow on Khrushchev, Truman Capote on an American traveling theater, George P. Elliott on the isolation of California from the rest of the world, Norman Mailer on himself as a hipster, Warren Miller on Cuba, Mary McCarthy on Venice, on painting, Harvey Swados on the airline pilot as a sporty organization man, and many others have rediscovered something which a short recent tradition of novelists since Flaubert seemed to have given up. This is the joy of speaking out straight the work of a mind.

There had been a pious renunciation for reasons other than purity and piety, I believe. There was a high motivation in passivity and self-denigration. The novelist took on the philistine view of his role—he was a minor, albeit a romantic figure; he could attain to "fame, riches, and the love of beautiful women," but not give evidence like the scientist toward a vision of reality. In a period of increasing specialization, and impressed by the corroborating prevalence of the notion of the artist as a man apart, addicted to his holy madness and irresponsibility, writers of fiction had seemed willing to leave philosophy to the philosophers, preaching to the preachers, and commentary to the commentators, many of whom express the act of thinking by looking thoughtful. This division of labor was not always the rule. It seemed to be for a long time. Specialization was accepted at a high penalty to both writers and audiences.

Why a change now?

A shift away from the art-for-art's-sake aesthetic has certainly been encouraged by some sharp commercial reasons, but also, I believe, it reflects an important shift in our states of mind in this time of special urgency and perpetual emergency. Let us dispose of the commercial encouragements at once: Magazines will print "articles."

Quick money there. A thirst for vivid and accurate writing has paralleled, let us say, the American middle-aged spread of junior colleges and adult education. Editors encourage novelists not to waste their talent in doing the major labor of their lives; they are asked to have their say, please, for immediate returns. Also, in some cases, there is a haste to bring mere face and opinion to the view of the public. The novelist is a fretful man who responds to seduction—like other men. A novel is a complex, artful way to say "Look at me!" while saying many more important things. The commitment involved in a noisy polemic is much narrower, the investment of character much less, and the reward in brief applause sometimes dizzying. Writers have no immunity against the temptation to display themselves like movie stars in a society which is avid to find new celebrities to devour. Many dangers here.

But the best of these novelists' essays—let us now frankly use that fine old word, which means roughly "a try" —is not merely a disguised fan interview in which the writer tells an as-told-to story to himself. This self-display is a symptom of hysteria, with the writer flying about in diminishing circles, divebombing the public with raw chunks of heart, until he disappears up his own soul. Something is expressed, but little is communicated.

The novelist-essayist, as I conceive him at his best, responds to a combative assertion that life is both terrible and full of delights, that the truth is both a joy and essential to the limited survival which we are allowed, that every man has an obligation to meet the facts of his time as directly as his powers permit. Having no power corrupts; a rational argument in the daylight is one way of asserting powers and possibilities.

It might be argued that the concentration camps and the atomic bomb are the cause of the revival of the serious essay by novelists. Of course, that would be simplistic; catastrophe is not a recent invention. Before these most total events, there was the War of 1914-1918, the convulsions to the East, the disasters in Spain and elsewhere. No one can record the specific date on which writers as a class suddenly cried out in chorus, "Enough of this timid abstention!" and began scribbling their moral and political views. But there has been a change from the time when novelists wrote their novels and an occasional review or a bit of fretful literary criticism, accepting politely the division of labor. The primitive need of the writer—to know, to master, to tell—has recaptured his intentions about himself. Along with speaking his mind by writing stories and novels, he has begun to speak his mind by speaking his mind. Some, like D. H. Lawrence, go on riding their obsessions and stomp over their audiences with a clatter of opinions about sex and politics. Some, like the contemporary writers already mentioned—and others come to mind at once—take the world curiously for what it is and make their passionate, delighted, or reforming projections of it. George Orwell has certainly been the most recent master in this vocation.

The long fantasy of permanent social security in an ivory tower has ended for most writers. For the best of them, of course, like James Joyce, this nonexistent dwelling was always firmly rooted on solid soil, with a winding stairway leading out into the city. Even dream towers cannot float in mere air.

As soon as the artificial isolation of the artist is broken down, the natural need to speak out in the man of ideas asserts itself again. The writer considers the world as the worm wriggles—with his entire body. Why stop this productive convulsion? No individual can escape the troubles of the world by armoring himself with silence and exile unless he is cunning enough to return to speech and fruitful connection with others.

The times are difficult, true. It is also true that the times have always been difficult. Even blind Homer would not have been Homer without the itch of unresolved doubt about the sense of our lives together on earth. (The hero, De Gaulle wrote in his memoirs, is always a natural melancholic. The writer, he might have added, is a man looking for ways to frustrate his natural melancholia.) But perhaps the times now are more than difficult, they are desperate. The novelist who once, to take a parody example, wrote from a comfortable weekend house near London, within earshot of the friendly crack of croquet balls on a lawn outside, now writes from within a buzz of implication: How long are we here? What about our children? Why do marriage and diplomacy and alcohol and money not perform their traditional soothing labor? Where is the work we like, the challenge we seek, the satisfying fulfillment in actions which can use us fully without destroying civilization?

Some of these questions have always played a part in the urge to invent stories. The lessons have been present and, if not solved, at least dramatized. The intelligent reader has always been purged of his congested desires by the experience contained within a work of art, however bemused he was by form and style. But now, in immediate need, many novelists no longer want to leave to others the formal judging and measuring of experience. The others just don't think well enough. Perhaps the novelists don't either. Nevertheless they travel the world, they read and study; most important, they are bitten by moral and metaphysical yearning. They have the vocation to pursue reality. They are not satisfied (few Americans are) by the answers washing over our heads in a flood of print. Therefore they are learning to speak out. In the United States they usually do this without official affiliation to party, doctrine, or church, although some of them occasionally take their supper at the White House of their choice.

What effect does this revived activity have on the reader? Well, at the very least, he is likely to find in the novelist's essay a superior variety of journalism, performed by a writer with a sense of pace and rhythm in prose and a vivid mission in his sense of life. Even when the novelist chops out a silly and self-important slice of punditry, he is likely to season it pungently. At his best, the novelist more than most people treasures his experience and husbands his memories; he keeps the doors and windows to feeling open late into his age; he keeps the fireplace burning.

Reader and writer together may rediscover in the essay the grand truths customarily drowned in a ruck of informational, speed-reading and speed-writing prose. The form of the personal essay demands risks and commitments never possible in its surrogates, the "fact piece" on one side and the inside-dope novel on the other.

What is the effect on the writer's art as novelist? This, when all is said, is still his primary concern. The chances are that he has always hectored the world in his notebooks and kept journals of travels, reading, conversation, and ideas. But the responsibility for these notes is very different when they feed explicit conclusions in argumentative prose. The dialogue is actual, not imaginary. The writer is committed to reasoning out his questions and answers. Certainly no pat argument can ever be made to the questions, What should a man do? Why are we here? How do we meet love and reconcile with death? But each man must, in one way or another, reconcile with these general questions which are implicit in every day's portion of experience. The writer, emerging from the privacy of his philosophical journal and the disguises of his fiction, commits himself to both rigor and risks in facing the world directly. Intelligence does not have to be contraband goods in the offshore islands of fiction.

The result, going full circle, might finally be to bring back into fiction the full weight and suppleness of the writer's original motivation. At his origins, the story-teller stood before the fire as singer, historian, philosopher, priest, mourner. Civilization gave him a peculiar sense of his limits, and lately held him in thrall with the notion of "objectivity" or of being an "entertainer." This is not the same thing as disciplining a gift. Now some writers, the best of them, are once again using both the story and the essay to tell the most that they can tell about all that they know. Artificial barriers of form have gone down. An article is really an essay, just as a story, too, is really a try at mastery of the sense of human life on earth.——HERBERT GOLD

NELSON ALGREN

Down with All Hands

At Pier 86 a blue-uniformed baggage hustler took both my bags and the electric typer off my hands, and I asked the elevator guy, on the way up, how much does a baggage hustler get per bag?

"He gets what you want to give in your heart," the guy instructed me.

"I don't want the man to starve," I explained. "How much does he get per bag?"

"Let me tell you something?" the guy asked, just as if I could stop him. "The intelligence you breathe, that you were born with, let *that* be your guide."

If I were going to keep a count of people I met who were in their right minds on this trip and those who were out of them, I decided, the kooks would already be out in front by one. I gave the baggage hustler a dollar and he looked unworried, so I knew I'd overpaid him. Well, easy come, easy go.

This was the first time I was crossing the Atlantic first class. My ticket assigned me to stateroom S-1, meaning sun deck and first to chow, but a man in a seafaring cap told me my home was now in U-68. I looked around to see if U.S. Lines had put me on a submarine by mistake, but the only raft in sight had three decks above water level, so I realized that what traveling first class means is that even if they put you down in the galleys you still don't have to row.

I kept going down stairs until I hit the engine room, and, as long as I was there, I felt I might as well inspect the turbines and the rest of that crazy stuff. The stuff looked to be in better shape for a crossing than I was, for I was a mite self-conscious about the pin that kept my topcoat from flapping against my knees. The bottom button had been missing for some time, so I went upstairs again to see if anyone would sew it on. In U-68 I found my bags, but nobody else was home. I went to sleep until I heard someone hollering, All ashore that's going ashore. Then I looked out of the porthole and saw the whole New York literary scene moving past.

I had seen it closer up than I'd ever see it again, and having come to know two crowds there, one around Broadway that takes a cut off the commerce in fighters and horses, the other that takes its cut off the commerce in books, I had found the track crowd a more trustworthy bunch than the "Have you read Norman Marathon lately?" crowd. Not only because they drank less and knew more, but because, by and large, they were more true to themselves than the bookmen. The sporting people seldom pretended to be something they were not, whereas I had never known a junior editor who knew who he was, and becoming a senior editor only seemed to compound the corruption. I mention this only to explain why the bottom button of my topcoat was missing.

As the sun sank slowly over Manhattan and I watched vigilantly for the Statue of Liberty out of the wrong side of the ship, a deck steward entered. I told him the object in the brown metal box was an electric typewriter so he wouldn't try to feed it, and he suggested I go up on the sports' deck.

"I didn't even know you had one," I told him, for the news came as a pleasant surprise. How the man could tell I'd played poker the night before I still don't know. I went up to look around.

Sure enough, there was a young couple leaning on the rail waiting for a game, so I just leaned on the rail beside them and didn't say anything. If they wanted a game, they'd have to make the first move. Neither one said anything, so I thought, You both look like poor losers to me anyhow, and went to a part of the rail I could call my own. There I looked down at the water and let memories flood in.

Like the time the MPs pinched the chaplain for auctioning off the ambulance, or the time in Marseilles, just before embarking, when I got the letter saying, Honey, don't come back. Well, absence makes the heart grow fonder for somebody else, is what I always say. But after a while I got tired of saying it, so I went back down to U-68 to see how much the steward had gotten for my clothes.

Apparently he hadn't even had a decent bid, because all he'd done was hang up my topcoat, a new experience for us both. If I had a needle and thread I'd sew you up myself, you sonofabitch, I told it, so at least you'd hang straight; you're trying to make people think I'm a bum. I went to the mirror and, sure enough, I'd made it.

It wasn't because I needed a shave so much that I made my next move, but out of curiosity about whether the electric razor would work on the bathroom current. It worked fine, so I cleared the dresser, took the typer out of its kennel, and plugged in. At the first jump of smoke I thought, Women and children first, but after I got the plug loose it kept jumping smoke at me, and if that wasn't lead I smelled burning I can whip Chico Vejar. A lucky thing I didn't bring a dish dryer, I thought, half the crew would have been washed overboard.

"Your dirty current blew up my nice typewriter," I accused the steward, but he looked as if he'd anticipated that event. "Lots of people do that lately," he assured me contentedly.

It just goes to show you, you can't plug a typewriter into the S.S. "Meyer Davis" and expect good results. It just wasn't a friendly ship, that was all there was to it.

Should evening ever bring you the need of an apple at sea, either go to bed or keep your fat mouth shut. All I did was to make some casual inquiry about where I might buy one and go for a short stroll, to find, on returning, a basket heaped with apples, three hues of grapes, pears, bananas, oranges, kumquats, and litchi nuts. My first thought was that I must have an admirer aboard, probably the captain.

Now, if I could smuggle this heap down to tourist class, I thought, I might make the price of my ticket back by the greatest seagoing financial coup on record. Finally, I felt I was being treated better than I, or anyone, deserved. A feeling from which I recovered swiftly by eating my way through the heap down to the wood. It didn't occur to me that this could happen twice in my life. Actually, it happened thereafter every time I left U-68. I couldn't take a ten-minute stroll without returning to find a basket of flora transported from the gardens of four continents to rot in my stateroom. Either I was being secretly watched or the stuff was growing out of the wall.

Once, however, I became accustomed to the admiration implicit in the presentation of these baskets, it was like a sudden backhand slap when one showed up definitely short one kumquat. Let the chef collar the clown who perpetrated this cruel mockery or come in and be flogged himself, was my thinking in the matter. Yes, and be damned to the cowardly rabble traveling second and third class over my strictly first-class sea.

Had I only been able to sustain this mood and had I only learned a few words of French, I might easily have qualified as a drama critic for *Partisan Review* or a mutuel clerk at a fifty-dollar window. I might even have been able to hold both jobs, because men are needed in both these lines. And not everyone is presentable enough to qualify. But the mood was melted by the strains, faint yet clear, of Meyer Davis' orchestra swinging *Drink, Drink, Drink to Old Heidelberg*—it was teatime in the cocktail bar and teatime in the lounge! Teatime in the powder room and in the hearts of men. For who can hold bitterness in his heart when music like *that* comes along?

"Oh, good for *you,* kindly Meyer Davis and your kindly orchestra," I thought and hurried to the lounge.

I loved that lounge because it was there that some of the most right-thinking people aboard were to be found, drinking tea just as that evening sun went down. I didn't even mind when the evening sun sank, because then the lights came up and I could see them all better. In fact, I was so moved by the consciousness of being among these great-souled men and women that, when the music stopped, I planted myself directly beneath the orchestra. "As for Meyer Davis' orchestra," I announced, "I say hurrah!"

The ladies joined me in three rousing cheers for Meyer Davis and I retired, assured that Mr. Davis was pleased to have found so frank an admirer aboard his ship.

Everyone wanted to know, in a sort of teatime huff, What is she so *quiet* about, Why don't she *say* something? Why they figured the poor broad should make more noise than anyone else because she was a duchess I couldn't quite catch.

But there she'd be, evening after evening, waiting for the duke to finish his creamed spinach so she could get started on her sirloin. The duke had had his quota of sirloins by the time she was born and must have been over the hill even then. Now only God and creamed spinach were keeping him pasted together. But, for some reason, he didn't want to fall apart till he was eighty-two. What his reasoning was, I don't know. But if he had more than three days to go, his reasoning was faulty.

Nobody held the duke's extreme age against him but myself. It was the little broad that had the nerve to sit there as if she wasn't yet thirty, when everyone knew she was every day of thirty-four, that made the ladies so salty. Myself, I didn't dare to say she hardly looked twenty-six.

In fact, I approved of the match from her standpoint, which seemed to be the only tenable one. What was the difference who spooned spinach to the duke the last week before he was buried? was how I felt. Either he had had it or he hadn't, and if he hadn't, not even Meyer Davis could help him. If I pulled a chair up beside hers to ask, "Baby, exactly what are your plans?", it would show her whose side I was on. But I never got around to it, being too diverted by the carryings-on of my own table.

At the head of it, in full command, was a seagoing Fatty Arbuckle, a ship's officer who looked like he'd lived on gold braid and some of the threads had caught on his sleeves. Since he was at the head and I was at the foot, there was no chance of pasting him one without knocking over the flowers. He took an immediate liking to me, too.

"Try the gin-ger, it's *tan*-gy." Fatty would recommend a dish of sweets to Mrs. Di Santos, and then leave his mouth hanging, tongue thrust into his cheek in a way that made me want to eat snake. The first time he pulled this on me I got a better grip on my fork in case he came closer. I thought he was after my salad. When you're a victim of overprivilege, you have to be ready for anything.

(The way you know you are traveling first class, *really* first class, is by the way the olive looks up at you, when the glass is gone dry, with a special appeal, saying, *"Please* eat me." Another way you know is by the way the waves back off, bowing, across a strictly first-class sea. It may look a bit rough and wild for the brutes two decks below, and if it isn't, the crew is entitled to knock them about a bit. Otherwise, what am I paying for?)

Mrs. Di Santos, a dazzling blonde from the headwaters of the Amazon, sat at the officer's right. She never showed up till evening, and by that hour was so zonked she had to be strapped into her chair. Everyone, for that matter, had to be strapped, with a view to prevention of personal-injury suits should the tub take a sudden dip, but Mrs. Di Santos would have had to be strapped even on a tennis court.

By the time she came to dinner she had just sense enough left to put stuff in her mouth—if it ran down the inside of her neck, she swallowed. If it didn't run, she chewed it. She was a healthy young sot who liked the stuff that ran down the inside of her neck better than the stuff she was forced to chew. I think she had real class when sober, but I never saw her asleep.

On Fatty's other side sat the Connecticut Child, a twenty-year-old of six foot one and a half, poor child, for I took her walking around the deck and she wasn't wearing high heels. My private guess was that someone had sent her in hope she might gain spirit and elegance. God knows she needed a touch of both. But I couldn't see how she was going to pick up either while she was sitting at our table. There was nobody there to pick up from. All she could learn was how to pass ginger.

Beside the Connecticut Child sat the Rear-echelon Radical, ever ready and always right, a real Fearless Philip, Boy Barrister, of a type usually associated as a junior member with a combination of barracudas called something like Greensponge, Perjuretz, Coldcalk, and O'Posse.

This was a judicial-type phenom, it became too plain, of the kind who sees nothing untenable in demanding that Fagin be presented on television as a Cockney because Cockneys have never suffered a pogrom like us, poor us, even though we were never there ourselves either. Yet we had relatives, we have heard, who were, thus entitling us to draw an exclusive immunity to practice cold-calking shysterism in a strictly legal tradition, poor us.

The Rear-echelon Radical was inevitably against any

form of censorship. He was for progress all down the line, of course. Yet you had to be careful about presenting Shylock, lest you give aid to the dark forces allied against Man. It made me wonder what made him think he was on the side of the forces of light. Particularly when he actually didn't give a hang, one way or another, about what happened to Man any more than he did what happened on the stage. But his operation, with a few loans made from banks at 4 per cent reloaned at 12, required a certain degree of protection, which he drew, as I've already said, in the tone of the most fair-minded of men, from the persecutions suffered by others. First class, I ought to have told you before, was purely loaded with liberals.

I like fair-minded people myself, so I felt right at home. In fact, I couldn't have picked a better table to study fair-mindedness in action. I had a ringside seat, as it were. Because nobody is more fair-minded than a fair-minded man deciding whether he wants Filet avec Champignons done medium rare or rare. And what I liked most about him was that he didn't mind keeping the rest of the table waiting at the chamber doors while he took the waiter into consultation. With one judicial finger on the menu designating the steak of his ultimate choice, the waiter leaning forward attentively, pencil in hand, the Rear-echelon Radical would frown in thought, while the tension around him mounted and spread, till even the duchess, at the next table, would feel it and crane her head about to see what was affecting her neck. When he had everyone's attention, he would hand his verdict down: "Meeeee-deeeee-yummm ray-err."

It was done. Tension relaxed, conversation picked up. He was the real thing in rear-echelon radicals all right. I wonder how he got his start.

Then it would be my turn, and since the Connecticut Child seemed to expect something from me, I put a bit of spit on the ball myself. I'd hold the menu close to my eyes, one eye nearly shut, and ask, "What is *poissonière*?" Immediately everyone would shout in chorus, "Fish!"—especially Mrs. Di Santos.

"Yeah," I'd answer shrewdly, "but which one?"

That menu was an honor roll of the Vasty Deep. Everything that disports itself in the trough of the waters or hangs upsy-downsy by eyeless suckers to the roof of the deepest sea-sunken cave, that scuttles sidewise across the sands, leaps in a spout of welcome and good cheer to swimmers off Cape Cod, or comes smiling down the Gulf Stream on its hunkers with no thought of tomorrow was on that card. Yet the best I could do, when I'd got through it at last, was to put it down and mutter, with a bored expression, "Nothing much in the way of sea food tonight, is there?" As if the one chance a person had for a decent meal aboard this tub was to harpoon something himself.

"Try the gin-ger," Gold-braid Fatty proposed, "it's *tan*-gy."

"What do we do now?" the Connecticut Child asked in a voice she had, for some reason, lowered.

"Jump ship and pan for gold," was the only solution I could think of at the moment.

Pale fruit, blue flowers, and spangled hats loaded the table where we sat, when the night of the gala Captain's Dinner came around at last. On the balcony just over our heads Meyer Davis and his aides stood ready. Gold-braid Fatty put on the most comical hat of all—and the fun even then had barely begun. I had never seen a table so loaded with favors since the last time I'd played pin the tail on the donkey.

This was it. We were traveling first class at last. We were almost too gay to bear.

Fatty himself, without removing his hat, began hacking at a swordfish as if it had tried to attack him. Mrs. Di Santos was dipping shark's fin with sherry down her neck in a way that made me glad they'd taken the trouble to pour it into a soup bowl instead of just handing her a fin and a bottle. Sharks wouldn't be in it with this one, I strongly suspected, if she ever got sober. While the Fair-minded Radical was inquiring about red snapper in a way that, had I been his waiter, would have caused me to inquire about *him* to a red snapper.

In an unprecedented action he had trapped himself between red snapper and lobster. Now he couldn't move either way because he was committed to lobster *if* the lobster were fresh and not frozen, and no one, simply no one, knew for an absolute certainty, beyond possibility of doubt, whether the brute was fresh or frozen. It seemed he would take it on contingency if it were, and that was contingent upon *how* fresh, and just as I figured to solve the whole matter with one straight shot to the jaw, Fatty dispatched the waiter to discover the hour at which the lobster's death had been registered.

The effect of this production on the Connecticut Child was disastrous, as it intimidated her to the point where she was afraid to order anything at all, lest she commit a misdemeanor. I told her everyone would be impressed if she ordered an eel, my private hope being that they might bring her a black snake by mistake. She liked the idea, but didn't know how to ask for one.

My own move would have been to go to the rail and holler—maybe one would come in and give himself up. Then the waiter returned with the good news for everyone: a dead lobster they had in there had been alive less than an hour before! In that case, the Rear-echelon Radical decided, he'd take it after all. Nobody stopped to ask the lobster how it felt about its choice of being scalded to death or frozen stiff. Well, that's how it goes when you're traveling first class.

Personally, I found myself wishing that the Rear-echelon Radical would make up his mind about his own life, which he seemed to be living out on contingency.

The remaining problem, it now seemed to me, was, Here it was only Tuesday, and with waiters clearing dishes covered with remains of haddock and whale, sole, clam, salmon, and eel, would there be enough left out there to go around by Friday? Well, no news is good news, and it takes two to tango.

Now, it turned out, Gold-braid Fatty had fixed things with the kitchen for the *surprise du chef*. I resolved quietly that as long as I remained able-bodied I wasn't going to be surprised by so much as a fry cook, not to mention a sea-going chef. But the big news was that the *surprise du chef* was actually Soufflé Grand Marnier, and upon that announcement Fatty took up a deflated balloon and began stretching it in a fashion that wouldn't have been so suggestive if he had kept his eyes open and his mouth shut, or the balloon had not been pink, as it was—the effect sustained was of a minor rapture. It really wasn't necessary, it seemed to me, to put all *that* into a simple thing like stretching a balloon. "You must have been at sea a long time, sir," I suggested, nodding toward the balloon to indicate that he couldn't have managed to stretch a balloon with such skill had he stayed on land.

For reply, Fatty blew the balloon up, tied it to keep it inflated, and then volleyed it toward me in a taunt as gentle as it was contemptuous. I had no choice but to volley it just as gently back.

"That was a good answer, Starbuck," I had to admit. "If I see white water, I'll let you know."

I fought down the temptation to push half a banana into his puss and say, "Call *this* tangy." The chief idea, I realized, was to get the hell out of there before the Soufflé Grand Marnier arrived, to be alone with the smoldering remains of my Smith-Corona, and I would have made it too, except for the straps of the chair. I was trying to get free without a waiter's help when Meyer Davis' orchestra swung into *Bluebird of Happiness,* the ship hit a long swell, the chair of our High Prince of Creamed Spinach went sliding backward from the duchess with the duke himself still in it. And bravely, proudly, he held his little dish firmly so as to spill none as he went, like a man who knows that no man ever knows how many dishes of spinach are left in his life, while two waiters rushed toward him—though it seemed to me they might just as well have walked. They had almost reached him when the ship rose in the swell and the duke promptly slid back toward the duchess, who hadn't yet missed him.

That was the moment, it seems to me now, though it is all made misty in memory for being so long ago, that Gold-braid Fatty rose in his seat with a fork gripped firmly in his hand and stabbed the pink balloon. It did not explode, though the faces of everyone at the table were fixed fast upon it. It gently deflated in mid-air, then turned itself into a tiny spill of green-gray dust, ceaselessly spilling over flowers long faded, fruit long decayed, and faces gone fleshless.

And lost and wandering through vast oceanic ages, the voice of the duchess came grieving to me forever:

"What are you plans *now,* Daddy-o?"

Then downward and down through deeps ever darker, dark-green to dark-blue to total black, I yet feel the impact as the S.S. "Meyer Davis" settled slowly upon the emerald sands.

The sea-sunken sea-drifted sands.

JAMES BALDWIN

Fifth Avenue Uptown: A Letter from Harlem

THERE IS a housing project standing now where the house in which we grew up once stood, and one of those stunted city trees is snarling where our doorway used to be. This is on the rehabilitated side of the avenue. The other side of the avenue—for progress takes time—has not been rehabilitated yet and it looks exactly as it looked in the days when we sat with our noses pressed against the windowpane, longing to be allowed to go "across the street." The grocery store which gave us credit is still there, and there can be no doubt that it is still giving credit. The people in the project certainly need it—far more, indeed, than they ever needed the project. The last time I passed by, the Jewish proprietor was still standing among his shelves, looking sadder and heavier but scarcely any older. Farther down the block stands the shoe-repair store in which our shoes were repaired until reparation became impossible and in which, then, we bought all our "new" ones. The Negro proprietor is still in the window, head down, working at the leather.

These two, I imagine, could tell a long tale if they would (perhaps they would be glad to if they could), having watched so many, for so long, struggling in the fishhooks, the barbed wire, of this avenue.

The avenue is elsewhere the renowned and elegant Fifth. The area I am describing, which, in today's gang parlance, would be called "the turf," is bounded by Lenox Avenue on the west, the Harlem River on the east, 135th Street on the north, and 130th Street on the south. We never lived beyond these boundaries; this is where we grew up. Walking along 145th Street—for example—familiar as it is, and similar, does not have the same impact because I do not know any of the people on the block. But when I turn east on 131st Street and Lenox Avenue, there is first a soda-pop joint, then a shoeshine "parlor," then a grocery store, then a dry cleaners', then the houses. All along the street there are people who watched me grow up, people who grew up with me, people I watched grow up along with my brothers and sisters; and, sometimes in my arms, sometimes underfoot, sometimes at my shoulder—or on it—their children, a riot, a forest of children, who include my nieces and nephews.

When we reach the end of this long block, we find ourselves on wide, filthy, hostile Fifth Avenue, facing that project which hangs over the avenue like a monument to the folly, and the cowardice, of good intentions. All along the block, for anyone who knows it, are immense human gaps, like craters. These gaps are not created merely by those who have moved away, inevitably into some other ghetto; or by those who have risen, almost always into a greater capacity for self-loathing and self-delusion; or yet by those who, by whatever means—World War II, the Korean war, a policeman's gun or billy, a gang war, a brawl, madness, an overdose of heroin, or, simply, unnatural exhaustion—are dead. I am talking about those who are left, and I am talking principally about the young. What are they doing? Well, some, a minority, are fanatical churchgoers, members of the more extreme of the Holy Roller sects. Many, many more are "muslims," by affiliation or sympathy, that is to say that they are united by nothing more—and nothing less—than a hatred of the white world and all its works. They are present, for example, at every Buy Black street-corner meeting—meetings in which the speaker urges his hearers to cease trading with white men and establish a separate economy. Neither the speaker nor his hearers can possibly do this, of course, since Negroes do not own General Motors or RCA or the A & P, nor, indeed, do they own more than a wholly insufficient fraction of anything else in Harlem (those who *do* own anything are more interested in their profits than in their fellows). But these meetings nevertheless keep alive in the participators a certain pride of bitterness without which, however futile this bitterness may be, they could scarcely remain alive at all. Many have given up. They stay home and watch the TV screen, living on the earnings of their parents, cousins, brothers, or uncles, and only leave the house to go to the movies or to the nearest bar. "How're you making it?" one may ask, running into them along the block, or in the bar. "Oh, I'm TV-ing it"; with the saddest, sweetest, most shamefaced of smiles, and from a great distance. This distance one is compelled to respect; anyone who has traveled so far will not easily be dragged again into the world. There are further retreats, of course, than the TV screen or the bar. There are those who are simply sitting on their stoops, "stoned," animated for a moment only, and hideously, by the approach of someone who may lend them the money for a "fix." Or by the approach of someone from whom they can purchase it, one of the shrewd ones, on the way to prison or just coming out.

And the others, who have avoided all of these deaths, get up in the morning and go downtown to meet "the man." They work in the white man's world all day and come home in the evening to this fetid block. They struggle to instill in their children some private sense of honor or dignity which will help the child to survive. This means, of course, that they must struggle, stolidly, incessantly, to keep this sense alive in themselves, in spite of the insults, the indifference, and the cruelty they are certain to encounter in their working day. They patiently browbeat the landlord into fixing the heat, the plaster, the plumbing; this demands prodigious patience; nor is patience usually enough. In trying to make their hovels habitable, they are perpetually throwing good money after bad. Such frustration, so long endured, is driving many strong, admirable men and women whose only crime is color to the very gates of paranoia.

One remembers them from another time—playing handball in the playground, going to church, wondering if they were going to be promoted at school. One remembers them going off to war—gladly, to escape this block. One remembers their return. Perhaps one remembers their wedding day. And one sees where the girl is now—vainly looking for salvation from some other embittered, trussed, and struggling boy—and sees the all-but-abandoned children in the streets.

Now I am perfectly aware that there are other slums in which white men are fighting for their lives, and mainly losing. I know that blood is also flowing through those streets and that the human damage there is incalculable. People are continually pointing out to me the wretchedness of white people in order to console me for the wretchedness of blacks. But an itemized account of the American failure does not console me and it should not console anyone else. That hundreds of thousands of white people are living, in effect, no better than the "niggers" is not a fact to be regarded with complacency. The social and moral bankruptcy suggested by this fact is of the bitterest, most terrifying kind.

The people, however, who believe that this democratic anguish has some consoling value are always pointing out that So-and-So, white, and So-and-So, black, rose from the slums into the big time. The existence—the public existence—of, say, Frank Sinatra and Sammy Davis, Jr. proves to them that America is still the land of opportunity and that inequalities vanish before the determined will. It proves nothing of the sort. The determined will is rare—at the moment, in this country, it is unspeakably rare—and the inequalities suffered by the many are in no way justified by the rise of a few. A few have always risen—in every country, every era, and in the teeth of regimes which can by no stretch of the imagination be thought of as free. Not all of these people, it is worth remembering, left the world better than they found it. The determined will is rare, but it is not invariably benevolent. Furthermore, the American equation of success with the big time reveals an awful disrespect for human life and human achievement. This equation has placed our cities among the most dangerous in the world and has placed our youth among the most empty and most bewildered. The situation of our youth is not mysterious. Children have never been very good at listening to their elders, but they have never failed to imitate them. They must, they have no other models. That is exactly what our children are doing. They are imitating our immorality, our disrespect for the pain of others.

All other slum dwellers, when the bank account permits it, can move out of the slum and vanish altogether from the eye of persecution. No Negro in this country has ever made that much money and it will be a long time before any Negro does. The Negroes in Harlem, who have no money, spend what they have on such gimcracks as they are sold. These include "wider" TV screens, more "faithful" hi-fi sets, more "powerful" cars, all of which, of course, are obsolete long before they are paid for. Anyone who has ever struggled with poverty knows how extremely expensive it is to be poor; and if one is a member of a captive population, economically speaking, one's feet have simply been placed on the treadmill forever. One is victimized, economically, in a thousand ways—rent, for example, or car insurance. Go shopping one day in Harlem—for anything—and compare Harlem prices and quality with those downtown.

The people who have managed to get off this block have only got as far as a more respectable ghetto. This respectable ghetto does not even have the advantages of the disreputable one—friends, neighbors, a familiar church, and friendly tradesmen; and it is not, moreover, in the nature of any ghetto to remain respectable long. Every Sunday, people who have left the block take the lonely ride back, dragging their increasingly discontented children with them. They spend the day talking, not always with words, about the trouble they've seen and the trouble—one must watch their eyes as they watch their children—they are only too likely to see. For children do not like ghettos. It takes them nearly no time to discover exactly why they are there.

The projects in Harlem are hated. They are hated almost as much as policemen, and this is saying a great deal. And they are hated for the same reason: both reveal, unbearably, the real attitude of the white world, no matter how many liberal speeches are made, no matter how many lofty editorials are written, no matter how many civil-rights commissions are set up.

The projects are hideous, of course, there being a law, apparently respected throughout the world, that popular housing shall be as cheerless as a prison. They are lumped all over Harlem, colorless, bleak, high, and revolting. The wide windows look out on Harlem's invincible and indescribable squalor: the Park Avenue railroad tracks, around which, about forty years ago, the present dark community began; the unrehabilitated houses, bowed down, it would seem, under the great weight of frustration and bitterness they contain; the dark, the ominous schoolhouses from which the child may emerge maimed, blinded, hooked, or enraged for life; and the churches, churches, block upon block of churches, niched in the walls like cannon in the walls of a fortress. Even if the administration of the projects were not so insanely humiliating (for example: one must report raises in salary to the management, which will then eat up the profit by raising one's rent; the management has the right to know who is staying in your apartment; the management can ask you to leave, at their discretion), the projects would still be hated because they are an insult to the meanest intelligence.

Harlem got its first private project, Riverton*—which is now, naturally, a slum—about twelve years ago because at that time Negroes were not allowed to live in Stuyvesant Town. Harlem watched Riverton go up, therefore, in the most violent bitterness of spirit, and hated it long before the builders arrived. They began hating it at about the time people began moving out of their condemned houses to make room for this additional proof of how thoroughly the white world despised them. And they had scarcely moved in, naturally, before they began smashing windows, defacing walls, urinating in the elevators, and fornicating in the playgrounds. Liberals, both white and black, were appalled at the spectacle. I was appalled by the liberal innocence—or cynicism, which comes out in practice as much the same thing. Other people were delighted to be able to point to proof positive that nothing could be done to better the lot of the colored people. They were, and are, right in one respect: that nothing can be done as long as they are treated like colored people. The people in Harlem know they are living there because white people do not think they are good enough to live anywhere else. No amount of "improvement" can sweeten this fact. Whatever money is now being earmarked to improve this, or any other ghetto, might as well be burnt. A ghetto can be improved in one way only: out of existence.

*The inhabitants of Riverton were much embittered by this description; they have, apparently, forgotten how their project came into being; and have repeatedly informed me that I cannot possibly be referring to Riverton, but to another housing project which is directly across the street. It is quite clear, I think, that I have no interest in accusing any individuals or families of the depredations herein described: but neither can I deny the evidence of my own eyes. Nor do I blame anyone in Harlem for making the best of a dreadful bargain. But anyone who lives in Harlem and imagines that he has *not* struck this bargain, or that what he takes to be his status (in whose eyes?) protects him against the common pain, demoralization, and danger, is simply self-deluded.

Similarly, the only way to police a ghetto is to be oppressive. None of the Police Commissioner's men, even with the best will in the world, have any way of understanding the lives led by the people they swagger about in twos and threes controlling. Their very presence is an insult, and it would be even if they spent their entire day feeding gumdrops to children. They represent the force of the white world, and that world's real intentions are, simply, for that world's criminal profit and ease, to keep the black man corralled up here, in his place. The badge, the gun in the holster, and the swinging club make vivid what will happen should his rebellion become overt. Rare, indeed, is the Harlem citizen, from the most circumspect church member to the most shiftless adolescent, who does not have a long tale to tell of police incompetence, injustice, or brutality. I myself have witnessed and endured it more than once. The businessmen and racketeers also have a story. And so do the prostitutes. (And this is not, perhaps, the place to discuss Harlem's very complex attitude toward black policemen, nor the reasons, according to Harlem, that they are nearly all downtown.)

It is hard, on the other hand, to blame the policeman, blank, good-natured, thoughtless, and insuperably innocent, for being such a perfect representative of the people he serves. He, too, believes in good intentions and is astounded and offended when they are not taken for the deed. He has never, himself, done anything for which to be hated—which of us has?—and yet he is facing, daily and nightly, people who would gladly see him dead, and he knows it. There is no way for him not to know it: there are few things under heaven more unnerving than the silent, accumulating contempt and hatred of a people. He moves through Harlem, therefore, like an occupying soldier in a bitterly hostile country; which is precisely what, and where, he is, and is the reason he walks in twos and threes. And he is not the only one who knows why he is always in company: the people who are watching him know why, too. Any street meeting, sacred or secular, which he and his colleagues uneasily cover has as its explicit or implicit burden the cruelty and injustice of the white domination. And these days, of course, in terms increasingly vivid and jubilant, it speaks of the end of that domination. The white policeman standing on a Harlem street corner finds himself at the very center of the revolution now occurring in the world. He is not prepared for it—naturally, nobody is—and, what is possibly much more to the point, he is exposed, as few white people are, to the anguish of the black people around him. Even if he is gifted with the merest mustard grain of imagination, something must seep in. He cannot avoid observing that some of the children, in spite of their color, remind him of children he has known and loved, perhaps even of his own children. He knows that he certainly does not want *his* children living this way. He can retreat from his uneasiness in only one direction: into a callousness which very shortly becomes second nature. He becomes more callous, the population becomes more hostile, the situation grows more tense, and the police force is increased. One day, to everyone's astonishment, someone drops a match in the powder keg and everything blows up. Before the dust has settled or the blood congealed, editorials, speeches, and civil-rights commissions are loud in the land, demanding to know what happened. What happened is that Negroes want to be treated like men.

Negroes want to be treated like men: a perfectly straightforward statement, containing only seven words. People who have mastered Kant, Hegel, Shakespeare, Marx, Freud, and the Bible find this statement utterly impenetrable. The idea seems to threaten profound, barely conscious assumptions. A kind of panic paralyzes their features, as though they found themselves trapped on the edge of a steep place. I once tried to describe to a very well-known American intellectual the conditions among Negroes in the South. My recital disturbed him and made him indignant; and he asked me in perfect innocence, "Why don't all the Negroes in the South move North?" I tried to explain what *has* happened, unfailingly, whenever a significant body of Negroes move North. They do not escape Jim Crow: they merely encounter another, not-less-deadly variety. They do not move to Chicago, they move to the South Side; they do not move to New York, they move to Harlem. The pressure within the ghetto causes the ghetto walls to expand, and this expansion is always violent. White people hold the line as long as they can, and in as many ways as they can, from verbal intimidation to physical violence. But inevitably the border which has divided the ghetto from the rest of the world falls into the hands of the ghetto. The white people fall back bitterly before the black horde; the landlords make a tidy profit by raising the rent, chopping up the rooms, and all but dispensing with the upkeep; and what has once been a neighborhood turns into a "turf." This is precisely what happened when the Puerto Ricans arrived in their thousands —and the bitterness thus caused is, as I write, being fought out all up and down those streets.

Northerners indulge in an extremely dangerous luxury. They seem to feel that because they fought on the right side during the Civil War, and won, they have earned the right merely to deplore what is going on in the South, without taking any responsibility for it; and that they can ignore what is happening in Northern cities because what is happening in Little Rock or Birmingham is worse. Well, in the first place, it is not possible for anyone who has not endured both to know which is "worse." I know Negroes who prefer the South and white Southerners, because "At least there, you haven't got to play any guessing games!" The guessing games referred to have driven more than one Negro into the narcotics ward, the madhouse, or the river. I know another Negro, a man very dear to me, who says, with conviction and with truth, "The spirit of the South is the spirit of America." He was born in the North and did his military training in the South. He did not, as far as I can gather, find the South "worse"; he found it, if anything, all too familiar. In the second place, though, even if Birmingham *is* worse, no doubt Johannesburg, South Africa, beats it by several miles, and Buchenwald was one of the worst things that ever happened in the entire history of the world. The world has never lacked for horrifying examples; but I do not believe that these examples are meant to be used as justification for our own crimes. This perpetual justification empties the heart of all human feeling. The emptier our hearts become, the greater will be our crimes. Thirdly, the South is not merely an embarrassingly backward region, but a part of this country, and what happens there concerns every one of us.

As far as the color problem is concerned, there is but one great difference between the Southern white and the Northerner: the Southerner remembers, historically and in his own psyche, a kind of Eden in which he loved black people and they loved him. Historically, the flaming sword laid across this Eden is the Civil War. Personally, it is the Southerner's sexual coming of age, when, without any warning, unbreakable taboos are set up between himself and his past. Everything, thereafter, is permitted him except the love he remembers and has never ceased to need. The resulting, indescribable torment affects every Southern mind and is the basis of the Southern hysteria.

None of this is true for the Northerner. Negroes represent nothing to him personally, except, perhaps, the dangers of carnality. He never sees Negroes. Southerners see them all the time. Northerners never think about them whereas Southerners are never really thinking of anything else. Negroes are, therefore, ignored in the North and are under surveillance in the South, and suffer hideously in both places. Neither the Southerner nor the Northerner is able to look on the Negro simply as a man. It seems to be indispensable to the national self-esteem that the Negro be considered either as a kind of ward (in which case we are told how many Negroes, comparatively, bought Cadillacs last year and how few, comparatively, were lynched), or as a victim (in which case we are promised that he will never vote in our assemblies or go to school with our kids). They are two sides of the same coin and the South will not change—*cannot* change—until the North changes. The country will not change until it re-examines itself and discovers what it really means by freedom. In the meantime, generations keep being born, bitterness is increased by incompetence, pride, and folly, and the world shrinks around us.

It is a terrible, an inexorable, law that one cannot deny the humanity of another without diminishing one's own: in the face of one's victim, one sees oneself. Walk through the streets of Harlem and see what we, this nation, have become.

East River Downtown:

Postscript to A Letter from Harlem

THE FACT that American Negroes rioted in the U.N. while Adlai Stevenson was addressing the Assembly shocked and baffled most white Americans. Stevenson's speech, and the spectacular disturbance in the gallery, were both touched off by the death, in Katanga, the day before, of Patrice Lumumba. Stevenson stated, in the course of his address, that the United States was "against" colonialism. God knows what the African nations, who hold 25 per cent of the voting stock in the U.N., were thinking—they may, for example, have been thinking of the U.S. abstention when the vote on Algerian freedom was before the Assembly—but I think I have a fairly accurate notion of what the Negroes in the gallery were thinking. I had intended to be there myself. It was my first reaction upon hearing of Lumumba's death. I was curious about the impact of this political assassination on Negroes in Harlem, for Lumumba had—has—captured the popular imagination there. I was curious to know if Lumumba's death, which is surely among the most sinister of recent events, would elicit from "our" side anything more than the usual, well-meaning rhetoric. And I was curious about the African reaction.

However, the chaos on my desk prevented my being in the U.N. gallery. Had I been there, I, too, in the eyes of most Americans, would have been merely a pawn in the hands of the Communists. The climate and the events of the last decade, and the steady pressure of the "cold" war, have given Americans yet another means of avoiding self-examination, and so it has been decided that the riots were "Communist" inspired. Nor was it long, naturally, before prominent Negroes rushed forward to assure the republic that the U.N. rioters do not represent the real feeling of the Negro community.

According, then, to what I take to be the prevailing view, these rioters were merely a handful of irresponsible, Stalinist-corrupted *provocateurs*.

I find this view amazing. It is a view which even a minimal effort at observation would immediately contradict. One has only, for example, to walk through Harlem and ask oneself two questions. The first question is: Would *I* like to live here? And the second question is: Why don't those who now live here move out? The answer to both questions is immediately obvious. Unless one takes refuge in the theory—however disguised—that Negroes are, somehow, different from white people, I do not see how one can escape the conclusion that the Negro's status in this country is not only a cruel injustice but a grave national liability.

Now, I do not doubt that, among the people at the U.N. that day, there were Stalinist and professional revolutionists acting out of the most cynical motives. Wherever there is great social discontent, these people are, sooner or later, to be found. Their presence is not as frightening as the discontent which creates their opportunity. What I find appalling—and really dangerous—is the American assumption that the Negro is so contented with his lot here that only the cynical agents of a foreign power can rouse him to protest. It is a notion which contains a gratuitous insult, implying, as it does, that Negroes can make no move unless they are manipulated. It forcibly suggests that the Southern attitude toward the Negro is also, essentially, the national attitude. When the South has trouble with its Negroes—when the Negroes refuse to remain in their "place"—it blames "outside" agitators and "Northern interference." When the nation has trouble with the Northern Negro, it blames the Kremlin. And this, by no means incidentally, is a very dangerous thing to do. We thus give credit to the Communists for attitudes and victories which are not theirs. We make of them the champions of the oppressed, and they could not, of course, be more delighted.

If, as is only too likely, one prefers not to visit Harlem and expose oneself to the anguish there, one has only to consider the two most powerful movements among Negroes in this country today. At one pole, there is the Negro student movement. This movement, I believe, will prove to be the very last attempt made by American Negroes to achieve acceptance in the republic, to force the country to honor its own ideals. The movement does not have as its goal the consumption of overcooked hamburgers and tasteless coffee at various sleazy lunch counters. Neither do Negroes, who have, largely, been produced by miscegenation, share the white man's helplessly hypocritical attitudes toward the time-honored and universal mingling. The goal of the student movement is nothing less than the liberation of the entire country from its most crippling attitudes and habits. The reason that it is important—of the utmost importance—for white people, here, to see the Negroes as people like themselves is that white people will not, otherwise, be able to see themselves as they are.

At the other pole is the Muslim movement, which daily becomes more powerful. The Muslims do not expect anything at all from the white people of this country. They do not believe that the American professions of democracy or equality have ever been even remotely sincere. They insist on the total separation of the races. This is to be achieved by the acquisition of land from the United States—land which is owed the Negroes as "back wages" for the labor wrested from them when they were slaves, and for their unrecognized and unhonored contributions to the wealth and power of this country. The student movement depends, at bottom, on an act of faith, an ability to see, beneath the cruelty and hysteria and apathy of white people, their bafflement and pain and essential decency. This is superbly difficult. It demands a perpetually cultivated spiritual resilience, for the bulk of the evidence contradicts the vision. But the Muslim movement has all the evidence on its side. Unless one supposes that the idea of black supremacy has virtues denied to the idea of white supremacy, one cannot possibly accept the deadly conclusions a Muslim draws from this evidence. On the other hand, it is quite impossible to argue with a Muslim concerning the actual state of Negroes in this country—the truth, after all, is the truth.

This is the great power a Muslim speaker has over his audience. His audience has not heard this truth—the truth about their daily lives—honored by anyone else. Almost anyone else, black or white, prefers to soften this truth, and point to a new day which is coming in America. But this day has been coming for nearly one hundred years. Viewed solely in the light of this country's moral professions, this lapse is inexcusable. Even more important, however, is the fact that there is desperately little in the record to indicate that white America ever seriously desired—or desires—to see this day arrive.

Usually, for example, those white people who are in favor of integration prove to be in favor of it later, in some other city, some other town, some other building, some other school. The arguments, or rationalizations, with which they attempt to disguise their panic cannot be respected. Northerners proffer their indignation about the South as a kind of badge, as proof of good intentions; never suspecting that they thus increase, in the heart of the Negro they are speaking to, a kind of helpless pain and rage—and pity. Negroes know how little most white people are prepared to implement their words with deeds, how little, when the chips are down, they are prepared to risk. And this long history of moral evasion has had an unhealthy effect on the total life of the country, and has eroded whatever respect Negroes may once have felt for white people.

We are beginning, therefore, to witness in this country a new thing. "I am not at all sure," states one prominent Negro, who is *not* a Muslim, "that I *want* to be integrated into a burning house." "I might," says another, "consider being integrated into something else, an American society more real and more honest—but *this?* No, thank you, man, who *needs* it?" And this searching disaffection has everything to do with the emergence of Africa: "At the rate things are going here, all of Africa will be free before we can get a lousy cup of coffee."

Now, of course, it is easy to say—and it is true enough, as far as it goes—that the American Negro deludes himself if he imagines himself capable of any loyalty other than his loyalty to the United States. He is an American, too, and he will survive or perish with the country. This seems an unanswerable argument. But, while I have no wish whatever to question the loyalty of American Negroes, I think this argument may be examined with some profit. The argument is used, I think, too often and too glibly. It obscures the effects of the passage of time, and the great changes that have taken place in the world.

In the first place, as the homeless wanderers of the twentieth century prove, the question of nationality no longer necessarily involves the question of allegiance. Allegiance, after all, has to work two ways; and one can grow weary of an allegiance which is not reciprocal. I have the right and the duty, for example, in my country, to vote; but it is my country's responsibility to protect my right to vote. People now approaching, or past, middle age, who have spent their lives in such struggles, have thereby acquired an understanding of America, and a belief in her potential which cannot now be shaken. (There are exceptions to this, however, W. E. B. Du Bois, for example. It is easy to dismiss him as a Stalinist; but it is more interesting to consider just why so intelligent a man became so disillusioned.) But I very strongly doubt that any Negro youth, now approaching maturity, and with the whole, vast world before him, is willing, say, to settle for Jim Crow in Miami, when he can—or, before the travel ban, *could*—feast at the welcome table in Havana. And he need not, to prefer Havana, have any pro-Communist, or, for that matter, pro-Cuban, or pro-Castro sympathies: he need merely prefer not to be treated as a second-class citizen.

These are extremely unattractive facts, but they *are* facts, and no purpose is served by denying them. Neither, as I have already tried to indicate, is any purpose served by pretending that Negroes who refuse to be bound by this country's peculiar attitudes are subversive. They have every right to refuse to be bound by a set of attitudes as useless now and as obsolete as the pillory. Finally, the time is forever behind us when Negroes could be expected to "wait." What is demanded now, and at once, is not that Negroes continue to adjust themselves to the cruel racial pressures of life in the United States but that the United States readjust itself to the facts of life in the present world.

One of these facts is that the American Negro can no longer, nor will he ever again, be controlled by white America's image of him. This fact has everything to do with the rise of Africa in world affairs. At the time that I was growing up, Negroes in this country were taught to be ashamed of Africa. They were taught it bluntly, as I was, for example, by being told that Africa had never contributed "anything" to civilization. Or one was taught the same lesson more obliquely, and even more effectively, by watching nearly naked, dancing, comic-opera, cannibalistic savages in the movies. They were nearly always all bad, sometimes funny, sometimes both. If one of them was good, his goodness was proved by his loyalty to the white man. A baffling sort of goodness, particularly as one's father, who certainly wanted one to be "good," was more than likely to come home cursing—cursing the white man. One's hair was always being attacked with hard brushes and combs and Vaseline: it was shameful to have "nappy" hair. One's legs and arms and face were always being greased, so that one would not look "ashy" in the wintertime. One was always being mercilessly scrubbed and polished, as though in the hope that a stain could thus be washed away—I hazard that the Negro children of my generation, anyway, had an earlier and more painful acquaintance with soap than any other children anywhere. The women were forever straightening and curling their hair, and using bleaching creams. And yet it was clear that none of this effort would release one from the stigma and danger of being a Negro; this effort merely increased the shame and rage. There was not, no matter where one turned, any acceptable image of oneself, no proof of one's existence. One had the choice, either of "acting just like a nigger" or of *not* acting just like a nigger—and only those who have tried it know how impossible it is to tell the difference.

My first hero was Joe Louis. I was ashamed of Father Divine. Haile Selassie was the first black emperor I ever saw—in a newsreel; he was pleading vainly with the West to prevent the rape of his country. And the extraordinary complex of tensions thus set up in the breast, between hatred of whites and contempt for blacks, is very hard to describe. Some of the most energetic people of my generation were destroyed by this interior warfare.

But none of this is so for those who are young now. The power of the white world to control their identities was crumbling as they were born; and by the time they were able to react to the world, Africa was on the stage of history. This could not but have an extraordinary effect on their own morale, for it meant that they were not merely the descendants of slaves in a white, Protestant, and puritan country: they were also related to kings and princes in an ancestral homeland, far away. And this has proved to be a great antidote to the poison of self-hatred.

It also signals, at last, the end of the Negro situation in this country, as we have so far known it. Any effort, from here on out, to keep the Negro in his "place" can only have the most extreme and unlucky repercussions. This being so, it would seem to me that the most intelligent effort we can now make is to give up this doomed endeavor and study how we can most quickly end this division in our house. The Negroes who rioted in the U.N. are but a very small echo of the black discontent now abroad in the world. If we are not able, and quickly, to face and begin to eliminate the sources of this discontent in our own country, we will never be able to do it on the great stage of the world.

SAUL BELLOW

Literary Notes on Khrushchev

KHRUSHCHEV, the heir of Lenin and Stalin, Malenkov's successor and the evident head of the Russian oligarchy, has stamped his image on the world and compels us to think about him. It is hard of course to believe that this bald, round, gesticulating, loud man may be capable of overcoming, of ruining, perhaps of destroying us.

"It's him, Khrushchev, dat nut," a garage attendant on Third Avenue said to me last September as the fleet of Russian Cadillacs rushed by. This time Khrushchev was a self-invited visitor. He did not arrive with our blessings, and he did not have our love, but that didn't seem to matter greatly to him. He was able, nevertheless, to dominate the headlines, the television screens, the U.N. Assembly and the midtown streets. An American in his position, feeling himself unwanted and, even worse, unloved, would have been self-effacing. Not Khruschev. He poured it on, holding press conferences in the street and trading insults from his balcony with the crowd, singing snatches of the *International,* giving a pantomime uppercut to an imaginary assassin. He played up to the crowd and luxuriated in its attention, behaving like a comic artist in a show written and directed by himself. And at the U.N., roaring with anger, interrupting Mr. Macmillan, landing his fists on the desk, waving a shoe in the air, hugging his allies and bugging his opponents, surging up from his seat to pump the hand of the elegant black Nkrumah in his gilt crimson toga or interrupting his own blasts at the West to plug Soviet mineral water, suddenly winsome, Khrushchev the charmer, not once did he give up the center of the stage. And no one seemed able to take it from him.

Balzac once described the statesman as a "monster of self-possession." He referred of course to the bourgeois statesman. Khrushchev is another sort of fish altogether. And since his début on the world scene shortly after Stalin died and Malenkov "retired," Khrushchev—running always a little ahead of Bulganin—has astonished, perplexed, bamboozled and appalled the world. If the traditional statesman is a prodigy of self-possession, Khrushchev seems instead to give himself away. He seems to be a man of candor, just as Russia seems to be a union of socialist republics. Other statesmen are satisfied to represent their countries. Not so Khrushchev. He wishes to personify Russia and the Communist cause.

Timidity will get us nowhere. If we want to understand him we must give the imagination its freedom and let it, in gambler's language, go for broke. Anyway, he compels us to think of him. We have him continually under our eyes. He is in China, he is in Paris and Berlin and San Francisco, and he performs everywhere. In Austria he inspects a piece of abstract sculpture and, with an astonished air, he asks the artist to tell him what the devil it stands for. Listening or pretending to listen, he observes that the sculptor will have to hang around forever to explain his incomprehensible work. He arrives in Finland in time to attend the birthday celebration of its president; he pushes the poor man aside and frolics before the cameras, eats, drinks, fulminates and lets himself be taken home. In America, on his first visit, his progress across the land was nothing less than spectacular. And no fifteenth-century king could have been more *himself,* whether with the press, with Mr. Garst on the farm, with dazzling dolls of Hollywood, or with the trade-union leaders in San Francisco. "You are like a nightingale," he said to Walter Reuther. "It closes its eyes when it sings, and sees nothing and hears nobody but itself." In Hollywood with Spyros Skouras, he matched success stories, each protagonist trying to prove that he rose from greater depths. "I was a poor immigrant." "I began working when I learned to walk—I was a shepherd boy, a factory laborer, I worked in the coal pits, and now I am Prime Minister of the great Soviet State." Neither of them mentioned the cost of his rise to the public-at-large: Skouras said nothing of the effects of Hollywood on the brains of Americans nor did Khrushchev mention deportations and purges. We who had this greatness thrust upon us had no spokesman in the debate. But then people in show business have always enjoyed a peculiar monopoly of patriotism. The mixture of ideology and entertainment on both sides brought about an emotional crisis on the West Coast, and it was here that Khrushchev was provoked into disclosing some of his deeper feelings. "When we were in Hollywood, they danced the cancan for us," he told the meeting of the trade-union leaders in San Francisco. "The girls who dance it have to pull up their skirts and show their backsides. They are good, honest actresses, but have to perform that dance. They are compelled to adapt themselves to the tastes of depraved people. People in your country will go to see it, but Soviet people would scorn such a spectacle. It is pornographic. It is the culture of surfeited and depraved people. Showing that sort of film is called freedom in this country. Such 'freedom' doesn't suit us. You seem to like the 'freedom' of looking at backsides. But we prefer freedom to think, to exercise our mental faculties, the freedom of creative progress." I take these words from a semi-official

Russian-sponsored publication. It does not add what some American reports added, namely, that the Premier here raised his coattails and exposed his rear to the entire gathering as he swooped into a parody of the cancan.

This, friends, is art. It is also an entirely new mode of historical interpretation by the world leader of Marxist thought who bodily, by the use of his own person, delivers a critique of Western civilization. It is, moreover, theater. And we are its enthralled and partly captive audience. Khrushchev's performance is, in the term used by James Joyce, an epiphany, a manifestation which summarizes or expresses a whole universe of meanings. "We will bury you," Khrushchev has told the capitalist world, and though it has since been said over and over that this is merely a Ukranian figure of speech meaning, "We will exceed you in production," I think that in watching this dance we might all feel the itching of the nose which, according to superstition, means that someone is walking on our graves. We would not be far out in seeing auguries of death in this cancan. The "culture of surfeited and depraved people" is doomed. That is the meaning of his brutal and angry comedy. It is also what he means when he plays villain and buffoon to the New York public. To him this is the slack, shallow, undisciplined and cultureless mob of a decadent capitalist city. Still, life is very complicated, for if the Hollywood cancan is poor stuff, what can we say of the products of socialist realism with their pure and loyal worker-heroes and their sweet and hokey maidens? Khrushchev himself is far above such junk. It is possible to conclude from this that in a dictatorship the tyrant may suck into himself all the resources of creativity and leave the art of his country impoverished.

It may, in fact, take not only Russia but the entire world to feed the needs of a single individual. For it can't be ideology alone that produces such outbursts; it must be character. "I have often thought," wrote William James, "that the best way to define a man's character would be to seek out the particular mental or moral attitude in which, when it came upon him, he felt himself most intensely active and alive. At such moments there is a voice inside which speaks and says: '*This* is the real me!' " So perhaps Krushchev feels himself, or attempts to reach himself, in these outbursts. And perhaps it is when the entire world is watching him soar and he is touching the limits of control that he feels most alive. He does not exhibit great range of feelings. When he takes off the rudimentary masks of bureaucratic composure or peasant dignity or affability, he is angry or jeering. But fear is not the best school for expressiveness, and no man could be an important party functionary under Stalin without the ability to live in fear. We cannot therefore expect him to be versatile. He had, however, what it took to finish the course, the nerves, the control, the patience, the piercing ambition, the strength to kill and to endure the threat of death. It would be premature to say that he has survived all that there is to survive in Russia, but it is a safe guess that in the relief of having reached first place he is whooping it up. Instead of having been punished for his crimes he has become a great leader, which persuades him that life is inherently dramatic. And in his joy at having reversed the moral-accounting system of bourgeois civilization he plays his role with ever greater spirit.

Our ablest political commentators have used theatrical metaphors to describe Khrushchev's behavior. Mr. Sulzberger in the New York *Times* speaks of the "fierce illogic of a Brendan Behan play." Others have been reminded of the Leningrad circus, and a British psychologist has suggested that Khrushchev may have made a study of Pavlov's conditioned reflex. After Pavlov had rewarded his dogs for responding to given signals, he scrambled the pattern and the animals suffered an hysterical breakdown. Our leaders, amid flowers and smiles and exchanges of charm, made appointments to meet Khrushchev at the Summit only to find that he had turned into the Great Boyg of the northern snows who deafened them with snarls and stunned them with ice. If Khrushchev had needed instruction in the technique of blowing hot and cold he could have gotten it from Hitler, who made a great deal of noise in the world, rather than from Pavlov, who made very little. From Hitler he might have learned that angry demonstrations unnerve well-conducted people, and that in statesmanship the advantage always lies with the unprincipled, the brutal and the insane. Hitler could at will convulse himself with rage and, when he had gained his ends, be coolly correct to his staff, all in a matter of moments. Khrushchev does not seem to have this combination of derangement and cold political technique which threatens the end of the world in fire and ice. But does he need lessons from Professor Pavlov in psychological techniques? Teach your granny to suck an egg.

No, the dramatic metaphor is the best one, and in trying to place his style, even before I had seen Khrushchev in action during his recent American visit, a short, buoyant, ruddy, compact, gesturing, tough man—it struck me that Marcel Marceau, another mime appearing in *The Overcoat* at a New York theater, and Khrushchev, at the other side of town, had both been inspired by the Russian comic tradition. The masterpiece of that tradition is Gogol's *Dead Souls*. From Gogol's landlords and peasants, grotesquely thick-headed or just as grotesquely shrewd, provincial autocrats, creeps, misers, officials, gluttons, gamblers and drunkards, Khrushchev seems to have taken many of the elements of his comic style. He is one of Gogol's stout men who "know better than thin men how to manage their affairs. The thin ones are more often employed on special missions, or are merely 'on the staff,' scurrying hither and thither; their existence is somehow too slight, airy and altogether insubstantial. The stout ones are never to be found filling ambiguous posts, but only straightforward ones; if they sit down anywhere, they do so solidly and firmly, so that, though their position may creak and bend beneath them, they never fall off."

When the occasion demands more earnestness he plays the Marxist. Speaking at the U.N. he made me think, when he called for colonial liberation, of Trotsky in the first years of the Russian Revolution and in particular of Trotsky's conduct during the signing of the Treaty of Brest-Litovsk. There to the amazement of the German generals, he delayed the negotiations in order to make speeches calling on the world proletariat to support and extend the revolution. Those days are gone forever, of course. They were gone even before Lenin died. And there is a great difference between the fresh revolutionary ardor of Trotsky and the stale agitational technique of an old party hack. Still, when it suits him, Khrushchev is a Marxist. Defending the poor working girls of Hollywood, he delivered the judgment of Marxian orthodoxy on their wriggling and kicking (more of the alienating labor imposed by capitalism on humanity).

There are certain similarities between Khrushchev's Marxism and the liberal ideology of Western businessmen. They make use of it at their convenience. Khrushchev, however, enjoys a considerable advantage in that the needs of Russian history and those of his own personality have coincided so that he is able at times to follow his instincts without restraint. He has besides a great contempt for the representatives of the West who are unable to do without the brittle, soiled and compromised conventions of civilized diplomacy. It is the great coma, the deep sleep, and he despises the sleepers and takes advantage of them. The pictures taken at the Summit reveal the extent of his success. General de Gaulle's mouth is drawn very small in a pucker of foreboding and distaste. Mr. Macmillan seems deeply hurt. Former President Eisenhower looks sad, but also opinionated. Things have gone wrong again, but it is certainly no fault of his. Together, the three must have seemed to Khrushchev like Keats's "still unravished brides of quietness." And it is not hard to guess what he, the descendant of serfs, risen to a position of such might, must have experienced. Confronting the leaders of the bourgeois West, so long feared and hated, he saw himself to be tougher, deeper and more intelligent than any of them. And, in expressing his feelings, more free.

It's hard to know whether the Khrushchev we saw banging with his shoe at the U.N. Assembly is the "real" Khrushchev. But one of the privileges of power seems to be the privilege of direct emotional self-expression. It is not a privilege exercised by many people in the West, so far as I can see.

"Men who have arrived can do what they like," declared the *Daily News* recently in one of its snappy ads. "There was a guy who liked spaghetti and beer, but when he became a junior executive, he thought it more fitting to order steak and asparagus. It was only when he became president of his company that he felt assured enough to go back to spaghetti and beer."

Such are the privileges of power, but bafflingly enough, apart from artists and tyrants, few people, even among company presidents, feel strong enough to tell the world how they feel. New York's Police Commissioner Kennedy, a man who has apparently arrived, could not, some time ago, express his honest views as to the religious convictions of the Jewish members of the force. Everyone knows that the commissioner is not anti-Semitic. Yet the New York Rabbinate felt compelled, as did Mayor Wagner, for formal reasons, to ask for a retraction. So it's not easy to speak one's mind. Even the artists have taken cover, disguising themselves as bank clerks and veiling their sayings. That leaves us with the tyrants. (Is it only a coincidence that Emily Post died during Khrushchev's visit?)

Masked in smiles and peasant charm, or in anger, the Russian Premier releases his deepest feelings and if we are not shaken by them it is because we are not in close touch with reality. In the West the connections between opinion, feeling and bodily motion have been broken. We have lost the expressive power. It is in the use of such power, falsely exploiting his Russian and peasant background, that Khrushchev has shown himself to be an adept. He has a passion always ready to exploit and, though he lies, he has the advantage. The principles of Western liberalism seem no longer to lend themselves to effective action. Deprived of the expressive power, we are awed by it, have a hunger for it and are afraid of it. Thus we praise the gray dignity of our soft-spoken leaders, but in our hearts we are suckers for passionate outbursts, even when those passionate outbursts are hypocritical and falsely motivated.

The best lack all conviction
While the worst are full of passionate intensity.

At times Khrushchev goes beyond Gogolian comedy; this is no longer the amiable chiseler who stuffs himself with fish or pancakes dipped in butter. Gogol's Chichikov, to congratulate himself when he has pulled a fast one, dances in the privacy of his room. But Khrushchev goes into his cancan before the world public with a deep and gnomish joy. Here is a man whom all the twisted currents of human purpose have brought within reach of world power. At a time when public figures show only secondary or tertiary personal characteristics, he appears to show only primary ones. He wears his instincts on his sleeve or like Dostoevsky's Father Karamazov, that corrupt and deep old man, he feigns simplicity.

When the charm and irony wear thin, he shows himself to be a harsh, arbitrary and complicated man. It was a simple enough matter for him to have joked contemptuously with Spyros Skouras; in debate with well-informed men who press him closely he becomes abusive, showing that the habit of authority has made him inflexible. He seems unable to discuss any matter except on his own terms. Nature, history, Russian Marxism and, perhaps most of all, the fact that he has survived under Stalin make it impossible for him to entertain other views. What amounted in Paris to ex-President Eisenhower's admission of a blunder must have seemed to him incredible. He lives under an iron necessity to be right. What he perhaps remembers best about men who were not right is their funerals. For him the line between the impossible and the possible is drawn with blood, and foreigners who do not see the blood must appear preposterous to him.

HERBERT BLAU

The Public Art of Crisis in the Suburbs of Hell

ABOUT THE TIME I started taking the theater neoclassically, for instruction as well as delight, I had just been hired to teach at a state college in California. While God and Man were being betrayed at Yale, the loyalty oath was being legislated in Sacramento. There were dark perturbations on campus, but in those pre-Birch and Goldwater balmy days, the accent was still on behavorial benevolence and the more clinical claptrapping of the doctrines of perfectibility—Deweyism, replete with reading laboratories and remedial writing. In the canons of "student-centered teaching" (liberal dogma caressing jargon in social contract) to call a student illiterate if he was illiterate was worse than calling a student a nigger if he was a . . . Well, you see the issue, words *do* fail. And there was reason in the surveys of "student needs," and something to remedy; even now, the laboratories continue, but with "stricter standards." The "goal": to get back to the subject through the student's problems. In such an atmosphere, no wonder the story arose about the freshman who, after a semester of self-searching—in psychology, creative arts, humanities, and even the social sciences, by Rorschach, true confession, by IBM—came to his instructor in English about a term paper, and said: "I don't know what to do, I can't find a subject, I've run out of problems."

The sputnik, great blast into the future, was grist for the New Conservatism. Could Johnny dare remain illiterate —lo! the Word made flesh, even among the psychological adjusters—if Ivan wasn't? Yet in the backsweep toward the McGuffey readers, there still survive, up to the college level, Home and Family Living, Bibliotherapy, Group Dynamics, Collective Fun and Creative Togetherness, and Deans who now believe in fraternities (those Platonic Ideas of what the NAACP is calling "Tokenism") as processes of Integration. And there is the semantic theory that all problems are merely verbal.

Sometimes this takes the form of reconciling opposites by canceling them: "They're saying the same thing in different words." Or, appearing to take opposites into account: "If Macomber could only communicate with Mitty, Mitty would understand." Yet even if Cow_1 is not Cow_2 (and I'm prepared to argue this), it is my contention—and the contention of the theater when it is not betraying its nature— that there are these possibilities, too: either Mitty is never going to understand Macomber; or, if Mitty comes to understand, it will be precisely what he understands that he won't like. Khrushchev, I contend, understands Kennedy. "We will bury you," he says, with minimal malice—sounding, for all the shoe thumping, like a genial and unobscurantist Genet.*

"O words," says Ionesco's Jack, "what crimes are committed in thy name." Which can be taken two ways: words

*A day or so after I wrote this, Premier Khrushchev said about President Kennedy's *Izvestia* interview: "When Mr. Kennedy becomes a Communist, we shall have a common language."

fail men, men fail words. We are—from the logical positivists to Antonin Artaud—too hard on words. Where words fail, they may fail at different limits. Lest we compound our crimes: Don't hesitate to call a spade a spade because somebody says it's a phoneme, or a well-wrought urn. You can't say the same thing in different words. Different words, different thing. Communication will not solve the world's problems, it may cause some of them. How sad to discover, for instance, that foreign students, after four years in American colleges, go away hating us for somewhat better reasons. As the world grows smaller and smaller, it also looms woefully large, so that while one of our recent Nobel Prize-winners, an expert on atomic particles, assures us we'll never see the end, we see all too clearly the scaly dragon of Communist China raising its sullen head; and we know, I fear, precisely what it wants. I think of Beckett's tramp, ruthless for recognition: "You're sure you saw me, you won't come and tell me tomorrow that you never saw me." There is a terrible innocence in the messenger from Godot, who says neither yes nor no.

As for the freshman, who had not yet developed techniques for seeing the whole world in a grain of sand, he was probably wrong, you can't run out of problems, one of the greatest being that when you examine the whole world in a grain of sand you see it isn't the whole world; that, Lao Tse, Swedenborg, Blake, and Alan Watts notwithstanding, a grain of sand is not an Empire. The least character in Shakespeare knows that: "I cannot draw a cart, nor eat dried oats./ If it be man's work, I'll do't." Or the other captain, who says about the military expedition of Fortinbras (who is not all that perfect a man of action): "We go to gain a little patch of ground/ That hath in it no profit but the name./ To pay five ducats, five, I would not farm it. . . ." Neither captain has entirely resolved the relationship between fact and fancy, but they each make reasonable claims upon the real. "Seeming, seeming." We may have to contend again with that old appalling possibility (suggested by Beckett and Shakespeare alike) that $illusion_1$ is no better than $illusion_2$.

Now the theater knows all this by instinct. Local habitation of illusion, the theater has conflict in its bones, and instead of doing away with it or pretending it doesn't exist or submitting it to panel discussion, it demands that conflict be brought to crisis. It is, indeed, the public art of crisis. (And that goes for the new "anti-drama," more crucial about crisis than any we have going.) In public life a condition of insupportable tension, like that of the Cold War, may be made livable by the illusions of greater production, more conspicuous consumption, the strategy of controlled depression, and the whole Disneyland of shelter programs and stockpiled weapons. In popular art, it leads to what Dwight Macdonald (himself not exempt) calls Masscult and Midcult, culture for the brainless and culture for the middle-brow and half-educated, such as Frank Baxter's TV Shakespeare or the suburban-egalitarian, theater-party, "Jews-and-Negroes-are-just-plain-white-protestant," orthodoxy of Broadway. (From *Under the Yum-Yum Tree* to *A Raisin in the Sun,* from *Gypsy* to *Gideon,* Paddy Cheyevsky's latest chapter from *The Greatest Story Ever Told,* one might do a study of public opinion on Broadway called "The Audience as Pavlovian Dog.") In real art, the same condition of insupportable tension, felt in privacy and cutting to the brain, is brought to even greater tension in the interest of *truth,* however unsayable, indefensible, or unbearable.

For people who don't understand the crucial concerns of the drama, who only think they believe in the dark at the top of the stairs, who are sure some guidance counselor or social worker or humane lady in slip or unbuttoned blouse will turn on the lights (or off; on or off, Love will out), there is secret wonder over the fact that neither Hamlet nor Oedipus was wise enough to consult a psychiatrist. But can you imagine either one of them going through a period of adjustment? "Why seems it so particular with thee?" asks

Gertrude, after the unnerving if common saw: "all that lives must die,/ Passing through nature to eternity." "Seems, madam! Nay, it is. I know not 'seems.'" Hamlet, a born New Critic, creates problems with a runaway tongue. A self-made Academy, he tries to keep the language alive by his talent for paradox and his insistence on the seven types of ambiguity as modes of salvation or, depending on your illusions, therapy. Hamlet knows all about "the tyranny of words," but when the wind is southerly he can tell a hawk from a handsaw. And his advice to the players shows he believes words to be the life of the design and that he distrusts those, himself included, who dishonor the words in their charge.

The dramatic character is beyond adjustment, as he is beyond bargaining—which is to say, whatever his social role, as dramatic agent he cannot be bourgeois. Lord of the bourgeois, the Troll King says to Peer Gynt: "Man, to thyself be—enough." But Peer, Don Quixote of Free Enterprise, is full of the momentum of a century ringing down the grooves of change; he cannot rest. Until he comes home roundabout or is gathered in the artifice of eternity, the dramatic character insists on following things out to their inevitable end, or to that unmathematical and ready middle of experience that resolves "To be or not to be" in "Let be." The motive: What? Will? Moral purpose? Fate? History? Providence? the Dignity of Man?—or all these working interweavingly and impossibly together, as in the mat-making incident of *Moby-Dick,* Chance, in the indifferent blade of the pagan Queequeg, having "the last featuring blow at events." The cost: mainly self-destruction—calamity, catastrophe, the fall of the sparrow, accidental slaughter, a plague on both your houses, the shadowy waters, the dark root of the scream, the mill race, Birnam Wood, and the bleeding eyeballs. The effect: catharsis? Maybe. More likely woe and wonder, the hieratic emotion of what the jazz addict means by stoned.

The excess of the instinct for bearing things out to the

edge of doom turns tragedy to comedy. We are in such a bad way now, with our cormorant Cold War. "What is right for us is comedy," says the Swiss dramatist Duerrenmatt. "Our world has led to the grotesque as well as to the atom bomb, and Hieronymus' madness is with us again, the apocalyptic vision has become the grotesquely real. But the grotesque is only a way of expressing in a tangible manner, of making us perceive physically the paradoxical, the form of the unformed, the face of a world without face; and just as in our thinking today we seem to be unable to do without the concept of paradox, so also in art, and in our world which at times seems still to exist only because the atom bomb exists: out of fear of the bomb." Dread prolonged *is* laughable—a commonplace long before Baudelaire, but a collective fact of our time. Or, as the banished Edgar, resting from his role as Mad Tom, puts it in *King Lear*: "the lamentable fall is from the best/ The worst returns to laughter."

If comedy is what happens when tragedy fails, tragedy is what happens when comedy fails. Duerrenmatt knows that the tragic (if not tragedy) may come out of the comic "as a frightening moment, as an abyss that opens suddenly"—as when Buster Keaton, directing the Rebel artillery with a sword that flies off the hilt, notices his comrades falling, mysteriously, one by one, about him. Discretion being the better part of valor, he runs, brandishing his terrible sword, blade leaving hilt in a high lyric arc, impaling a Union sniper. At the limits of the credible, the absurd, an *O altitudo!* in reverse. "The point about tragedy," says Harold Pinter, "is that it is *no longer funny*. It is funny, and then it becomes no longer funny."

Whether crisis produces woe, wonder, or laughter, it is always in the interest of some Higher Self, one's god, or oracle, or essence, the deified *persona,* the grand mask of the comic animal. If it is not true, as the Greek choruses intoned, that Wisdom comes of suffering, then, maybe, as the Renaissance proclaimed with death's head intuition, "Ripeness is all." Ripeness: maturing, coming to fruition, the image drawn from nature, suggesting fulfillment of the human, achieved only in crisis and hastening, teleologically, to an end. "Blest fig's end," says Iago. One forgets there follows upon the wondrous idea of Ripeness in *King Lear* a sense of its absurdity, in Gloucester's equivocal remark: "And that's true too." Something like the enigmatic comedy of the gesture, no less spiritual for its scatology, of Leonardo's young Saint John the Baptist.

If in Socrates the unexamined life is not worth living, in Shakespeare it is the uncontested. Even in the sonnets, the boughs do not quiver in the cold, they *shake against* it. The serenity of *The Tempest* and the green world of *Cymbeline* follow the blood and blackness of *Macbeth,* the dazzling scrofula of *Troilus,* and the misanthropy of *Timon.* Even when terror undergoes a sea-change, strong in the memory of the Brave New World is the mudcaked animality of Caliban and all the assimilated rage of the great tragedies, up to the very horror of that "kill, kill, kill, kill, kill, kill!" Even from his grave, Shakespeare speaks like a dramatist:

> Good friend for Jesus sake forbeare,
> To digg the dust encloased heare;
> Blessed by ye man yt spares these stones
> And curst be he yt moves my bones.

That last warning struck me all the more when I saw the same epitaph in the parish church of Chipping Camden, the curse removed, as the eighteenth century revised away the "multitudinous seas incarnadine" and the almost unimaginable horror of Cordelia's death. I had visited Holy Trinity in Stratford on a day in late autumn. Leaving the grave, I returned to the churchyard, a perfect sonnet of morning frost and bare ruin'd choirs. There, looking toward the Avon, I saw in the middle of the gentle river—like a footnote from the Underground—a large sign in red block letters: GREAT DANGER, WEIR BELOW.

Great drama is committed to that DANGER, and to the mystery of that WEIR. The dullard Kuligin, in Chekov's

The Three Sisters, tells the story of a schoolmate who was "expelled from the fifth form because he could never understand *ut consecutivum.* Now he is frightfully poor and ill, and when I meet him I say, 'How are you, *ut consecutivum*?' 'Yes,' he says, 'that's just the trouble—*consecutivum*' . . . and then he coughs. . . ." The anecdote is part of that whole mystique of malfunction and irrelevance that gives Chekov's studies of provincial life a longevity that *Middletown* and the Kinsey reports will never have. Words, words, words. "Balzac was married in Berdichev." (*Pause.*) Nothing is more real than nothing, says Beckett after Democritus, defining the formal principle of the following sequence:

ANDREY. In Moscow you sit in a huge room at a restaurant; you know no one and no one knows you, and at the same time you don't feel a stranger. . . . But here you know everyone and everyone knows you, and yet you are a stranger—a stranger. . . . A stranger, and lonely. . . .

FERAPONT. Eh? (*A pause.*) And the same contractor says—maybe it's not true—that there's a rope stretched right across Moscow.

ANDREY. What for?

FERAPONT. I can't say, sir. The contractor said so.

ANDREY. Nonsense. . . .

For all his virtues in the enlightenment of a *non sequitur* reality, such a passage makes about half of Ionesco obsolete. Moreover, though Nothingness is confirmed, neither Andrey nor Ferapont is denied; the one's intelligence and the other's innocence come to the same end. The drama occurs at that impasse of human relations, no less human for the impasse, where the rest is silence, for the time being. History remains, a vague possibility. "It doesn't matter, it doesn't matter," says the doctor, reading the newspaper and humming "Tarara-boom-dee-ay!" "If we only knew, if we only knew!" says Olga, the music of the military band fading. Andrey pushes the perambulator in which Bobik is sitting. *Consecutivum*—that's the trouble, not stasis. WEIR BELOW.

However it ends, drama begins with those who won't

"Let be." *"L'audace, encore l'audace, et toujours l'audace."* Not all heroes are up to Danton's ethic, and if Hotspur is not entirely right that "out of this nettle danger we pluck this flower safety," at least we pluck from the drama's dedication to danger the courage to live in peaceful coexistence with the irremediable. "What do we do, Kate, when the visions fail us?" "We kneel down and pray, Mr. Blake." The prescription is lyric, the response dramatic. No mere quietism here, that voice expects results. In drama—how often have we heard it?—action is all. Though it may return us, inevitably will, to the mystery of that weir.

Andrey's lament to Ferapont is echoed by a village woman, cautioning her child at the end of John Whiting's *Saint's Day,* a bizarre, incoherent, and lovely play set in the English countryside: "Stella! We are strangers here, Stella." The child is performing a "grave dance" around a corpse who bears her name. It is impossible to say what it means, nor to resolve it, nor is it necessary. Among the new wave of English dramatists, socialist or angry or both, Whiting has not been searching for causes, because he believes all causes are failures. There is an Eliotic fall in the assertion of one of his characters that "it is not a question of finding but of losing the pieties, the allegiances, the loves"; but the final consideration for Whiting is not a matter of ideologies or postures or platforms, rather, literally, life and death. With or without the Bomb, "our fear is that the unknown hand is already at the switch." The sin of previous generations, with their passion for social exposé (the play's chief character is an octogenarian muckraker, now disgraced), was misinformation on the human condition, the failure to remind us as we convert history to the service of men that "the purpose of any memory—of any experience [is] to give foundation to the state of death." Truth and glibness mixed. Whiting knows that one of the chosen voices of intellectuals in this century is that which seems, prematurely, to have passed through nature to eternity. We have grown too chummy with Yorick's skull. The sin of the present generation is the disaffiliation it brings on, and which Whiting shares. *Saint's Day* reflects in action, and in a certain anarchic failure of form, the cost of setting limits on obligation, the risk of neutrality on aesthetic grounds, and the catastrophe of partial commitment. "There is always the responsibility—it must rest on someone."

Where courage fails, society like nature revenges itself. Disaffiliation invites the demonic. Indifference, recoiling into action, becomes the dupe of accident, as after the graveyard scene of *Hamlet*. The result: promiscuous slaughter. Today, in mass withdrawal from the horror behind we are almost passive before the horror ahead. Camus said the great philosophical problem of our time is suicide; the great practical problem is how to avoid deferring to solutions that are suicidal. Or, as Gerard Piel, publisher of *Scientific American,* said recently in San Francisco, we become victims of "the authors of frauds by computers. . . ." Nothing will come of nothing. Yet where to begin? Every profit a loss, every deterrent a possible disaster. Our reality is creepy. Literally. Think of the boon of penicillin bugged by the counter-revolution of staphylococcus. Would that the mystifications of modern society were even so imaginable as that weir. One hears the splashing of Grendel's dam everywhere, within and without. Whatever there is of "ontological anxiety" passes over to the structures we create, so that we find paranoia and schizophrenia in institutions. Heorot quivers in the cold. Is there some grim poetic justice in the fact that Mies van der Rohe's bronze consummation of the Bauhaus, which aimed to turn the blight of industry to art, was built for Seagram's? The whores sing in *The Rise and Fall of the City of Mahagonny*: "We must have whiskey, O you know why!"

In our time who can avoid serving the enemy? (I am not alone in having enjoyed the discomfiting benevolence of a grant from one of the mortal enemies of my childhood.) If Ionesco's *Rhinoceros* had the full courage of its excellent conceit, Berenger would have gone on protesting his humanity while changing, willy-nilly, into a beast. The comedy would have been realer if more repellent by denying egress to those in the market for evasion. We all go under. It is the way we go that counts. One hopes he will go when he goes like Ahab's Pequod, taking a living piece of heaven with him. But there we have it—that skeleton-beneath-the-skin-sensibility, part of the higher criticism and one of the clichés of chaos, missing the issue in its own way, dodging crisis. (It is curious that President Kennedy, after the Cuban rout and the Berlin hostilities, picked up the down-turned tone of the disciplines of despair, the realistic promise of his Inauguration speech returning, somewhat, on a tour through the Midwest.) If T. S. Eliot taught us anything of value, it is to learn to live with illusions by improving their quality. Not what do we do as we go under, but what do while we're here, I'd say, on the assumption the going under (yes, Old Possum, we must still give foundation to the state of death) will take care of itself.

"Nothing to be done." That's hardly the way a play should begin. However, a generation of incinerators, Hiroshima, and deterred deterrents lies between *Waiting for Lefty* and *Waiting for Godot*. And one of the illusions we've had to improve the quality of is that social problems are social. They are that, perhaps, but more than that—and it was not Dag Hammarskjöld but Jean Genet who gave us the better report on the Congo, a virtual prediction of the recent murder and dismemberment of thirteen Italian soldiers. (Recommended reading: *The Maids* as a minority view of our relations with Cuba.) It may be all right in wish fulfillment to get rid of social evil, as Giraudoux's Madwoman does, by pushing all the capitalists into the sewer, but it's another thing to get them anywhere near it so it can be done. Odets was saying: "Come on, let's do it—*now*!" But it was done when it was done, and done imperfectly. The New Deal was negotiated by experts, but it was improvisation nonetheless. Giraudoux, an elegant ironist, was saying, "Wouldn't it be nice if. . . ." Which is a way of putting the real issue into somebody else's head. Genet is saying, the issue murderously out in the open, "Look out, it's going to happen, it *is* happening—those knives are real." Only Genet, like the Envoy in *The Balcony,* is a master of obfuscation, and a pervert to boot. Can things be really that bad? we muse, fingering the selvage of *his* illusions, safe as only voyeurs can be.

"Security some men call the suburbs of hell,/ Only a dead wall between," says a Genetic character out of Jacobean drama. Look at our situation in Berlin, that dead wall. Any first-rate dramatist would nose out one of the greatest ironies in the crisis, the fact that when the Krupp munitions empire was put up for sale, nobody had enough money to buy it out. So it was restored to its proper owner and recently celebrated its 150th Anniversary. The New York *Times* reported, "Everyone,"—ministers, ambassadors, employees, and two thousand invited guests—"had kind words for the House of Krupp." Theodor Heuss, former president of West Germany, was the main speaker. He said there was nothing "basically sinful" in the firm's past. Only "hatred spurred by war" had created an image of Krupp as an "annex to hell" while huge munitions firms abroad were seen "in the hands of heavenly angels." I don't know what company Mr. Heuss keeps, but outside of Shaw, and except by indirection in defense planning, I've never heard a good word for munitions makers anywhere. For propriety's sake we generally keep them out of the way, like the Mummy in Strindberg's *Ghost Sonata.* May choirs of angels sing around them all, for as to a properer disposition of the House of Krupp, I'm not qualified to offer an alternative. I'm not sure, in fact, there is one. I do know that the theater cannot afford to put up, however, with the weird proposal that Germans, denazified, are just like other people; no more than it could put up with the equally astonishing idea that nobody is incapable of becoming a Nazi. I am. I insist upon it, like Berenger, *yet* there but for the grace of God and historical circumstance go I. There is an enormous conceptual difference between the Karamazovian idea that "we are all murderers" and that we are *nothing but* murderers. If the theater brings conflict to crisis, it's because our conflicts are aggravated by the plague of choice, the most tortuous of which is, indeed—in an age where everything, not only the nefarious but the benign, conspires against it—the choice to remain human. Which includes facing up to crisis without hypocrisy and without snap judgment.

Where drama really takes place, judgment stops short. The Eichmann trial, which sent Portia packing back to Belmont, demonstrated this in an unexpected way. One could be predictably stupefied by Eichmann's discriminating between the assertion of one witness that it was four million and another that it was five million Jews he was responsible for killing. What monster was this? Yet when the prosecutor Hausner asked Eichmann whether he was guilty, the trial took a sharp turn into the special stupefactions of drama. Eichmann, with wondrous control it seemed, started to distinguish between moral and legal guilt, whereupon Hausner raised a finger at him and thundered: "Answer yes or no!" I don't know to what perverse instinct I may be testifying, but *at that moment* loyalties were annihilated for me, and I was with Eichmann.

Drama being a perpetual present moment, it may cut *you* to the brain. You are there, defenseless, guilty creature sitting at a play. What you lose by way of status and self-possession (*Einfühling* or *Verfremdung,* drama sucks you in), you make up by full exposure. You are confronted with —what else?—yourself. That doesn't mean everybody else is excluded; if they were, you could escape the issue by claiming discrimination. The theater is nothing if not universal. Yet in a real Theater—I am not speaking of that politic convocation of worms where people meet for self-edification and digestion's sake—there is no safety in numbers either. Death or a lemon pie, you must face the issue. You are responsible for your foolishness as for your atrocities, and you may be horrified at the way one brings on the other, as when Lear asks his daughters to say they love him.

And there is sorcery in the way, facing it all, brought nearly to exhaustion as *Lear* brings you, you become more available to yourself.

"You live badly, my friends. It is shameful to live like that." The charge may be gently reproachful, objective, as with Chekov. It may be partisan and partial, as with Arthur Miller. "Attention must be paid!" You may hear a false accent in the voice, but you pay attention because the play insists on forcing its conflict to crisis, as when Biff forces Willie, already half-beaten, to confront himself. Whipping out the gaspipe, Biff says: "All right, phony! Then let's lay it on the line." The drama might be deeper if Miller did the same for Biff, who is clear about his failure but a little woolly about his aspirations. Still, we may be thankful for half-truths in a world of manifold illusions. Real drama, at some point, insists on laying it on the line. O'Neill's Hickey won't let the bums be content with their pipe dreams, to the misbegotten limit of his own delusions; nor, for all his massive clumsiness (about which we are sometimes too facile), would O'Neill be content with his own. If there is evasion in the confessions of *Long Day's Journey into Night,* it is beyond O'Neill's control, and he knows it, painfully: "The *makings* of a poet. No, I'm afraid I'm like the guy who is always panhandling for a smoke. He hasn't even got the makings. He's only got the habit. I couldn't touch what I tried to tell you just now. I just stammered. That's the best I'll ever do. I mean, if I live. Well, it will be faithful realism, at least. Stammering is the native eloquence of us fog people." Its pathetic, but we have nothing more honest in American drama.

Though recently we have acquired another sort of voice. "I'm crazy, you bastard," says the psychopath in *Zoo Story,* at the dead level of conflict. In drama, either that's my bench or yours, however we may be taught, and believe in, the value of sharing. There is a sense in which that line speaks for modern art, which has at its best been predicated on theories formulated by sinners and strangers, apostates and traitors, perverts and sickmen, and by all the holy demonism that is our romantic legacy and agony.

It's a wonder we don't run away. Some do. Given the strategies of demonic art, the drama takes their flight, with Ubuesque pride, as a mark of *its* efficiency. Which speaks in the language of excommunication. It's funny, but then it's no longer funny. Ubu mourns, and becomes Clov. The laughter turns elegiac. A friend of mine once objected to Beckett's *Endgame* because "you can't call the characters on the telephone." True. But if you could, you'd only be talking to yourself. *Endgame* is the crisis of exhaustion playing itself out in the suburbs of hell. It has the eloquence of blood below the eyelids of the nearly dead. It comes into the world of men and affairs like a scarcely audible bell out of the enshrouding fog—no less alarming for its remoteness. It is just such a story as Horatio might tell if he tried to fulfill the impossible burden placed on him by Hamlet in those exquisite dying lines: "Absent thee from felicity a while,/ And in this harsh world draw thy breath in pain/ To tell my story." How tell it? Where that story really took place, Horatio never was. To tell it, he'd have to re-enact the play, he'd have to *become* Hamlet. But wasn't it he who said, " 'T were to consider too curiously to consider so." Failing to tell the story, he'd become Hamm.

In such a play, rehearsing visions of greatness around "the insane root," the magic is blacker than we might like; but you can't run away because where in the world would you go? No modern drama comes closer to making you feel what Socrates meant when he said: "There's a doctrine whispered in secret that man has no right to open the door and run away; this is a great mystery which I do not quite understand." I don't presume to understand it either, but it is a mystery which informs all the great drama I know, and which constitutes for me the true condition of theater. It is this sense of the theatrical event that must have kept the audience in their seats at the first performance of Euripides' *Trojan Women,* one of the bravest plays ever written. In full daylight, Euripides said to the assembled Athenians, a people proud of being the most civilized in the world, that they were essentially a bunch of barbarians. They had just finished the siege of the innocent island of Melos, which they had assaulted for commercial reasons. Not content with victory, they had sacked the place. The play's prophecy of retribution on the Greeks (it dealt with the Trojan War, but the prophecy was writ large and contemporary) was actually fulfilled in the Sicilian expedition, virtually the end of the Athenian empire.

All the traditions of the Greek theater permitted Euripides to deal with such a crisis, because that theater, as we have been told, was central to the culture. Now that theater is only marginal, it may have to clamor more to get at the issues, but it will be worthless if it doesn't. The so-called Theater of the Absurd has been fighting a guerrilla war. It is the form of the Resistance, coming up out of Kafka's Burrow. Its passion is bare survival, and it uses every beanbag, brassknuckle, and Molotov cocktail that can be salvaged from the wreck of theatrical history. It has the scapegoat *noblesse* of the Underground. And it awaits the time. The theater, it knows, needs more than piddling heroes and tight little emotions; it needs actors who, honoring that other, more inhibited, underground activity of the studio, *can* tear a passion to tatters, and it needs plays with a wildly civilized insurgence. It must seize with exuberance the task of being the public art of crisis in an age where crisis is a social and moral norm. And it must not merely escape into the apparatus of ritual and incantation, compounding the spiritual plague by making a ceremony of it. One can be as square in ritual as in realism, and the best of those dramatists whose guardian angel is Artaud avoid the deadbeat of an easy demonism. The theater needs to learn again to contend with the world out of which history is made, men creating events, events determining men; a world of realpolitik, sneak attacks, and holy wars, no less hieratic for its industry and no less hallucinated for its systems and categories, bureaucrats and dossiers.

As a public form, the theater has an illustrious history that is by nature opposed either to false silence or false security; it is a place where, strictly speaking, secrets are illegal. It knows about crisis as other forms don't because it is virtually a State of Crisis—material, time-serving, collaborative, and adulterated by competing aesthetic claims as by competing temperaments. More than any other form, it calls constantly for its own purification: Eleonora Duse wants to kill all the actors; Gordon Craig wants marionettes and towers of light; Jacques Copeau wants to sweep the boards or take young blood into the country to kiss the soil again. They never succeed, but they live out the issues. Because it aspires to function, however marginal it may temporarily be, at the dead center of the community, the theater is more subject to compromise and adjustment than other forms. That is its shame and—when, somehow, in the strange bipartisanship of personal will and cultural ripeness the theater's inherent corruption is mastered—the source of its formal glory.

The theater has greater possibilities than other forms because it takes greater risks. This is a question of nature as much as choice. As it moves toward popular acceptance (and note the way even the anti-drama is becoming fashionable), it must beware of an excess of its own communal instinct. It must not be cabined or confined by demands for conformity, even to its own techniques of outrage, and all the other conspiracies of social approval; nor must it be tamed by good will and benevolence. God bless the medium, it is individual and protestant to its corporate bones and cannot help but look for trouble. For every saint who wants to purify there are a thousand who think they love the theater and unwittingly, or pusillanimously, betray it. You who work in the theater: learn to trust the trouble as it sings! For the real theater, memorializing another Golgotha, cannot be appeased by either false optimism or facile anguish or official realism. "After all, life—public or private—can often be carried on," says the Prime Minister of England, "with reasonable satisfaction on what a cynic once called a healthy basis of mutual distrust." In the theater, distrust is distrust, there is finally no hidden agenda. The theater is responsible to that distrust—where it comes from and what it does, its real sources, its real motives, its real consequences. Those declared, the theater leaves us—as far as humanly possible —to our own resources.

GEORGE P. ELLIOTT

Why Are They Driving Me Crazy?

SOME PEOPLE do not believe in California. I do. There are now anonymous signboards in Iowa announcing "There is no California." I don't go along with that. Some people grant that there is a California, all right, but wish there wasn't. Las Vegas is sort of the chrome-plated toilet of Southern California, and last fall the sheriffs over in Nevada were talking about setting up machine guns at their border to keep out Californians fleeing the bomb to come. I don't go along with that either. California isn't essentially different from the rest of the nation. It's the same, only steeper. This state at the brink of the country is so steep that change roars over it as over rapids.

The devices the world is throwing at me aren't so new—follies, lies, murders, that sort of thing—but some of them are new *to me* and they're certainly coming at me a lot faster than they used to. They didn't all happen in the last six weeks. Neither did they happen just in California. But I've been gone six and a half years, and here and now is where they're getting to me.

I keep wondering why people are trying to drive me crazy. Not more than a handful of them know that I exist, but they're after me all the same. Some of them want to get it over with quick and kill me. Here are some of the reasons I think so. I didn't make up any of these facts. Nearly all of them are to be found in the newspapers. The rest I picked up from friends, professors, reliable witnesses. It's just the way I interpret the facts that shows how crazy I am.

Everybody expects lunacies to happen down in Southern California. But this Christmas there was a new one which got to me. They put little Christmas trees on graves—plain trees, trees sprayed blue, beballed trees. Why? What earthly reason? Maybe they did it so I'd go batty trying to figure out why. That's as good a reason as any.

Half the people in Southern California make their living off the war to come. When you talk to them they don't seem to want a war. They expect lots of people to be killed in it, themselves included unless they're lucky. Do they oppose the coming of a war? Not at all. Their life work is devoted to bringing the war about. Why? Why? The best I can come up with is that they would rather go along with things—make a lot of money, have fun, do what they're told good Americans ought to do—than survive. Anyone can see it is insane of me to think such thoughts. Surely it makes no sense to say that lots of ordinary people prefer a wall-to-wall TV home to the continued existence of their city, their family, themselves. But what the hell ARE they up to?

A friend of mine in Los Angeles was one of several actors who read the Birch Society Bluebook over an FM station. The purpose of doing this was to give people a chance to see what the Birch Society is like in its own words. His house was threatened with bombing. The police said they would not protect his home till after it had been bombed, as two ministers' homes were. You see what they're up to? Driving me crazy trying to figure out whose side who is on. The L.A. police now—they're tricky. When it became publicly known that private guards had been hired to protect this actor's home, the police came around after all and guarded it for the rest of the week free. I'm still guessing.

Last Fourth of July, the climax to the fireworks program on the Marina in San Francisco was a mushroom-shaped cloud. Hurray for the red, white and blue—BOOM. Still, as you'd expect, *most* things aren't so obvious up around the Bay Area, especially in that citadel of reasonableness, the University of California. But they're peculiar.

A few weeks ago some earnest students decided they wanted to hear a talk by Gus Hall, head of the U.S. Communist Party. The University YMCA is hospitable to serious discussion groups. The man in charge of the Y belongs to the logical class of madman: he believes that freedom of speech applies not only to the right but also to the wrong and the left. A meeting was scheduled and announced. A considerable fuss was made in the papers over the event. An old alumnus had previously announced that he had intended to bequeath the University a million dollars; now he said that he would withdraw the money if Gus Hall was allowed to speak on campus. (The Y is neither part of the University nor on the campus.) In the evening of the meeting, the room filled to capacity well before the scheduled time. Gus Hall gave his talk and answered questions; the meeting as such was unexceptionable. Afterward a good many students stood around chatting. The millionaire alumnus joined then, and they talked with him. A week or so later he announced that he had changed his mind; he was bequeathing several million dollars worth of real estate to the University, and no strings attached.

So what do *I* dwell on? Less on the fact that the old geezer was able to change his mind than that he almost didn't. Hadn't he ever listened to a Communist before? Anyway, he hasn't changed his mind all that much. Now he declares a course on Communism should be given at the University—by a certified anti-Communist. Even the Berkeley

High School students recently knew enough to reject a propaganda course like that. Also I dwell on the poetry prize he donated separately from his millions. Being a poet, he wanted to encourage poetry; he is giving an annual two hundred dollars which will be divided five ways among the student poets. How do I, a poet and a friend of poets, react? I look this millionaire's two-hundred-dollar five-way gift horse in the mouth and hereby, on behalf of nobody else, kick it in the teeth as hard as I can.

Or take the case of many hundreds of Cal students rioting this semester to get into a course in introductory physics. Lots of them lined up all night, camping out in sleeping bags. They mobbed the doors in the morning. Girls fainted, vomited over themselves and their neighbors, were knocked down and trampled on. Who teaches the course? The only man most of them will ever have seen in the flesh who is trying to kill them, Edward Teller. Why are they crowding to him? To shame him with forgiving glances? No, they are not Jesus-Christians. To stab him to death? No, not knife-Christians. Then why? To kiss the hand that promises to kill them? Maybe, but that's not what they said when asked. A lot of them said they wanted to get into the course (enrollment was to be limited to 900) to get a snap C or an easy A. An official said the whole thing was insignificant. A faculty member said the main motive of the students was to oppose an unpopular science requirement. A couple of the students who were there told me it was obvious that many of the students in the mob were enjoying themselves, were doing it to enjoy themselves. I'm dizzy.

The crowd to enroll in Freshman English trampled a girl into the hospital. The same variety of speculations: the kids did it to have some excitement, to get the teacher of their choice (whom they seldom knew), out of existentialist boredom, to defy the administration. This last explanation particularly makes my gears clash: because they resent the administration, they hurt one another. In my day we burned effigies.

In both these incipient riots the police were alerted and present, but did nothing to keep order. Was it from the natural stupidity of policemen? Was it personal incompetence? Was it because of orders from above? Whose orders? Why given? No more speculation! One thing I have learned from *them*: the simpler the better. The simplest explanation of this is that it was done to drive me crazy. The only question that matters is why this huge waste of effort was made. It would have been much more efficient to kill me outright.

I keep telling myself it's not just California. It was in another, unspectacular state that a sporting goods store advertised: "As an extra precaution for Civil Defense we would recommend that you investigate a .22 cal. hand gun as a potential survival weapon." Falloutshelterism was stimulated by the President of the United States and neighbor-shooting was blessed by a priest of the largest Christian church. It's not just California, but here and now is where my neighbors are, and they look like the Kennedy-type bomb-Americans to me. Most of them are Christians but they don't look like Jesus-Christians to me, they look like pistol-Christians.

There's a writer around town who tells people I used to be a Card-Carrying Member of the Communist Party and that he has seen a letter I wrote denouncing him to the FBI. (I wonder how the letter went. "Dear J. Edgar: Keep an eye on Joe Blow. He's a 100% unAmerican Commie-lover. *I ought to know*. Patriotically, John Doe, CCMCP.") This writer is a very intelligent man, moderately famous, much admired by many followers; he has strings to his bow. I never hurt him. I scarcely know him, met him twice, once 22 years ago, once 15 years ago, both times at parties. Yet he bothers to slander me. Maybe I wrote a letter to the FBI in my sleep, the way I used to walk in my sleep. How can I trust myself? Maybe I joined the Communist Party in my sleep and lost the card before I woke up.

Eight years ago we lived next door to the Tellers. My daughter played with Dr. Teller's children. I sometimes wondered gloomily what they were putting together in the toy closet. Vest-pocket H-bombs? What a vile mind I have. According to *Life,* which is a good place to learn about *them,* Teller made up alphabet rhymes for his children when they were little. "A stands for atom; it is so small No one has ever seen it at all." Guess what B stands for. I never really talked with Teller. All the same, I got a strong impression of his sincerity: he wanted to kill me for my own good. It's an impression which his recent book hasn't changed a bit.

My office is in Dwinelle Hall, a ten-year-old classroom and office building. It is modern and soulless, as one would expect, but also it was laid out by a man whose intention was to drive all its occupants batty. One friend has been quartered there from the beginning and has yet to remember the rationale of its arrangement, even the way the rooms are numbered, and she has tried. A bit over a year ago a former acquaintance and present colleague, whose office is now across the hall from the one I'm in, was talking with his teaching assistant when a former student appeared in the doorway. He pulled a shotgun from under his coat, shot the teaching assistant dead in the back, and blasted the professor in the left jaw. The man had come intending to kill only the professor, who he thought was a Communist. He shot both to be on the safe side. He had food cached away in the hills —premature falloutshelterism—and thought he was starting World War III.

You might immediately think, as I did when I heard about it two thousand miles away, that it was clearly the murderer that was mad. Wrong again. It's me. To a demented glance like mine, a chief of campus police would seem to be there partly to prevent men with shotguns from shooting professors and students and certainly not in any way to encourage attacks on them. Not a bit of it. This one let the reporters understand that the professor had been associated with all sorts of inflammatory causes. (He was publicly opposed to idolaters of big-time collegiate sports, and had been scurrilously attacked for this opposition. He had supported the Cal students who had the year before been manhandled by the San Francisco police for demonstrating against the House Un-American Activities Committee.) The worst of the local papers the next day gave the impression that the killer was a man of respectable family whose excessive zeal had been inflamed by an egghead opponent of anti-Communists. Maybe my shot colleague is the same kind of Communist that McCarthy used to hint that he saw and that the Birchites say they see—a Communist like Eisenhower, for example, or Truman.

How do I know what he does in his sleep? How can any of us know what we join in our sleep? Maybe that's why I've been sleeping badly lately. If only I would quit trying to oppose their driving me crazy: then I could at least do what I like in my sleep, as they do wide awake.

Like this shooting business again. It *still* seems to me that an important official of the University should instantly have come to his defense with a public statement. Wasn't the shotgun attack on his body enough? Does he merit the least slur on his reputation? The President of the University was petitioned to come to the professor's aid with a public statement. He did not, though after a few days, when the killer had been caught and had confessed, even the worst of the papers allowed that he was mad and the victims both innocent. I've heard of an explanation for the President's silence, given by a philosophy professor who fancies himself as an *eminence grise* and who is a mouse behind the throne. "The main duty of the University is to keep out of the papers." In spite of the strain it puts me under, I continue to think the main duty of the University is to teach and to do research and, in this particular case, to support one of its own. But no. They know better. Maybe someday I will too.

I'm far enough gone so that the notion has occurred to me that some bomb-American might read this piece and show up at my door one afternoon intending to start the Third World War on me. Why not?

I'm even far enough gone not to care which of them

starts the next war, or why, or how. A psychopathic Russian lieutenant in a missile station, a submarine U.S. captain with a faulty trigger, De Gaulle, Macmillan the gray—what difference does it make to us corpses-to-be? Yet it seems to matter a lot to *them*.

I hope soon to be far enough gone to understand why it matters so much to them who starts the next, last war. Maybe then I could care too. If only they would make an actuality out of the master idea of Dr. Teller. (I am sure he shares my views on private bombings and the assassinating of Cal professors.) If only there were fifty thousand trucks roaming the highways day and night, each capable of firing a nuclear bomb, each manned by a carefully screened lieutenant and sergeant, both of whom would be trained to operate the mechanism. Then there wouldn't be anything else worth worrying about.

HERBERT GOLD

Death in Miami Beach

THE STATE OF MADNESS can be defined partly as an extreme of isolation of one human being from everyone else. It provides a model for dying. Only an intermittent and fragmentary awareness of others interrupts the black folding of the layers of self upon each other—this also defines the state of that dilemma known as "mental health."

There is a false madness induced by the accidents of isolation which prisoners, travelers, and the very ill may sometimes experience without giving up their return ticket. Surely you out there all know what I mean from your own troubles and painful decisions. To say that it is false madness does not soften its extremity. The mask of existence fits harshly on your skin, but it is in fact your only skin; and when harshly your skin is peeled off—beneath it you are naked and your naked isolation is no joy to you.

During a period of work on a long job of writing in the winter of 1958, I deliberately withdrew myself from all those who knew my name and traveled by automobile in slow stages through the deep South to Miami Beach, Key West, Havana, and finally back up toward Detroit. No one asked me to write a novel, no one asked me to go away; but I did anyway. I was tempted by the prospect of dreaming through my story amid a pleasant chaos of sun and sea, all other responsibilities suspended, and so I arranged it for myself.

Work is very fine, but after the day's work, isolation, silence, and death seemed to follow me through the zazzy carnival of Miami, the casual resort indolence of Key West, and the smoky, blistered elegance of a tourist's Havana. In Havana, from the rooftop of the Ambos Mundos Hotel, I could see Batista's police loafing with their weapons in front of public buildings; occasionally there were bombs; once a body happened to be left in the street and people hurried by as if they knew nothing, nothing, nothing at all but the next step before them.

At Key West, a few days before Christmas, I visited the turtle slaughterhouse. It is one of the few tourist attractions on this spot of island, "North Havana," raised far out into the sea off the coast of Florida. Visitors take their kiddies by the hand and lead them to see the nice turtles.

Before being killed and canned, the turtles swim in dense kraals, bumping each other in the murky water, armor clashing, dully lurching against the high pens. Later, trussed on a plank dock, they lie unblinking in the sun, their flippers pierced and tied. The tough leather of their skin does not disguise their present helplessness and pain. They wear thick, sun-hardened accumulations of blood at their wounds. Barbados turtles, as large as children, they belong to a species which has been eliminated locally by ardent harvesting of the waters near Key West, but the commercial tradition still brings them here to be slaughtered. Crucified like thieves, they breathe in little sighs, they gulp, they wait.

At a further stage, in the room where the actual slaughtering occurs, the butchers stride through gore in heavy boots. The visitor must proceed on a catwalk; a misstep will plunge him into a slow river of entrails and blood. Because it was near Christmastime, the owners of the plant had installed a speaker system for musical divertissement of the butchers, and while the turtles dried under the sun or lay exposed to the butchers' knives, Christmas bells tolled out, electronically amplified, *God Rest Ye Merry, Gentlemen,* or the Bing Crosby recording of *Adeste Fideles.*

These commercial details are not intended to support a special plea on behalf of the humane harvesting of Barbados turtles. In fact, let me grant that I sought out this scene and visited the abattoir without having any proper business there at all: merely curiosity and the need to confirm my imagination about it. I should be judged for vulgarity by the man who chooses out of purity not to follow me, not by the man I saw lurking outside, with a face ravaged by the horrified fascination which makes it impossible for him to visit his dreams. What had I done which he could not permit himself? Was I filthied, was I weakened by pleasure but obscurely nourished, was I fed on coveted turtle joys after trampling in turtle blood? Had I asked permission from the butcher and plied a knife with my own hands on the belly of one of the slow, unblinking, dragon-headed, ancient seabeasts? And did it arch its graceful dragon neck in reproach as I stabbed? He stared at me like a jealous lover, imagining my wickedness, rabid and hopeless, wanting to bury his head in the reek on my hands.

Most of us turn from the vision of death only out of weakness, and this is no turning from death. Serve up your turtle steak, gourmet friend, with no protest from me; I'll eat at your table. ("A nice rendition," one gentleman said of Bing Crosby to his wife.) Turtle is tasty, somewhat gamy meat. Protein nourishes the brain—brings oxygen and freedom.

A few days later, in Miami Beach, I participated in two trivial accidents. My hotel was in one of the oldest, therefore least expensive, parts of the town, only a short block from the sea and a short block from restaurants and therefore very convenient to my casual schedule: breakfast at Whelan's, a stretch of writing, a long swim, lunch, a pleasant bit of loafing on the beach, then perhaps some sun-baked work at my typewriter on the tar roof ("solarium"), and another swim before dinner. I had the habit in the morning of disregarding the elevator, hurrying down a back stairway of the Webster Hotel, through an alley, and so shortcutting to the drugstore. One day, wearing tennis shoes, I felt an evil slide and crunch underfoot, and knew first by the shrinking in my heart and then by simple inspection that I had stepped on a small animal.

It seemed to be a variety of tropical cockroach. It had been perhaps an inch and a half long, longer with its wings spread, and it had strayed from the raised platform nearby where the hotel stored its rubbish. Now it lay twitching, legs scrambling in the air without moving, and a yellow ooze seeped from its body within the crushed carapace. I suppose it was already dead despite all this nervous movement. I went for a walk, told myself that this was a silly matter to be fretful about (I was merely isolated), and finally took my habitual breakfast: orange juice, scrambled eggs, toast, coffee.

An hour later the dead beast was glued by its own innards to the paving of the alley; the Florida sun was moving through the sky above it. But now there was also a row of ants leading to it, another leading away, like twin caterpillars dissembling their unity of purpose. They were not merely eating, of course, they were carrying off the meat to their hill someplace. But the dead roach still twitched, and when the tickling jaws struck, it fluttered, squeezed, blindly pushed in its place. The ants went scrambling away, each carrying its minuscule steak.

All afternoon the shell of the roach lay there. Its row of legs no longer waved of their own power, but there were still tremors as the eating ants tugged at it. Unfatigued and busy, they were determined to wipe this slate clean.

Shortly before dark I again came down the back stairway. Now the familiar arena had changed. Another foot had struck, more strange and haphazard than my own. The shell of the roach was destroyed; there were also dead ants freckling the stone; stillness and death. The ants were suddenly individual in death; the undulating columns were erased. And the work of eating was permanently interrupted for both eaters and eaten.

The next morning when I walked through the alley no sign remained. A sweeper had done her work; there were straight, mechanical striations—a friendly broom. Good. But I bent to look for some sign or memorial to the departed beast on this stretch of alley which I now knew very well. There was none. Marks of broom; new arrangements of pebbles and dust; history here had entered upon an epoch which was strange to me.

Then finally a homely death entered what might pass for society in my isolated Miami Beach—the world of the soda fountain at Whelan's, where strollers came into an air-conditioned place to shake off the sand of the beach, sip a Coke, buy lotions and plastic sunglasses, and sometimes order a quick meal.

I was taking my breakfast, according to my habit, on a stool at the counter. By this time I was acquainted with Frank, the short-order cook, who had emigrated from Second Avenue in New York twenty years ago for his health and, for sweet health's sake, still managed to cover the leathery pouched skin of age with a fierce Miami tan, despite his long hours in Whelan's service. It relieved the silence to exchange a few morning words with a man who by now knew my face: "Two scrambled light."

"Same as yesterday, Mister."

"Yes, like yesterday." (Triumph in my voice: He remembers me!) "Whole-wheat toast. You got marmalade today?"

"Marmalade." Frank knew my face and my eggs.

Other eaters, like me, were forking up eggs and grits

and sipping their Cokes or coffee when the woman entered. She was blotched with sunburn, had a swollen nose, and a mouth open so wide for noise that all her features were distorted. Emitting emergency alarm signals, turning her head and staring, demanding passage, demanding attention, a shouting vehicle, she pushed a stumbling old man along with her. "Ohh," she screamed, "a Bromo! For God's sake a Bromo! My husband is dying, a Bromo, for God's sake!"

The man's face was blue and he seemed barely conscious. He swayed stiffly as she steered him toward a stool near me.

"Oh, a Bromo right now, please!" she wailed.

Frank, behind the counter, looked sideways at her, pretended the impossible—that he did not hear her—and went on making a bacon-lettuce-and-tomato sandwich on whole-wheat toast, light on the mayonnaise.

Two or three of us jumped up to support the old man. His skin had a thick purple glow that said death to all our eyes.

"Oh, have mercy, a Bromo for my poor husband!" the woman screamed. "He didn't do nothing to you! For God's sake why don't you give it to him?"

Floundering, I watched Frank finish the bee-ell-tee, slide it onto a plate, and hand it to his customer. The hot-rodder bent his head to the spilling sandwich and ate as if his life depended on it, thrustingly. In the meantime, the pharmacist, a short man in a white coat, sweating profusely despite the air conditioning, came bustling from his cubicle and said, "Heart attack? You want I should call a doctor, Missus?"

"Ohh, please, dear God, a Bromo!" she shouted.

"I'll call a doctor, he'll be right over."

"Bromo for a dying man! Why don't you give it to him? Mercy, mercy!"

The pharmacist was on the telephone and the howling woman subsided in shrill spasms. Her husband swayed on the stool, his eyes shut, while his wife leaned sobbing against his back to keep him from toppling onto the ground. She refused to let anyone touch him in order to lay him out on the floor—someone's idea—as if this ministry would commit him once and for all to the hands of death. Naturally, my innards shrank from this; the layers of the self closed tight; the flower of feeling was shut, sealed. I wanted to rush in some place, rush away; strike, destroy, *run*; kill Frank, kill the hotrodder, because a man was dying and nobody could do anything. Thus righteousness substitutes for being straight with the world. I was sly and scared. Thus I occupied myself with rage at my friend Frank, who pretended to hear nothing and stubbornly refused to make the glass of Bromo Seltzer.

During the five minutes before the doctor arrived, the scene altered rapidly and tensely. Of course, all the breakfasters but the determined hotrodder stopped their eating. The kid in the leather jacket asked for pretzels with his Coke for sustained strength behind the wheel. The rest of us drifted, lurking behind the sick man on his stool. His wife wept and cursed and heaved out her sobs because no one would supply a Bromo.

Then abruptly the man shook himself and opened his eyes and tried to stand up. He stumbled; his wife pushed him back onto the stool. He shook his head and mumbled. Then rapidly the purple color diminished; his eyes stopped their blind rolling; he began to talk with his wife. He was returning to the living. He and his wife had a whispered consultation. She nodded rapidly at him, like a bird.

Suddenly she alighted and flew out the door. The man, left behind on the stool, said hoarsely, "Lemme have a glass of water, will you, pal?"

Frank gave him the water.

Now the doctor entered, rolling his sleeves down and carrying his black bag open. He had apparently run a block in the tropical morning heat.

"Haha!" said the formerly dying man. Just like that: "Hahaha! Hi, Doc!"

"You're the sick man?" said the doctor. "Let's see now—"

"Hahaha! Don't touch me, Doc," said the old man, leaning away. "Listen, Doc, it's a funny thing. My wife gets herself all excited—aggravated."

"You mean you're all right?" the doctor said.

"Just like a little attack was all I had, hahaha," said the old man.

"You're okay?"

"Look, Doc, I ain't been eating right, you know, enjoying myself, hahaha. A little attack. I get them sometimes. Like a little attack is all."

"Okay," said the doctor firmly, "you don't want me to look at you? Okay." He nodded briskly to the pharmacist, said, "I've got a patient in my office," and trotted off again into the heat.

The old man smiled and gazed without malice at Frank, who had refused him the Bromo. Instead of leaving a tip he left him one word of explanation before he headed off after his wife. The word was deposited on the counter behind him with an apologetic smile: "Constipation."

Eggs in the plates of all the late breakfasters were left cold and shiny. The hotrodder alone had finished his sandwich, Coke, and pretzels, and left whistling. Angry at last, I discharged an unformulated hostility on Frank: "Why the devil didn't you give the man his Bromo?"

His reply seems an obvious bit of logical disquisition at this remove, but there in the shadow of panic and crisis it struck me with the force of revelation. Rubbing a dirty cloth on the counter—formulating and reformulating a smear of grease before me—he said, "If he was dying of a heart attack, what good would a Bromo do him? And if he was not dying, what good is a Bromo?"

"Yes, but."

"So I have to do my job, but I don't have to listen to nuts."

"But you didn't say anything! That woman was hysterical."

He looked at me with undisguised pity for my ignorance. "That's why I didn't say anything. I been in trouble for saying things before, I learned."

He went back to work; the pharmacist was back in his cubicle, counting pills into a bottle; the doctor had returned to his office. It was eleven o'clock and Frank took down the sign about the breakfast special. A man came in frightened to ask for the special, and Frank pointed to the sign, which was upside down on the counter, and said, "It's five minutes after eleven already. But I'll give it to you." The look of despair faded from the man's face.

In a few days I finished my own job and began the long drive out of the false Florida summer into the northern winter, my heels passing over all sorts of unfelt beasties, my gullet accepting steaks and chops, my heart leaping with no better welcome to death than before. In Detroit my daughter asked me, "What's God's last name? How big is the whole world? Where do you go when you die?"

The foregoing inconclusive words were written two years ago. Now I have seen fit to return to my cafeteria-and-old-folks slum on lower Collins Avenue, and ostensibly for the same lure of cheap sun, sky, water, beach, boredom. I write, I swim. I stroll on Lincoln Road, I eat steaks and pizza, I sniff the sea with my sunburnt beak, I suck in my belly and run barefoot on the sand, I sleep, I write. In front of one of the new hotels I found a nude in plaster, beckoning, with her hand lifted as if hitching a ride. All aboard, you masturbators. Some of the fruit juice and hamburger stands have disappeared; new ones have opened. The Ellis Department Store, Here Since 1919, is closed, looks ransacked, has a box of Fruit of the Loom T-shirts spilled in the window and a U.S. Federal Court bankruptcy notice affixed to its sealed door.

I met a waitress in a restaurant which advertises nine-course dollar dinners. She has a pretty, lively, thirty-five-year-old girl's face, with all the black brightness of eye a man could want; she turns out to be Corsican and we speak

French; an artillery sergeant brought her to Florida and apparently tired of her brightness of eye. She has a rattling Corsican accent, likes Edith Piaf records, and gives me extra shrimp bits in my shrimp bits salad. So some things change. Last time I heard no Edith Piaf and earned no extra forkfuls of shrimp. The sirloin steak she brings me spreads its wings and seems ready to flop off the plate. My gut talks French and I take ease in the flattery of food. I wait and at last she slips into my booth with me and sighs. It is eleven o'clock, time to begin real life. Her history is sad. I feel obliged to offer some recompense for the evil done her by men and luck, and so I listen, wondering how her eyes can remain so bright as the disasters and disillusionments unroll.

When I said good night, she replied with a funny, rapidly fiddling, diddling, twenty-one-fingered gesture at her mouth. I asked what it meant. "Fun and glee!" she said, "fun and glee! *Maintenant je suis une vraie Américaine.*" Her eyes burn like stars, but like the stars, she has darkness between them.

A day and a night and another day. The first week passes.

I eat salty bagels in the sun, I listen to the teenage girls after school with their curious mixture of Florida cracker and Bronx accents. I go back into the damp of my room—the peculiar dank assault of cheap tropical bedrooms—and think my novel through once again, examining the pile of manuscript with my intentions in motion like a column of ants working over the struggling body of an insect. And when the life seems to weaken, I leave it and go out onto the beach or into the street.

Madness consists partly in an extreme of isolation? Partly. But the demented tumble down from their associations and memories into other associations and memories; they are sent away into the future with a map of the past which conforms to no agreed past and to no other map—and yet it is their only chart, their history and route, their needs which are unfailingly present. The lonely traveler also brutally inflicts absolute possession of his movements upon the endless day, and the novelty of what he sees joins him in yet another way to his deepest desires and dreads. He returns, he never lets go. There is no escape even in isolation; there is no isolation, merely interrupted and distorted association, until death claims us. Then every man is an island entire of itself.

In love, we seek freedom and purity even more than the comfort of diminished isolation. Those few fortunate ones who have the talent can bear the paradox of love. The rest of us are harassed by our contradictory demands—*join me, make me free*. With age and aging, the model of all voyages (learn and grow, diminish and weary), comes final approach to the ultimate simplicity which love seeks to confound—death. A paradox forever out of balance to answer a grave black simplicity: *we are ill used*. The facts we make for ourselves disappoint the intentions with which we make them. The opposable thumb, which is said to be responsible for civilization and history, gives us no answers here, though with it we can grasp our pens and break insects in our hands. Finally we die, opposable thumbs and all.

In the meantime, I visit my story. We exchange visits. I laugh over it, frown and worry over it, and urge it forward. Then I leave it for the Miami streets. The book follows me; it does not let me visit unaccompanied; it enters me instead and I try to shake it off as an adept at voodoo fights against possession by the importunate god. The opposable thumb is of no use in this contest; both the prize and the weapons have reached beyond tools, even tools of thinking; I am the quadruple god's horse—dream of love, hope of meaning, joy of power, relish in being. Too much burden on one soul. Who asked me to feel sorry or glad for others? They were merely pious who asked me. Why follow their orders? I decide: I *won't*. But I cannot escape my self, which also gives orders. The flower of feeling opens; the flower shuts; it obeys the freshness of weather. All emotion flowing from health or illness partakes of the pathetic fallacy, identifying moral value with the gifts of nature. My feet want to run; I am wearing Keds, and feel light on the foam rubber soles; but the heat of the sun holds me to earth.

There is a hotel on Washington Boulevard which specializes in "economical, comfortable living for the retired." It is a huge dark building like the Women's House of Detention in Greenwich Village, but without the bars on the rooms, and there are purple lights playing on the palm trees outside, soft music piped throughout the grounds, and the frequent blare of a loudspeaker: "Missus Goldberg to the telephone! Missus Goldberg! *Sadie, answer the phone!*" when the children call from New York. The streets of the neighborhood are filled with the chattering of mournful elder statesmen, mostly losers after sixty years of continual negotiation, men with chagrined pouches slipping sideways beneath their eyes, women with hair bursting onto their cheeks and upper lips, as if all at once, near the end, they have decided to make a final try at being better men than their husbands.

To walk through the crowd during the hour following their afternoon naps is to wade in senility. There is a deep-sea lack of light despite all the sun and brisk resort clatter; you gasp for life and run to look in a dusty window. Narcissus wants to be just thirty-five, *"nel mezzo del cammin di nostra vita,"* and not seventy, not seventy! The crowd flutters by. "She thought she could be my daughter-in-law! A girl like that! To be my daughter-in-law! And you know what? Now she is." "I used to be in business. I had a good business. It was a nice store, good location. Furniture. I should have kept my location." "What does the weather report say? Does the weather report ever say anything but the weather?" "Moishe died. He had an attack. Well, we all got to go."

Is it the same voice, the same rhythm? It is the same crowd—grief, isolation, death. There almost always seems to be an ambulance pulling up or pulling away.

It is fine to tell a story, which feels like affirmation, but afterwards, after the morning's writing, then what? Writing is an expression of affirmation, power, longing, but not a proper cause of these emotions in the writer. He is a guide into delight and dread because he can escape victimization (he thinks); he has left a little trail of paper behind him as he threads his way into the maze, and can find his way back (he believes—though the roar of the maze sets up a disarray in anything as fragmentary as his intentions about return). He tracks the minotaur with an open mind. "Maybe I'll like it," he says, "and maybe I won't. At least I'll see." He initiates passion only because he has it—otherwise self-delusion and covetous self-therapy. And so it is not good to be alone for long, entirely alone.

But at least for a time, until they dim out, loneliness sharpens the eyes. I feel like a safecracker; loneliness has also sharpened my fingertips, and my entire body throughout feels the clicking tumblers as I yearn toward the combination. I come to focus, I work. But afterwards, then what? I have retreated from the distractions of Manhattan. There are no telephone calls. No friendship, no duties, no hazards of pique or pleasure. I shall work till the battery runs down, frozen and stilled by this busy emptiness under the sun. I ask myself: Can the silent column of ants reconstruct the living roach at its leisure underground? No, only a tree can make a tree, only a winged roach can make a winged roach. A column of ants works by an invisible will which resides in no one of its jointed parts, but only a swollen green ant can breed an urgent ant.

As I walk on Lincoln Road, the smart shopping area of "the Beach," I ogle the oglers, the sunburned sun-worshippers basted with oil, cream, tonic, and lotion—the touts, boxers, fairies, grandmothers, exiled Cubans, local hot-rodders and their gumchewing molls, sportsmen, natty invalids in gabardine, drunks, stockbrokers, antique collectors, Semites and anti-Semites all taking the air together on Lincoln Road. Hill people, swamp people, and ex-pugs sell newspapers flown in from all over—New York, Chicago,

Los Angeles ("Smogsville!" cackles a refugee). And New York is harried by flu and Chicago is black with coal and damp. And here we all are on Lincoln Road, with a delicious breeze, courtesy of the steakhouse pumping cool air into the street. So let's buy the hometown paper to see how miserable we might have been, for others are.

On Lincoln Road, fair Lincoln Road in Miami Beach, the Negroes have been freed; freed of existence, that is; only a few black ghosts slip discreetly by. Even if they were not so discreet, they would be invisible, though for a new reason: they are going someplace, namely, to work, or at another hour, home. For them, Lincoln Road is a mere artery for transit, while for the others, Lincoln Road is parlor, sunroom, promontory into health and beauty. For the visitors, Lincoln Road is a slow matter, a recipe for yearned-for slowness, sloth, strolling ease, delicacy of control. The cocky Broadway chapparoonies are wearing their new pleatless "Miami-Tailored Daks." Their bellies do the work of belts, hiding the place where belts would be. Now I'm so slow I don't need a belt, the pants proudly announce; I'm just walkin' along, just struttin' down the avenue, just here and pleasant with myself, and when I take a breath, the expandable elastic waistband expands with me. In the men's room of a bar off Lincoln Road, hung with photographs of wrestlers, there is a curious vending machine which is decorated with a crown and raised scepter and submits a product called DE-LA: "Say Delay, a light lubricating ointment designed to aid in the prevention of premature climax. Odorless. Safe. Stainless. Easy to apply. Directions on package. 50¢ coins only. Machine does not give change."

Machine makes comment, however. Machine is trying to tell us something.

The Negro girl who cleans my room gets yelled at, screamed at, all morning. "Stupid, stupid, stupid! A single room only gets two towels, one face, one bath!" She smiles slyly to herself as if she knows where the manager's DE-LA is hidden. This is the southland, I am reminded, where we have grits for breakfast. But it is not quite dat ole Dixie, boss, which changeth not, nor can age alter it. It is Miami Beach. The Sholem Aleichem Literary Society ("Managed by Tourists—Managed for Tourists") has a For Rent sign on it. "Owner Will Remodel for Any Business."

I decide as I walk: I'll write my book till the battery runs down, though distraction seems necessary; other duties, friends, "real life."

The sirens of the police ambulances work up and down the Beach all day and night, announcing the news as they carry away the attacked, the fallen, the stroked, the perished. A population of the aged sheds its members at the merest trifle of an excuse—a bottle of cold pop in the sun, a skipped nap, somebody raising his voice suddenly—or no excuse at all. It touches life and someone dies. It treads carelessly and someone dies. The sirens whir and howl and Negroes courteously open the back door for the corpse. For some reason people smile at the ambulance as they stroll, sucking ice cream. Perhaps they dream of an accident, a distraction: *Siren meets white Thunderbird, boy of forty cut off in his prime, had a girl in there with him, not his wife.* Perhaps thinking: *Not me this time.*

One of those impossible coincidences. Today I met Dr. Meyer leading his blind wife. He was our family doctor in Cleveland, addicted to practical jokes, who always said he wanted to do research, and in fact he had some sort of connection with one of the important drug laboratories. When he retired from practice, he announced to my parents over a bottle of wine that now he would begin his true life's work. I had decided that his practical jokes, bought in Jean's Fun House on East 9th Street—buzzers, false flies, stomach noises, leaky cups—were a symptom of childish anger at adult responsibility. But now that he could retire from practice and try his hand at research. . . . It turned out that his wife had inoperable cataracts; she went blind fast, and he went sour, quiet, mean; and they left Cleveland for Miami Beach, where I saw him leading her, walking with the stiff, frightened step of the unaccustomed blind. He is shrunken; only today do I notice that he is a small man—when I was a boy, he was immense. At present, and forever until the very end, his life's work is to steer his wife to the beach in the morning and sit with her to describe what he sees. He has replaced both practical jokes and dreams of a laboratory with loyalty to his wife, but virtue has made him a furious runt.

Fantasies of thighs, breasts, bellies as I nap on the beach. I awaken, sticky with salt. My nose is peeling. Shall I visit the Corsican waitress again tonight? Shall I ask the Meyers to dinner? But I have made this disappearance into Miami Beach in order to avoid the troubles of others and of myself. I swim again. I doze again. I dream of sex with a woman I overheard describing the proper way to kill a chicken "so it don't suffer. You ask anyone, they'll tell you. And there's nothing like fresh-killed chicken. You can't trust the butchers."

A man in the coffee shop later said to the cashier: "I been sick, that's why you ain't seen me. Doctor said coronary thrombosis. You ever heard of that?"

"Naw. Lots of people got coronaries, but that thrombosis, that's a new thing. The docs keep finding new things so they can charge us."

"Well, I'll tell you, it left me feeling pretty weak."

I went one night to see a road company version of *My Fair Lady* at the Miami Beach Auditorium, which more frequently provides hospitality for wrestling or boxing matches. A maggoty, bored imitation of Rex Harrison, a thick Eliza without any bounce. The audience is quietly taking in the famous sight. They write on their postcards home: Tonight we saw a Broadway show, but the girl was fat.

Crazy Louie on the beach—a frantic grandfather with Latin records, maracas, castanets, silk Cuban shirts, feathers, straw skirt, rubber Halloween masks, a huge earring loosely hooked to his ear by a bent hairpin, thick glasses sliding down his nose, leathery withered legs, dancing and dancing, all sinews and grins and shakes to some inner song while the portable phonograph goes rattle-and-scrape, screech, rattle, and scrape. Amazingly, the crowd which regularly gathers on the sand nearby seems to enjoy his music; some of them shake, too, dreaming of the days when they had lust to squander on their legs. Dr. Meyer's wife smiles as he describes the scene. "Are you smiling, Meyer?" she asks. He says yes, but is lying. Crazy Louie bangs his castanet under her nose and screams *"Olé!"* and she jumps. At last Dr. Meyer smiles.

Then he tells her that sometimes the beginnings of arteriosclerosis can be detected at age twenty-five. "Cuts off the blood supply to the brain. The psychiatrists think they're smart, but they can't do anything about the histological system. The brain dries up like a scab."

"Meyer, you shouldn't use such language."

"You mean histology?"

"I mean scab, Meyer."

Crazy Louie is dancing and cackling, kicking sand. The old ladies in their bathing skirts fan themselves contentedly as he enters his Afro-Cuban apocalypse. On the beach there is a rural, village tolerance of madness. Louie doesn't do any harm. His children sent him down. He is new since my last visit.

And where are my old friends?

The cockroach in the alley is long gone, of course, and its grandchildren unto many generations. But I have found cheap sun again for my sinus, and white ocean breaking against the distractions of Manhattan in winter, spring, summer, fall. I think of a friend, a Jewish chauvinist, arguing with his girl: "When your people were still living in trees and hitting each other with sticks, my people already had sinus trouble."

The Spinoza Forum is gone, replaced by a motel. Dr. Wolfson still goes to the beach every afternoon. But the neighborhood is changed. He has nothing to say to me except that raw beets, honey, and tangerines keep a man virtuous and healthy, no matter what his age.

The woman who knew Thomas Wolfe—did I forget to mention that last time?—and swam as if she wanted to die, and worked as a B-girl . . . gone. She wanted to reconstruct some cabin-in-the-woods dream of perfection, but she could never find the missing pieces. Life is not a jigsaw puzzle; once it has been scrambled, the old picture is gone.

The racing-car driver with whom I chatted a couple of times at breakfast—gone.

The column of ants at the cockroach—gone.

The drummed-up acquaintances—even their names forgotten.

The hotel clerk who wanted to explore in Guatemala —perhaps he is exploring in Guatemala. The new manager of the hotel has never even heard of him.

And the man who died—dead.

I know this for certain, for I have finally discovered an old friend. Frank, the gray bozo behind the counter at Whelan's, is still there. I had taken up new eating habits and did not return to Whelan's during my first week in Miami Beach, but then I did and found him, still building hamburger platters and scrambling eggs. At first he did not remember me. He never knew my name. When I reminded him of the incident about the man who died, and of our long breakfast friendship, a look of irritation captured his face—demands were being made on him—but then his cross mug creased into a smile. He did remember me! He only needed to be reminded!

"You know that old fool," he said. "Later really did die. He's dead. Later died."

There was a new cat in the store. A new special on toothbrushes. A new pharmacist.

I had a hamburger on our old friendship, and Frank put an extra slice of tomato on the side to *prove* that he remembered me. But why should he? He had been an experience for me—the same now, with balder eyebrows—

but what was I to him? For me he existed as an example of something, a moment of frightening history, a troubled memory which I had set down in words. I had needed a friend then, but he did not. I was frightened by death then, and worse, by a way of receiving death, but he was not and perhaps never admits that he might be.

Why does he stay in Miami Beach?

Yes, for a job. Yes, for the sun. But why there?

All right, then why not there?

Why do I go back?

Why did I go back? What happened to those dead and dying ones? They died and were dead; they were swept away. I thought, the first time I went to Miami Beach, that I had made a free choice to be isolated, but I discovered that everyone comes to the state of isolation in time—though not freely. What I did out of apparent health and youth, in the pleasure of work, those others did in sickness and age, in the anxiety of boredom. But eventually work is done, health turns to decay, youth turns to ripeness turns to age; feebleness and dying must precede death except for fighter pilots, who are anachronisms. Miami Beach is an extension, adult education course in how to die, pursued with great seriousness by the enrollees. The old folks work at it with deliberate and modest intensity, in group sessions, complimenting each other on their tans, their sport shirts, their postgraduate skill at finding a proper weather. The young vacationers flush in on packaged tours, immerse themselves in the ceremonial indulgences of resort hotels, eat, swim, and enjoy their honeymoon wrestling, take in Eartha Kitt or Leo de Lion, sigh with boredom and excess, buy bottles of Man Tan at the air terminal ("Arrive With Fresh Sun On Your Cheeks!"), and flee back to real life with a secret conviction that this is leisure? Strictly for the birds, brother.

That first time in Miami Beach, I was a curious observer, obscurely moved, with the face of a man who fearfully unwinds a rope as he visits his dream of the turtle slaughterhouse. The second time (the last time), two years' change had begun to discover my implication to me; I broke the rope; the model of death is real; the dream of dying is real. The tanned, reduced, heliotropic Doctor Meyer recognized me despite his wife's blindness ("Hannah! Look who's here!"), and when I spoke to her, she gropingly embraced me. This was why I went back—to feel Mrs. Meyer's arms hotly convulsed about my neck, as if I were still a boy in Cleveland, and to know that I was not a young man from Cleveland visiting Miami Beach as he had toured carnivals, the war, the Caribbean, Europe, and taken the boat ride around Manhattan. I was a winter visitor, tired of town, come for the sun, who had been there before.

Am I now satisfied with what I found? Which is: "Later really did die. Later died." Just as in the alley two years ago, in that swept space where there was no longer any roach and no column of ants, history enters upon new epochs which begin to grow familiar to me.

PAUL GOODMAN

The Devolution of Democracy

DEMOCRATIC POWER springs from an enlightened electorate. The neglect of this possibility in America, the failure to protect and advance it with new form and content during a century and a half of expanding area and population, of complicating economy and frequently revolutionized technology, and broadening relations with the rest of the world, has resulted in an electorate so demoralized that it is a question if it is possible to govern democratically at all. We tend to take lightly Jefferson's famous remark about the necessity for a revolution every twenty years, every new generation, but it is probably literally true, to renew democracy as he conceived it. (Jefferson was not, in fact, given to ill-considered slogans nor even dogmatism; but in stupider times his Enlightenment daring seems outlandish.) Meantime, during that century and a half, while the democratic power was being corrupted and was dwindling, other kinds of power and inertia have boldly filled up the vacuum, up to our present feudal system of monopolies, military and other bureaucracies, party machines, communications networks, and Established institutions.

The Kennedy Administration came in—one speaks as if it were there a thousand years; will we get out of it alive? —after a marvelously established regime of business as usual. And it was going to "make America move." It would be a rule of things by active personalities instead of a bureaucratic staff; it would be a "disorderly" Administration, in the sense that ideas and people could leap-frog the chain of command and clash and have it out; it would be rich with ideas, as guaranteed by putting in or near power such notorious thinkers of new thoughts as academics from prestigious colleges. What the activity and thought were to be toward, what the purpose was, was not clear—there were no issues in the campaign, no effort to enlighten the electorate —but it was called the New Frontier. Now in this essay I want to show that this *image* of a government, of active persons with no idea, indeed fits the real situation better than its only rival did, and the voters were aesthetically wise to choose it—by a squeak.

After a year, including a Hundred Days and everything, and having learned that it is powerless and irrelevant except to "lead" in an intensified Cold War (which is itself, of course, powerless and irrelevant to any human good), the boyish *élan* is more sober. A philosopher close to the President now explains to me that the best to be hoped from government is to "mitigate the evils of modern life." This Niebuhrian political theory is not very wise, for if the aim is *merely* to mitigate, and not attack the structure and causes of the evils, one will not *even* mitigate, for the structure aggrandizes itself and produces new evils. It is as with civil liberties: if one merely protects them, without increasing the opportunities of freedom, one loses them. So I demur. I am then lectured to the effect that "if you had lived in the Administration of Jefferson, you would have been dissatisfied in the same way." That is, after a year in "power" under the present conditions, the Administration has begun to rewrite American history and prove that democratic power is a myth.

Since, by this philosophy, man is incurably stupid and his institutions evil, we must not get too hot to reform this or that present evil. And so they think. For instance, when three or four of us ask another Harvard professor to put a little zip into counteracting the nausea of the mass-media —we propose to him a couple of excellent libertarian plans and are even ready to write the legislation and outline the campaign to arouse public opinion—we are treated to the popular wisdom that "people get what they want" and "what great art was ever produced by subsidy?" (Needless to say, however, when Cultural Freedom and the Encounter of Ideas are instruments of the CIA, means have been readily found to subsidize intellectual groups, even though nothing could be more treasonable to cultural freedom and the encounter of ideas.) But the problem, it seems to me, is an existential one; how does the professor, as an intellectual individual, keep down his nausea in front of the TV screen and not *have* to change? Presumably it is a government of men, and not an automatic machine, or what is the professor doing there?

Finally, on December 10, 1961, we have the answer in the Washington *Post:* Scholars in government "are good for ungarbling what thinkers on the outside have written . . . and tabulating the points" (Prof. Schlesinger). I am breathless with the thought that Walt Rostow, etc., or even Arthur Schlesinger, imagine they can write more clearly than thinkers on the outside; but I am indignant that such good talents should be misused for writing *précis;* it's like the waste of skills in the Army.

After a year, the conception of a government of active personalities and disorderly clash has crystallized into the doctrine of the "Web of Tensions," the use of internal conflict to generate ideas. This Hegelian notion is psychologically correct. In the present ground-rules of the White

House, however, it works out as follows: (1) There is a careful preselection of the combatants, so that no too obstreperous voice will disturb the proceedings, or laugh. (2) If anyone *in* the debate does disagree in a way awkward for the Cold War policy—and especially if his predictions prove correct—he is dropped. (3) At best in a megalopolis like the United States government, the Web of Controversy is far removed from even its own staff-workers, who nevertheless have to provide relevant materials and know what they are doing when they execute orders. To these workers the effect of the Web of Tensions is confusion, the feeling of purposelessness or divided purpose, of being out of contact and therefore absolutely frustrated when their earnest efforts are disregarded for reasons that cannot be explained to them. They then naturally withdraw into the usual bureaucratic apathy, now not even orderly. (4) Nor is this difficulty helped if the tense thinkers are by disposition in-turned, unfriendly, and unpragmatic. (5) Last but not least, the inventive out-going moment of the Tension, the reason for it altogether, is horribly inhibited by the fact that the thinkers don't have any power anyway. As one critic has observed, the Web of Tensions simply means that they are getting more tense.

I don't want to be unfair, though it is hard not to be sarcastic. In the centralized power-complex that these people are committed to, and with the baroque conception of national sovereignty that they represent in a world that has come to have a different nature, it is probably impossible to govern. Both vested interests and the social-psychology of the people (and the influence of the vested interests in the social-psychology of the people) are fixed on the Cold War. Even the coalition that put Kennedy in office is too varigated to be maintained, and I shall try to show that he is re-forming that coalition to be a better Cold War "leader." The kind of revolutionary attitudes and do-or-die attempts at education that would make for government and tend again toward democratic power, are beyond the talents of these people;

nor, of course, do they want them. They did not run, they were not elected, to thwart the "industrial-military complex," as the departing President called it: to make peace and internationalize the world; to diversify and decentralize our economy; really to help backward peoples according to their needs and customs rather than for our own profits and war-aims in alliance with their ruling cliques; to revive civil liberties and try to improve the quality of American life. They did not campaign for these purposes, but I am puzzled why, except for the politicians, they did campaign.

II

To get a better view of Washington after a year, let us turn from these Top philosophers to those who are not in the Web of Tensions, though not a thousand miles away. Here is a collection of comments:

"Lot of activism: action for the sake of action." "The way they want to get something moving, you feel that they need to overcome something 'static' that is threatening to engulf them." "They don't know the difference between real power and the juvenile trappings of power." "You say that the Americans in general have a neurotic feeling of powerlessness, but you don't realize that those in power are equally frustrated." "As a matter of fact, there *is* a lot of loose power around, in Congress for instance, but he doesn't wield it." "If some Congressmen had monkey-glands—"

"This Administration is peculiarly humorless, like phony actors. At least Eisenhower was a genuine Rotarian." " 'Posture' is the favorite word. The preposterous syntax in the President's speeches: 'Ask not—' 'Let no one think,' etc., especially when he occasionally mispronounces common words." "The worst was the speech to the Latin Americans, peppered with Spanish quotations but nobody taught him how to pronounce the words. It was embarrassing." "The Roman style is highly esteemed: tough, terse, we play for keeps." "I think they were badly stung by that remark last spring that they were great dribblers but never made a basket. I think that the need to produce at all costs was one reason for the Cuban goof." "Kennedy took full responsibility for it, like a Roman—and made full use of the scapegoat that he had poor Intelligence. But Bobby shut up the ones who apparently had more accurate information."

"They act on schematic preconceptions, with a crazy emphasis on Analysis and Facts; completely unpragmatic." "They have a justified contempt for the 'fuzzy liberals' who spout generalities that have nothing to do with the concrete situations, but they don't understand that to get anywhere, you have to have an ideal, a pragmatic-end-in-view."

"Naturally, being unpragmatic, they are continually projecting and finding scapegoats, rather than having real obstacles to overcome." "They talk about the dilemmas inherited from Eisenhower; but how is their own policy any different?" "They are apprehensive of obstacles that don't even exist, for example, opposition in the Appropriations Committee on issues where there is no opposition. In my opinion, they do the same with the Russians. They never think of clearing up an ambiguity by going and asking; they always figure it out by Analysis and guessing. This isn't helped by an Intelligence that feeds them false facts." "They try to circumvent the preconceived obstacles by tricks. You get a memorandum an hour before the meeting, so there's no time to research it and back up your opposition. Perpetuation of errors."

"He is astoundingly sensitive to criticism in the press. Unlike Roosevelt who got mad and told them off. But Kennedy says, 'Now Jimmy Reston shouldn't have said a thing like that.' " "He calls in *Life* to explain himself to *them!* So it becomes a symbiosis: since he takes them seriously, they are flattered and give him a good press, and he gets sucked in." "Is he still worrying about the close vote? Or maybe doubtful he should be there at all? By the way, why should he?" "Kennedy believes that there is a terrific force of reaction, that mustn't be confronted too fast, and one mustn't go too far."

"Of course, in an enterprise this big there's bound to be confusion and bad communications. But it doesn't help when they play it cool and by ear. Take the private-shelter story in *Life:* a press-officer gave it out and there was a howl afterwards." "In the Eisenhower chain-of-command routine, there was at some level a definite decision, also routine and usually lousy. But here one doesn't know *what* has been decided, if anything." "If he had a policy, why didn't he fire them all and put in his own people to pursue his policy? How much obstruction can you put up with? In three years Chile will be Communist even without Castro." "The difference under Roosevelt was that the Secretary would draw everybody together and inspire them with a pep talk; so that in *spite* of the bureaucracy they pulled together and got going." "Well, in my agency the chief complaint is that there isn't any contact with the bright young men who have access to the White House. You ask, what do they talk about in the White House? Oh, everything."

Finally, "There you are. All this talk around here finally tends to revolve around what He is like, and that's boring. Is it boring because we're sick of talking about personalities instead of issues, or is it boring because Kennedy is boring? It comes to the same thing. Kennedy seems to me to be simple." "Maybe the chief use of this Administration, especially after the last, is that it shows that livelier, better educated, and more likable people are even more boring in this situation, unless they stand for something."

III

This is not a happy spectacle. Let me point out, however, that it pretty accurately describes the behavior of a crew of hipsters, as Mailer called them in 1960, not foreseeing the consequences. It is the cool and activist role-playing of vitality in a situation of impotence. (The impotence is caused partly by obstacles and partly by their characters.) Like the artist and live person he is, Mailer responded accurately to the type during the campaign; he missed its meaning because he is (transiently, I hope) a chump. He is a great one for the style, the *nuance,* of life; he failed to remember that, as Kant said, a characteristic of art is to be *Zweck ohne Zweck,* purposive without a purpose. More serious has been the error of the liberals who were "realistic" and who, instead of going about their business of dissenting and building a movement that they believed in, supported Kennedy on the theory that, once elected, he would drop the morals and techniques that got him the nomination. But to no reasonable person's surprise, the Administration proves, after the election, to have the same basic character as when the candidate was wresting the nomination and waging an uphill campaign. Being in office, however, is less favorable than campaigning for the display of jumpy vitality well-heeled, morally uncommitted and intellectually shallow. Unfortunately, the end is not yet.

Of course I am judging by a high standard, but otherwise why bother? Why should these people seek office unless they had a useful idea and felt indispensable to execute it? Omit Kennedy and ask about the professors. They have given up citizenly independence and freedom of criticism in order to be servants of the public and friends of the cops. Presumably this is for the utility of power rather than the vanity of power. What? how? The answer is Analysis and Tabulation. In like manner, the scientists make bombs and missiles, but they do not make policy and they do not strike to enforce peace.

IV

The impotence of the administration is due, I have said, to the past down-slope of our history and its present irrelevance to world history-making. These causes are intrinsically related, for if the United States were not the kind of society it has become, its Administration could work toward a world order. Our emergency is not in Berlin, etc., as the newspapers keep proclaiming but in the economic, social, and psychological need for the Cold War. (Thus, if I were asked how to save us from Russian bombs, the first step would be to free the TV channels, for real controversy and true reporting on international affairs, for criticism and programing in our municipal and vocational lives, so that people would have to face the things that matter.)

With whatever hopes and purposes the Administration came in (and, as Oscar Gass has pointed out, these were already quite marginal and inoffensive to anybody), it has met the massiveness of the status quo and its established powers, venal, blimpish, police-ridden, prejudiced, and illiberal; officially existing in the Pentagon, the Treasury, the FBI, the Civil Service, the Scientific corporations, a large part of Congress. Eisenhower's Administration, in its personnel and motives and chain-of-command staff-work, rather simply expressed these underlying existing forces and inertias; it therefore had—especially in the retrospect of having survived it—a certain solid impressiveness. The picture on the box was the same as the contents. With the best will in the world, the status quo is a rocky mass to move; but of course the son of Joseph Kennedy had no such foolish idea. His first official act was to continue the existing FBI and CIA, and that was already the end of working toward a new America or a new world. The Wall Street stalwarts—Dillon, McCone, Foster, etc.—were brought back as they would have been if Nixon had won. The Pentagon could become only more so. Inevitably the subordinates of the agencies would be unchanged, but in a large number of cases the same types were returned to make policy, or obstruct "policy." (Foreign Aid is a sad example, as if the racketeering governments in the aid-countries were not intractable enough; and although, politically, even the Cold Warriors rightly fear that these countries will be "lost.") Must we not assume that "tragic" bureaucratic mishaps and failures-to-communicate are importantly due to the persistence of forces that want no change?

So we are presented with the embarrassingly *un*impressive spectacle of impotence among men who, by their personality, intelligence, and freer methods have promised to make America move; an irrelevant activism, a "tough" "hard" "posture" (it is necessary to put every word in quotation marks), and an astounding timidity that results from trying to be different from their own class-strength and class-needs, although they have neither a new idea to give courage nor a revolutionary will to make a change. That, on the domestic scene, there *is* no such new idea nor will to useful change, you can observe by looking out the window or thumbing through *Life;* the scene is, as might be feared, the same, only a year more so. More big money, more unashamed tax-dodgers, more cops, and more army. The war-budget is at least 25 per cent more than Mr. Eisenhower's last; but otherwise the "public sector," that Ken Galbraith was vocal about, is not further nourished. Some in Washington say that the Education bill was beaten by a "tragic" combination of perplexities—Negro-white, parochial-public, poor states-rich states; others, however, say that Dillon could afford it, that it was legislatively handled precisely in order to lose, and what evidence *is* there that Kennedy cares anything about Education? The New York *Times* has editorially described his interest as "tepid." That is, the program for a better quality of American life was fairly trivial to begin with (the liberals claimed that this moderation was necessary in order to win the election), but the will to achieve even this program has been lacking.

The field of action has been international affairs. It is estimated that three-quarters of the President's calendar is devoted to foreign and military matters, and certainly other matters are considered in this light, as fits the budget. The address to the Manufacturers strongly makes this point: when business is good, we look good in the world. Civil Rights for Negroes are never spoken of as social justice but always as enhancing our Image in Africa and Asia. (I asked a young Ethiopian what *was* the image of America in Ethiopia; he said that the vast majority of his people had never heard of America.) The pressing problems of Youth are recognized by the Administration either as delinquency to be handled by the Justice Department or in terms of the few thousand, FBI screened, in the Peace Corps.

Yet here too, because of circumstances, action is impotent—except for the one grim potency of destroying everything. At present the administration of any sovereign State can make world-sense only by fitting into and furthering the inevitable development of the world community, and indeed by relaxing its own sovereignty. The interesting and long-range movement of the world has to do with increasing communications, exchange of people, the vanishing of colonialism and the rise of backward peoples from poverty, regional economic cooperation for mutual advantage. These secular movements occur, of course, according to their own laws, independent of Washington. A powerful national government can act in them only by contributing to them, perhaps leading. But an American administration is bedeviled in these things by business as usual and militarism, provincialism and jingoism. We cannot exchange goods with half the world; we cannot even talk to the Chinese. We cannot feed famine, though we have a surplus; we cannot give help to peoples except through our "friends," their rulers who rob them; and if a region is not a battleground, it is not considered useful to help at all. We put an ex-FBI man in charge of immigration. We cannot educate without propagandizing. We cannot engage in space-exploration without competing, nor develop modern technology without polluting the atmosphere. We cannot strengthen the parliament of nations lest it evade our grip. And of course the behavior of all the other sovereignties—including new-fledged cannibals and feudal lordlings as well as tall generals and ideologists even crazier than our own—confounds the frustration.

The sphere of free action diminishes. Even Latin America is increasingly frustrating. The chief current idea seems to be the perfecting of the arrangements, begun by Truman and continued by Eisenhower, with the big new power associated with the Common Market. As McGeorge Bundy put it on December 6, 1961, "It would be better if Western Europe were one great power . . . with the economic strength, the military self-confidence, the political unity of a true great power"; and on the same day the President plugged for trade arrangements with Europa. (By the way, what will prevent French rights and German skill and money from becoming a third nuclear giant?) Bundy warns that our rapprochement with Europa might amount to a Rich Man's Club against the rest of the world—yes, so it might; but in terms reminiscent of the White Man's Burden, Walt Rostow mentions the responsibility of the "North" for developing the "South." In my opinion this allied policy is better than Barry Goldwater's isolated fortress of America, but it will not exactly kindle the enthusiasm of the nations toward the peace and unity of the world.

But the chief outlet for frustrated action is, of course, armaments and threatening postures. Oscar Gass deliciously reports the expression "posture of sacrifice" as a threat. Most often, the style is that of a frustrated juvenile delinquent who fears he might be judged inactive and probably powerless. This is younger than hipster, but it must be remembered that in international affairs statesmen always regress to more adolescent attitudes, whether friendly or hostile. We play the game of Chicken. There is gloating that our "tough" "hard" "policy" has "won" in Berlin. Soldiers are mobilized and will perhaps be demobilized. We will have Bomb Shelters and defy them. Walt Rostow is training guerrillas, since Castro did so well with them. (This is puzzling. Into what friendly countryside are the American guerrillas supposed to melt? Surely he means commandos?) The more hip age-level of the same frustration-syndrome is Game Theory applied to war. In Game Theory, the Web of Tensions is finally isolated completely from any contact with common reason, biological safety, or even any opponent except one's projections. All members of the Administration are experts in Game Theory.

A necessity for maintaining the Roman or cool posture is to have the situation always under control and not to be embarrassed by a goof or booboo. Unfortunately, this entails many contradictions. Since slant-eyed peasants are not really under one's control; since often one's best-considered efforts, as in Venezuela, work out opposite to what one planned; since from the beginning one is operating by a preconceived scheme, there are bound to be blunders and the threatening posture renders them more disastrous and more embarrassing. It is not possible to relent, atone, make amends, for these postures are "weak." On the other hand, to alibi, to be touchy to criticism, apprehensive of being misunderstood, fearful of future criticism, timid of commitment, forced to be consistent—these postures are also glaringly "weak." (One had the impression that Cuba, etc., was intimidating in this way, as if a gang suddenly realized they were on a tougher block than they had been brought up on.) There is then nothing for it but to strengthen reprisals and enlarge the arsenal. This is called the Cold War, and of course this has become the greatest frustration of all, since the final and only proof of power, to fight and win, entails suicide and losing. That is, the outlet for frustrated activity is a scene where activity is frustrated.

Gordon Christiansen, the chemist, argues that the newer tactics of the Cold War are *solely* for home consumption. Since the bomb shelters are scientifically fraudulent, they will not deceive the Russians; so their purpose, he says, must be a calculated deception of the Americans, to prepare for our making a first strike. This is too shocking to believe; and also, I think, it is too ill-considered as a political policy for such astute politicians. Given the rising protest of so many respected scientists and students and even children, and many mothers, pushing the Civil Defense might result in riots on the streets. It is simpler to take it as the inevitable accumulation of frenzied expedients, as with the beast in *The Burrow*. But of course this comes to the same end result as Christiansen fears. The breakdown of common sense and morals in the continuing Cold War makes it more and more indifferent who will be "guilty."

V

As is apparent from all the foregoing, the demography of the Administration consists of the Status Quo, the Coalition on which it was elected, and is own characteristic groups, viz.:

(1) Wall Street Republicans, continuing.

(2) The Pentagon, continuing, in which we must include the aristocrats of military science in Rand and Aerospace. These latter, since more mentally busy, are more bellicose than professional generals whose aims, on retirement, seem to be intensely economic and therefore they have an incentive to retire alive.

(3) Bureaucracy and Civil Service in the other agencies, also mostly continuing.

(4) FBI and CIA, continuing. These are, again, activist-violent in disposition. The FBI is more lower-class, the CIA more middle-class. But the aristocrats of the violent-minded are the new-come professors from the old OSS, trained in the prudence of Strategic Bombing. About half a dozen members of this Club have access.

(5) The fuzzy liberals, part of the coalition who don't really belong. But even Harriman would be called a liberal. (Reuther, of the UAW, is said to be a useful friend.)

(6) The professors. These are characteristic and fall into various types: e.g., Schlesinger, Wofford, or Galbraith more for thought and speeches; Rostow more for power postures; Bundy more for administering.

(7) A number of genuine intellectuals, interested in prudent and ideal action. These are mostly younger men—like the young instructors or assistant professors at universities, who suggest curriculum changes. This group is also characteristic of the Administration and gives it a livelier tone than its predecessor.

(8) The President's entourage for special assignments, with Irish names that roll on the tongue. We may here include Robert Kennedy. These are called, probably unfairly, the Irish Mafia.

(9) Besides, there is an unofficial night-life circle, generally upper-class and violent-minded. Important is Joseph Alsop who is said to leak hard-to-get data in order to push his activist policies and interests, e.g., the National Estimate of missiles. Alsop's tack is as follows: two years ago he said there was a missile gap, so we had to build fast; now he says that the gap was exaggerated, we are way ahead, so we can take risks. This gets you coming and going.

As might be expected, the glossary and style have strains of (1) Madison Avenue: e.g., "hard" and "soft" are applied to research; "hard" research contains numerals. "Shop," as "over in Charley Hitch's shop." "Sanitize" is very good: it means to doctor a report, as to Congress, to take out the virulence. (2) Rand Corporation: "escalate," "hardware," "parameters"—"what are the parameters of the problem?" A horror is "wargasm," meaning all-out retaliation, which I recommend to Mailer for his hipster-theory. (3) Armed services: "tough" and other terms of panic about masculinity. (4) Lionel Trilling-literary, especially "posture."

A curiosity that deserves special mention, however, is "exercise," as "A crude propaganda exercise," referring to a Soviet complaint about a Nazi in NATO. (British? I read in R. H. S. Crossman, "The aim of the exercise is clear," referring to a book he is reviewing.) The denotation is that the activity is only practice, it is not the real thing, it is not for keeps. Addressed to an inferior in a bureaucracy it can be crushingly one-up, for it means that there are grown-ups who do real things. But when used generally, as it is, it connotes that oneself is not *yet* altogether for real, one is waiting to graduate and get to work. (This is strictly the Cold War situation.) The next meaning—reinforced by the academic metaphor itself—is that *all* activity is merely academic, detached from any serious possibility of life. Since it is necessary to put up an appearance of being alive, one then adopts a posture or stance. *But such persons could commit suicide.*

Finally, I must call attention to words like "discipline,"

"sacrifice," "responsibility," and "challenge," which in Kennedy's mouth have a special stoical-Catholic tinkle. ("In this grave period, labor must discipline itself—" "The press must discipline itself and assume responsibility—") This is not the Catholicism that was touchy during the campaign, the prospect of Pope John in the White House (oh, to have had that fat man instead of Kennedy or Nixon!). It is the more moral Catholicism of the little boy who disciplines himself from masturbating and checks off his victorious days on the calendar. Masturbating proves you are weak and makes you weak. In this context, "challenge" is the kind of strenuous excitement possible to persons who, having given up their internal spontaneity, rally to an external demand; and then (as Murray Kempton judges) Kennedy is animated, genuine, physically courageous, and even unselfconsciously humorous.

(To my ear, in the rhetoric of Kennedy's big set speeches, there is an incompatibility between the two strains of the stoical-Catholic and the figure-of-history. The sense of duty does not seem to be himself, but his submissive—and evasive—obedience to some grown-ups; one is not convinced of his moral courage. The call-to-glory is warmer and more personal, but it is juvenile. How can a figure-of-history be spiritually inhibited? He cannot grow his myth but must finally manufacture it. With the best efforts of Madison Avenue and the History Department, such prose will not turn to poetry.)

VI

This brings me to the main theme of these reflections, the possible future of this character of Administration in our present democracy, the formation of what I shall call a New Consensus. We have now had the Cold War for fifteen years and it is about time that it became politically domesticated, with its own ethos and personnel. In the present Administration we have a remarkable and *organic* amalgam of the heirs and co-workers of America First and McCarthy and the heirs of Democratic Liberalism. This has an historical meaning. I cannot agree with otherwise excellent observers that we can write off the New Frontier as simply another sell for business as usual, for history does not simply repeat. Let me revert to my opening sentence, the failure of democracy by neglecting to improve the electorate. We then have, in scheme, the following devolution:

(1) For Jefferson, the chief use of democracy was *to* improve the electorate and so itself; people learn by deciding, including making mistakes. He championed decentralization, for people can reasonably decide only what they know about intimately. Madison hit on federalism as a revolutionary device for experimentation, for if the small group made a mistake, it did little harm to the whole; if it found something useful, it could be adopted by others and benefit the whole. One is struck by the pragmatism of such political thought, transforming the town-meeting into an experimental, self-improving unit with provision for expanding society. Any basic function could be the principle for the small political unit; e.g., to provide primary education, Jefferson suggested the militia-company or hundred. Applied to industry, the unit is the soviet. The political units select their federal delegates; this is democratic centralism from below.

(2) With the Jacksonian revolution, as De Tocqueville was quick to see, the democratic idea was already abandoned, for the power now resided in the majority of people *as they were,* with their passions and prejudices uneducated by the responsible give-and-take in a face-to-face meeting that had to make practical decisions and use tax-money. Instead, the people would merely vote on issues and party-programs. This was an invitation for demagogues and party-leaders to get power, and for lobbying interests, that could deliver votes and cash, to influence the politicians for their own power.

(3) Through the 19th century, these nonpublic and nongovernmental powers, bankers and industrialists, vastly

increased their influence. Attempts to control them, e.g., by silver legislation and trust-busting, themselves centralized and increased the governmental power. But what was tragic was that grass-roots politics, like the agrarian and labor movements, also followed the centralized bureaucratic style. And of course the stresses and dislocations of war speeded up these processes. It is said that one reason Woodrow Wilson hesitated to declare war was that he knew that the industries vastly expanded and empowered by war could never be displaced from power after the war.

(4) The imminent breakdown of the system in 1929 brought back a surge of popular participation in some respects not unlike the age of Jackson. But this was soon re-integrated into the bureaucratic central government by the paternalism of Roosevelt and his Agencies. Economic controls, social insurance, and other welfare began to break down altogether the formal division between government and the monopolies and other great powers of society. All this was regularized after the Second World War; by the 1950's there existed one massive Organized System, inert or expanding by its own law, immovable by any political public power, and administered, rather than governed, by the administration of Eisenhower.

(5) The election of 1960 was remarkable in that now there was not even the semblance of issues or programs for the voters to decide between. The election was importantly decided by the contrast of personalities on a TV screen. It was the end of the Jacksonian idea, since with mass-communications and national commodities, people's passions and prejudices were themselves nationalized. There had ceased to be a democracy even in form. The Administration would be, however, the necessary *symbol* of government. (For a rough analogy, consider the Roman "Republic" and its senators and consuls during the early Empire.) Now what are the characteristics of such a symbolic government, and what might be its future development?

VII

Eisenhower was unsatisfactory in many ways. With all his solid virtues and genuine Rotarian togetherness and Everyman's ignorance, he was often ludicrous as a Chief of State. Newsmen had to edit him, satire had to be suppressed, lest the image of government break down altogether. Culturally, he was out of place as the head of a Great Power. But most important, his regime was universally regarded as dangerously boring. For two reasons: first, the public will to politics, whether or not it was possible to exert power, had absolutely no object on which to exercise itself. Discussions of domestic "policy" fell to an all-time low; and instead, there sprang up a vast literature of criticism of the System en bloc, of the Cars, the Organization, the Suburbs, etc., etc. Most of this was a one-upping cynical product of the system itself, yet it did not express dissent and was disillusioning to the young. The later years of Eisenhower were marked by a resurgence of Youth, acting now in parapolitical movements, Birchite or Beatnik or Pacifist. But secondly, and most important, the adequate administrative inactivism of Eisenhower was symbolically quite inadequate for the affluent rigors of the Cold War. The old-fashioned diplomacy of J. F. Dulles, as brinkmanly as it was, still did not provide sufficient popular identification for so immense and continuing a deadlock. People began to join SANE.

It is essential to consider the social psychology of the Cold War. Robert Engler has recently written a fine study of the cultural effects of the Cold War; but we must ask also what are the moods and paralysis *in* the culture that demand such a sustained, pointless, menacing, and potentially catastrophic enterprise. I have gone into this subject frequently elsewhere—the exacerbation, in modern conditions, of masochistic violence, Enemy-projection, and paralysis—but let me here especially mention the public mood of powerlessness, powerlessness on the job, in the bureaucracy, before the TV screen, in politics, with the police; the sense that "nothing can be done." This powerlessness projects itself in the fantasy of the Big News on the Front Page, the terrific Drama of We and They mutually frowning for absolute stakes. But for this fantasy to thrive, there must be adequate Actors. Nixon plugged as hard as he could his *ad hominem* clash with Khrushchev, and indeed thereby almost won the election.

In all these respects Kennedy's Administration is a find. Kennedy can take care of himself in public and with his peers. His musicale has been praised by Paul Henry Lang who was so brutal to Ike. He is his own Secretary of State. His jaw is commensurate with General MacArthur's.* (Russian generals scowl; ours tend to jut the jaw.) He is vigorous and has physical courage. His lack of moral courage is no defect because, with Franco, Chiang Kai-shek, and tommy-gun-defended bomb-shelters, we are far beyond principle anyway; and on the contrary, a slippery idealism, in the style of Luce, makes a good hipster. We have seen that the Administration of active personalities *is* good; unlike with Eisenhower, the Game Theorists now seem at home. Yet the President himself is also a serious man, *sage* in the French sense, commensurate with the need for caution in the Emergency. He does his homework and learns the Facts. He is intelligent—not in the sense that we speak of our friends as intelligent, but in that he can read rapidly through a reasoned memorandum and catch the drift. Though he is high-toned himself, het has a nice family; his brother and sister-in-law have formed a study group in Fairfax county across the Potomac, and Professors Walt and Arthur are going to give weekly lectures.

Most important of all, finally, with the Kennedy Administration there emerges for the first time the possibility of a National Unity to "wage" the Cold War. There is no other figure whose background encompasses McCarthy (and

*In the East Wing of the White House hangs a picture of the Great Stone Face. Considering the theme of Hawthorne's tale, this is really carrying the profiles of history to the point of juvenile *hybris*. Like asking Frost to alter his poem at the Inauguration.

so guarantees that he is not soft on communism) and the Liberal Democrats (and so guarantees that there will be no wage-cuts during the war-economy). For the remainder of this essay, let us trace the lineaments of the New Consensus as a further devolution of American democracy.

VIII

A new Center is necessary. We saw that it is in the nature of the Cold War, where there is aggressive activism without pragmatic power, then there must be blunders, embarrassing at home and abroad, and even economically injurious and so leading to panic among American businessmen who are notoriously unable to take the long view. Such things jolt public identification. Also, the present Administration came in not only with a tenuous majority but also by a coalition—e.g., of urban Negro preachers and Southern politicians, of leftists and financiers—quite impossible to maintain. Within three months of being in office, Kennedy had lost the more earnest liberals who had supported him anyway only because of their congenital obsession not to leave a blank space on a ballot. He has lost the professors, scientists, etc., who protest the nuclear insanity. Youth has held on a little longer—with the Peace Corps and all—but is pulling away fast in all directions. (A gentleman high in the Administration has said that "Youth is not a class"; he is in error.) On the other hand, stalwart party liberals like Gov. Lehman and Mrs. Roosevelt—and apparently even Bowles and Stevenson—*never* quit when there is the appearance of "influence" (they supported Wagner, and Mrs. Roosevelt is now for bomb-shelters if they are community bomb-shelters!). So the Center can go this far left. On the other hand, from the beginning, Kennedy visited Nixon and Eisenhower and as far as General MacArthur. The plan for the New Consensus, therefore, emerges as follows:

(1) To drop the trouble-making liberals as quietly as possible.

(2) To exclude and ridicule the Extreme Right. The official stamp on this policy was the remarkable statement of J. Edgar Hoover condemning the rabid as unwitting fomenters of Communism. He sounded like the anti-anti-Communists of 1953.

(3) By a modest social legislation and a modest advance in Civil Rights, to hold the unions and organized Negro groups, while reassuring business and convincing the Southerners that, in our world position, a progress toward desegregation is inevitable. With the stepped-up production of military hardware, there ought to be no increase in unemployment, even a decrease. Given this much and the continued support of, for example, Senator Humphrey (the Senator is alleged to have said, "When I accepted the leadership, I gave up liberal principles"), the Administration can rely on the ADA milieu of the New York *Post,* without impeding further gains.

(4) The true grandeur and security of the New Consensus come from these further gains: it is beginning to captivate the mass of lower-brow readers of the New York *Daily News* and the educated suburbanites who read Luce magazines and egg on their sons to get good grades and make the prestige colleges. These are the solid centers of Cold War fervor and Cold War mentality. The strengthening of the FBI suits both the righteousness of the stupider and the conformism of the brighter. For the *News* readers, there is an advantage in the friendly ambience of Catholic humanism-plus-discipline, quite oblivious of any notion of civil liberties or social change; for the college-bound, the professors are reassuring of tolerance, and their schools are among the most prestigious. The amalgam of Murrow and Luce in Information has been masterly. To the horror of John Birch, Inc., the TV attitude toward the Communists is often understanding and almost admiring—they are a powerful enemy, we shall have to confront them for "a generation and maybe two generations"—(I quote from a TV documentary called *The Remarkable Comrades*). It is now

only the young pacifists who are treated sharply as naive, misguided, and dangerous idealists. Persons like myself and my friends are gently encouraged as "utopians."

IX

What is the intellectual Idea of the New Consensus? Let us go back to the Professors, who are not now class-objectionable because, in principle, everybody who is not underprivileged goes to college. First, they are not eggheads. An egghead is one who, seduced by intellect and truth, might by chance say something inexpedient or something poetical that illumines the scene. Also, they are not brain-trusters, pragmatists who might come out with future-thinking like the TVA or the uncensored WPA. Rather, as we have seen, the Professors do Analysis and Tabulate Facts. As philosophers, they affirm a broad tolerance of ideas and an absolute pessimism about ideal or "utopian" action. Thus, via Dr. Niebuhr, the sage of *The New Leader,* we get the astoundingly un-Protestant rapprochement of Harvard and the neo-Jesuits!

Washington at present has a pleasantly free atmosphere of discussion. (Naturally I do not know the tone in the middle of the Web of Tensions.) Unlike the previous crew, the professors know from experience that propositions do not bite, and they do make the best conversation-pieces. I myself have been urged, by one who has access, to continue my indispensable "role of dissent." That is, we are the Jester. What is puzzling, however, is that the Administration is continually plaintively asking for ideas; the President asked even the NAM to send him ideas. The implication is, partly, that the carping critics really have no alternatives to suggest. The important fact is that, since the Administration neither can nor is willing to make structural changes, these people would not recognize an idea if they saw it. The openness to ideas, the hunger for ideas, in fact works out as follows:

When a radical reform is proposed—e.g., a concrete

plan to countervail the technologized FBI or the mass-media —at once one hears the most subtle niceties of definition and an amazing purity about constitutionality, possible corruption and abuse, the right of the public to "choose," etc., etc.; and anyway, as the clincher, Congress will never appropriate money for such a purpose. (As a critic has observed, "The wisdom of a policy is measured by the opinion of Mr. Oren Harris of Arkansas.") But if it is a matter of lending a much greater sum to a railroad that every banker has rejected as a bad risk, then there is no difficulty, there is a much looser interpretation of the public interest, and the Administration is willing to push. In the welfare state, there is a nice discrimination between expenditures that subsidize large enterprises and those that are worthless or peanuts. If the Public Sector means roads for General Motors or Urban Renewal for Webb and Knapp, it is attended to; if it means community experiments, work camps for youth, public defenders, or even primary education, it is nicely scrutinized. (But of course this double standard of scrutiny has long been familiar to us in the mysterious law of Economics whereby expenditures in 000,000,000, for armament, are never questioned with regard to nine or ten figures; expenditures for highways, in 00,000,000 are rarely questioned for eight or nine figures. But expenditures for useful domestic purposes, in 000,000 or even 0,000, are most strictly scrutinized; and, as poor people know, expenditures in 00 or even 0.00 require a means test and a quiz on morals.)

"Wagner is a hopeless boob!" exclaimed the Professor. "Then why did you support him?" "It was the chance of getting the Democratic machine away from De Sapio." "But it's *my* city!" I cried, "and you killed a strong reform movement." . . . Yet De Sapio *did* deliver New York City in the nominating convention, after oddly backing Symington, although any honest poll would have given most of the city to Stevenson. There's loyalty! To learn this kind of practical wisdom, you do not need to go to Harvard; you can get it in a pool-room.

Let me illustrate the Higher Science from Aerospace, a wholly government-supported corporation. Attacking Kefauver's anti-drug-monopoly bill, the spokesman of Aerospace explained that it would retard progress in space exploration, e.g., in developing medicines for victims of nuclear fallout. (Washington *Star,* Dec. 10, 1961). Aren't these people shameless?

Since I am nervous about the self-discipline entailed in the New Consensus, I ask about Civil Liberties. I am told, "Bobby Kennedy is not *against* civil liberties, he does not have any notion of what civil liberties *are.*" I did not have the chance to see Harris Wofford, the adviser on Civil Rights, since he was out of the country. (There is no adviser on Civil Liberties.) Wofford is an excellent and thoughtful man; he has even written for *Liberation* about civil disobedience. But he is a professor from Notre Dame and his view on civil disobedience is that we cannot take away a man's God-given right to rot in jail (he does not go on to Hobbes' dictum that the State breaks the social compact if it jails you, and it's your natural duty to escape). But to my mind the most alarming clue of what the Administration promises on civil liberties was its bland, and entirely innocent, proposal to raise the news-rates in order to make the Post Office pay for itself! (This had to be dropped by Congress.) Yet one might have expected it: these people, professors of law and government and history, apparently do not have any notion of what the democratic idea *is.*

X

The New Consensus is an ignoble prospect. It could also be dangerous; for if such a national unity can fully form, we shall drift into a kind of fascism of the majority. If there were then a major reverse—supposing Brazil, Chile, Venezuela would follow Castro—the United States would be a police-state.

Robert Engler speaks of the society of the continuing

Cold War as a "garrison state." I don't think so; it doesn't look like that. Rather, just the tightening of the existing suburban conformism, grade-seeking education, FBI protection, and mass-media, with a little addition of "discipline," "responsibility," and "sacrifice." This would be literally the despotism of the majority that Mill feared, manipulated by a popular Administration to meet chronic Emergency.

In my opinion, the present Administration is committed to the Cold War (despite some evidence, I cannot believe it plans a first-strike nuclear war). It has no other economic plan than a war economy, no foreign policy outside the CIA, and no domestic idea at all.

If the Cold War is to be relaxed and catastrophe prevented, we must do it by action outside of their politics, by every means and on every relevant issue. There is already agitation for peace throughout the world, sporadically, with increasing frequency, and by increasing numbers.

ELIZABETH HARDWICK

The Life and Death of Caryl Chessman

THEY RODE together in harmony, Abraham and Isaac, until they came to Mount Moriah. But Abraham prepared everything for the sacrifice, calmly and quietly; but when he turned and drew the knife, Isaac saw that his left hand was clenched in despair, that a tremor passed through his body —but Abraham drew the knife. Then they returned again home, and Sarah hastened to meet them, but Isaac had lost his faith. No word of this had even been spoken in the world, and Isaac never talked to anyone about what he had seen, and Abraham did not suspect that anyone had seen it.

Kierkegaard, *Fear and Trembling*

The "abominable and voluptuous act known as *reading the paper,*" Proust called it. In a bleary, addicted daze I followed the last years in the life of Caryl Chessman and, with increasing interest—or *consumption,* perhaps one should call the taking in of the flesh and blood of a person through the daily press—his last months. After the shock of his pointless execution, after his exit from the front pages, Chessman still did not entirely remove himself from public contemplation to make room for the young criminals who seemed to spring from the earth just as his bones were lowered into it. Even during the triumphal procession, soon after his death, of Tony and Margaret—the short, little couple, their hands raised as if in a benediction—the ghostly, beaky, droopy, heart-shaped face remained, creating one of those accidental juxtapositions whose significance is everything or nothing.

I wondered how Chessman had appeared in the newspapers during his arrest and trial as "the red light bandit." I went back to the files of the New York *Herald Tribune* and looked up the dates of his tragic history. January 23, 1948, when Chessman was arrested in a stolen car and identified as the man who made assaults on two women—there was nothing in the paper; May 18th, 1948, when he was convicted on seventeen of eighteen charges—nothing; June 25, 1948, when he was given two death sentences—no mention of the case; July 3, 1948, when, at the age of twenty-seven, he entered Death Row in San Quentin prison —blankness in the *Herald Tribune* on this matter. To the East at least, Chessman had been nonexistent as a criminal, as a case, as a doomed young man. He had to bring himself forth from the void of prison, from nothingness, from nonexistence. This condition of his nothingness, his nonexistence, makes his remarkable articulation, his tireless creation of himself as a fact, his nearly miraculous resurrection or birth—which it was we do not know—a powerfully moving human drama. With extraordinary energy, Chessman made, on the very edge of extinction, one of those startling efforts of personal rehabilitation, salvation of the self. It was this energy that brought him out of darkness to the notice of the Pope, Albert Schweitzer, Mauriac, Dean Pike, Marlon

Brando, Steve Allen, rioting students in Lisbon (Lisbon!) —and, perhaps by creating his life, Chessman had to lose it. The vigor of his creation aroused fear, bewilderment, suspicion. As he tells us in his accounts of his fellow convicts on Death Row, it is usually the lost, the cringing, the deteriorated who are finally repieved. A man needs a measure of true life in order to be worth execution.

People on the street, talking about the case, found Chessman's energy, his articulation of his own tragic trap, his stubborn efforts on his own behalf, truly alarming. These efforts were not mitigating; indeed they were condemning. He had trained himself to sleep only a few hours a night so that he could write his books, study law, work on his case. But suppose another condemned man wanted his sleep, couldn't bother to work on his own destiny, hadn't the strength or the talent to bring himself from darkness to light —what then? Lest his very gifts save him, some people wanted him executed in order to show the insignificance of personal vigor before the impersonal law. And, true, his energy is very uncommon among habitual criminals. "Flabby, bald, lobotomized" Lepke; dreamy, paretic gangsters; depressed, deteriorated murderers; goofs putting bombs on planes. Chessman was a young hoodlum who was able, in the last decade of his life, to call upon strange reserves of strength. His early violence and his late effort at personal integration seem to have come from the same mysterious source. Life is haunted by one so peculiarly instructive, a history so full of fearful symbolism.

Cell 2455, Death Row, Chessman's autobiography, is a work of genuine and poignant interest. (Its faults as literature are those almost inevitably found in naturalistic first novels by young men who are writing from harsh experience: occasional sentimentality, strained efforts at rhetorical decoration, cultural pretentiousness. Its virtues are of the same genre—power, natural expressiveness, authenticity.) This is an oddly American book. The need to confess violent thoughts is softened by the cream of despairing sentiment, remembered hopes, perfect loves, and the incongruent beauties of the jungle. I had not thought of reading it until after the execution. It had not seemed likely that Chessman would have sufficient objectivity to tell us what we wanted to know about him; or that, if he had the intention to give a serious picture, he would have the words at hand. Almost unwillingly one discovers that he really had, as he said, a great deal to tell. The life of a chronic offender, existence reduced to chaos or ruled by tides of compulsion, reform school, jail, parole, jail once more, and death at the end of it—that history he is abundantly able to record.

The aim of this aching revelation was to save the author from the gas chamber and that it did not do. Its other aim—to picture the life of a young criminal—is accomplished with exceptional truth. Careening cars, gun fights, arrests, escapes, loyalties and betrayals, horror, confusion, defiance, manic decision, hopeless cruelties: there it is. But it is not a collage. In the center is a person, young, monstrously careless, living in hell, acting out these sordid images and twisted yearnings. Chessman is himself and also a national and international phenomenon of our period. Someone like him will be in the news tomorrow in New York, in Paris, in Moscow. His story has an uncanny application at a hundred points. You never doubt his existence or that of his companions, desperate boys named Tuffy or Skinny, and coarse girls, defiantly self-debasing. These are harsh portraits, very unlike the social worker's case history, the TV delinquents, who cannot avoid a false tidiness and handsomeness as they sweat to render an image not their own. The kindly, manly interviewer, the restless kid, the nagging, hysterical parents—the truth is so much worse than the "problem." We know convicts and condemned men are people, but we are always certain they are not the people in the movies. Their restless, self-devouring emptiness, so like our own, has an unbearably great importance because of their crimes against others and their torture to themselves. Chessman's books, particularly *Cell 2455,* and many passages from his other books about his case, could not possibly be negligible because of the information he was peculiarly able to impart. And beyond that, the fact that he, from whom nothing could have been expected, was able to write them at all is a circumstance of compelling interest. It seems to suggest that only through "art," through some difficult and utterly personal expression is reclamation and prevention possible. This is a world beyond the therapy of the basketball court, the recreation center, the social worker's hopeful sympathy. Its energy alone could only be used up in some violent dedication.

The Story: Chessman's family, his early years, are not what one would expect. He was an only child who loved his parents and was loved by them. Perhaps this love lends itself to interpretation because of his tendency to idealize his parents and his failure to make them real. About his mother: "Hallie was a dreamer, at heart a poetess with both feet firmly planted on the ground and her soft, searching blue eyes in the heavens." In any case, the affection on both sides was real and lasting. Chessman was spared the blight of neglect, abandonment, beatings, drunkenness; his severe delinquency does not easily yield its secret and the family situation is a clue to his strength rather than his weaknesses. His parents urged him to "do the right thing," to return to reform school when he had escaped and so on, but he does not record any pressure more coercive than their mere hopes and pleas. They were feeble trusting people. The believed whatever excuse their son gave for staying out all night and were always surprised and dismayed to learn he had been "getting into trouble." Chessman's schemes, his plans, his hopes, all expressed in the vigorous distortions of his own personality, were of a degree of vitality and daring beyond anything the parents could call upon. They were frail, harmless branches blown about by a genuine tornado. To the tornado, they are the idealized calm, pitiful and innocent. He defends and destroys them at the same time. After he was grown, Chessman learned that his mother was a foundling. She did not know who she was. He set out to find her. With the money he got holding up brothels, he hired a detective to trace his mother's origins. Nothing was discovered.

Early, he contracted bronchial asthma. He was nursed and protected by his parents, but in his own mind the asthma was a profound indication of weakness and shame. "The need to be strong became more demanding with each passing attack." A few years later, an attack of encephalitis left Chessman tone deaf. "The disease ravaged [his] personality as well as his physical self." This was followed by tantrums at school, cruelty, and hatred of himself because of aggressive feelings. His mother was injured in an automobile accident and became permanently paralyzed. Disasters multiplied. All the family resources were spent on the mother's illness. When Chessman was fifteen, his father attempted suicide, "with a prayer for forgiveness." The family went on the dole. With the humiliation of food packages, Chessman began his criminal activity. He told his credulous parents that he had a paper route and got up early in the morning to rob stores of provisions left outside. The dole, the food packages, the search for new doctors and new operations for the mother are pretexts for crime; he does not pretend they were more than that.

All pretexts are gradually discarded. Motivation is hidden and justification is not even attempted beyond the hunger of vanity and the compulsion of destructiveness. "He committed nine burglaries, he purchased food with forged personal checks and got, in addition to the food, a dollar or two back in cash." Because of his childhood illnesses and physical weaknesses, Chessman convinced himself that he wouldn't live long and that his thefts and forgeries would be punished by God. His guilt was relieved and, waiting as he was upon his final and eternal judgment, he could hope his parents would not discover his misdeeds. Not long after, he went to a doctor for a simple stomach ache and had his illusion of imminent death destroyed. He was told he was sound and healthy. "These words had an almost paralyzing effect. . . . They meant he wouldn't die!" His parents, after all, would have the sorrow of his disgrace. "God had no right to punish his parents for what he had done! Already they had been made to suffer too much. Already they had made too many sacrifices for him. He, alone, deserved punishment." (These are youthful sentiments, recalled later. Chessman died an atheist, rejecting religious rites and burial and saying that for him to call upon God would be hypocrisy. One of his lawyers thought this his worst trait of character.)

It is hard to avoid the thought that Chessman's conscious feelings about his parents masked other feelings of great distress to himself. Shortly after his discovery that he would have to live, he began to risk everything. And the story of his life, at the point of its greatest recklessness and violence, becomes more truthful. Self-knowledge increases, as nostalgia, adolescent emotions, acceptable fears and longings withdraw.

Cars: "That night he stole two cars and committed three burglaries." The young offender's dreams are alive with the embraces of warm, fat, forbidden cars. The car is freedom, power, exhilaration, madness. "Driving was a joyous form of creative expression. Driving made him free. Driving was his personal, triumphant accomplishment." Yet, the pleasure of driving is no greater than the joy in wrecking. ". . . he practiced driving or 'tooling' these hot heaps. He learned to corner, to broadside, to speed and snap-shift them. He purposely rolled and crashed them. He sent them hurtling through traffic at high speeds. He sought out patrol cars and motorcycle cops and taunted them into chasing him, just for the thrill of ditching them, just for the hell of it, and for practice." The car is escape—and capture. No sooner are Chessman and the other reform boys out of jail than they are in a stolen car, running through a stop light, alerting the police, who start after them and put them back in jail. The car is not stolen, altered, driven, to provide accommodation for the criminal on the run. It is wrecked just when it would be most useful. It is driven conspicuously, not stealthily.

Capture: Capture is courted with all the passionate energy that just a few weeks previously went into escape. "I stepped into a stolen car the Glendale police had staked out and was promptly arrested by two detectives with drawn guns." Or "I wanted peace and I unhesitatingly declared war to find it. I wanted to get even, to have one last defiant fling, and to go out in a blaze of ironically stolen glory." There is no meaning, no purpose, no gain. "Repeatedly we had had it impressed upon us that the road we followed led not to riches but to prison or the grave. Soon we reached the point where we were unable to justify the continuation of our collective effort without frankly admitting that our goal was merely to raise as much violent, dramatic, suicidal hell as possible. . . ."

He was put in reform school, released in April, 1937. He came home to his weak, lenient, kind parents. "The next day he was home and his homecoming was a happy one. . . . Not a word of censure did he hear. His parents' sole concern was for his future and how it could be made a success. And they were immensely pleased at how sturdy and healthy he appeared." Freedom is brief. The need to get back in conflict with the law begins almost at the prison gate, after the handshake with the paroling officer, after the lecture. Paroled in April, in May he had stolen a car and more armed robberies began. All this culminated years later in his arrest and identification as the "red light bandit," an armed robber who flashed a red light into cars parked on "lovers' lanes," robbed the couple, and twice sexually assaulted the women. "After nine years of criminal violence and penal servitude following his release from reform school, he had come to the condemned row at San Quentin prison, twice condemned to death."

San Quentin at last. Prison is a part of the cycle; escape and capture alternate back and forth, "naturally." Capture is rest from the manic push. The glum, exhausted face of the young outlaw is as revealing as his arrogant, excited mask during the chase. There is no sensible plan, no criminal organization; it is crime and punishment, escape and capture, parole and violation. San Quentin, the ultimate, the final, appears early in this grim dialogue. With Chessman, the exhilaration of violence gives way to extraordinary exertion in handling the fact of imprisonment.

Cruelty and threats have no meaning to men who live by cruelty and threats. They merely provide self-justification. The desire to be strong, not to bend under punishment, keeps criminal defiance alive. "I preferred to stand on my own feet, even if it was in hell." Independence, fearlessness, distorted into horrors, have a monstrous power over the convict. Chessman certainly died with "dignity," and that was the best he could do for himself, even if his kind of fearlessness is a tragic example of strength. Even his last words make much of the crippling "courage" he had lived by. "When you read this, they will have killed me. I will have exchanged oblivion for an unprecendented twelve year nightmare. And you will have witnessed the final, lethal, ritualistic act. It is my hope and my belief that you will be able to report that I died with dignity, without animal fear and without bravado. I owe that much to myself."

The woe of his crimes and the waste of his life lay upon Chessman's soul. He feels that society does not understand the young criminal. It is his mission to explain. "It is the story of a grinning, brooding, young criminal psychopath in definitely willing bondage to his psychopathy." The fate is personal, mysterious. "My father had failed to grasp the real reason for my many clashes with authority. He would never understand what drove me. He never would be fully aware of the jungle."

And what drove him? What was the jungle? "I ventured the thought that perhaps after one spends a while in a jungle world he gets so he cannot or does not want to believe there is anything better, or that it is attainable in any case. Maybe hate has a lot to do with it. Hate for everybody, for himself."

"But there are periods of self-doubt when you know yourself for what you really are—an angry, hating, fighting *failure*. Usually then you curse your doubts and blaspheme the imagery [*sic*] of the self you see."

His history is appalling. "Yes, I have been in reform schools, jails, and prisons most of my life. Yes, I had committed many, many crimes and had ample warning of what to expect if I kept on. Yes, I had kept on nevertheless. No, I was not guilty of the crimes for which I was sentenced to death. I was not the red light bandit. . . . Yes, I would say I was not the red light bandit even if I were."

The Thing is describable but inexplicable. "I was one of the trees in this dark and forbidding forest. I knew what it meant to live beyond the reach of other men or God. I had 'proved' everything I had felt the need to prove: that I couldn't be scared or broken or driven to my knees, that I didn't give a damn. But here is where the tragedy lies: this felt need is compulsive and negative only. It is a need to prove one can do without—without love, without faith, without belief, without warmth, without friends, without freedom. This negative need to prove becomes progressively greater and greater . . . the ultimate (conscious or unconscious) need is to prove that one can do without even life itself."

How is society to heal such a desperate sickness? Chessman puts himself in the position of a leper who is also a physician. He studies his own pains and deformations; he does not find the answer. Each offender is different from every other. The salvation of the meanest or the mildest is as complicated and difficult as the life of every noncriminal man. It is tedious, discouraging, even hopeless. Society is too dull, too rigid, too tired to make the effort. We do not even want to reform the criminal because of our anger that we have sometimes tried and failed. Every account of jails, of guards and matrons seems to show that reform is not believed in or encouraged. If a man might be saved by eight hours at the piano, the warden is sure to put him in the jute mill to teach him his lesson. The senseless determination of the prison officials to keep poor Chessman from writing is one of the most depressing and telling aspects of this sad case. One of the wardens at San Quentin, admitting that Chessman was not a difficult disciplinary problem, said, "So far as I'm concerned, our only problems with him have been literary."

The case: There was a large element of the sacrificial in Chessman's execution. Even if he was absolutely guilty, the way of stating the charge and the decision to give the death penalty were severe beyond anything we are accustomed to. Further, the fact that the unusual severity of the sentence, in a case where murder was not involved or kidnapping either in any sense in which the world understands the term, could not be modified after exhaustive litigation suggests again the sacrificial and symbolic nature of the case. In Mark Davidson's study in *The Californian* he says, ". . . Chessman was not convicted of rape, because in both of the robbery-attack offenses for which he was condemned, the victims persuaded the bandit not to pursue coitus. The bandit instead had them perform *fellatio*. . . ." It has been widely suggested that Chessman's execution was society's punishment of its own perverse sexual wishes or deeds.

The mystery and force of Chessman's character were probably more outraging than the sordid crime itself. This older juvenile posed the question for which we have no answer. Why had he been a hoodlum at all? His cockiness, his loquaciousness, his cleverness, his energy, his talents only made his life more mysterious and more repulsive. His command of the word repelled the jurors. One of them twelve years later told a reporter that Chessman was just "as vicious as ever." When asked how she could know this, she replied, "After all, I seen his picture in the papers and he still has that same mean look, don't he?" He went on talking, defying, acting as his own lawyer, writing books, trying society's patience more and more. His life represents our defeat, our dread of the clear fact that we do not know how to deal with the senseless violence of the young. It is not too hard to understand organized crime, but how can you understand two young boys who kill an old couple in their candy store for a few dollars? In our rich society, the smallness of the sums for which people are killed shows a contempt for money as well as for human life. The nihilism at the bottom of Chessman's fate, his brains, what the newspapers called his "evil genius," made him a fearful and dreadful example. His cleverness undid him. His fight for his life was stubborn, cocky, pugnacious—and defiant.

In a sacrificial death, the circumstances that the mass fears and dreads and violently condemns may arouse involuntary feelings of wonder and grief in others. There was something almost noble in the steely, unyielding effort Chessman had made to define and save himself. He was a real person. He had breathed life into himself. One could only say that when he died this poor criminal was *at his best*. It was dismal to think his struggle counted for nothing. His ordeal was a tangle of paradoxes. He had spent twelve years in the death house because the law hesitated to deny him every possibility for reversal of the sentence. Those were horrible years, awaiting the answer. Would it have been better if he had been executed six months after his sentence? No, it would not have been better. And yet twelve years are twelve years, a unique suffering that cannot be denied. Somehow a justice complicated enough to delay twelve years to study the "technicalities" should have been complicated enough to refuse death simply because so many delays were legally possible. A part of the protest was a cry against rigidity and against the element of meanness in the law's refusal to place the case in a human context. And there was the *feeling* that Chessman might be innocent.

The claims for innocence: 1. The transcript of the trial was deeply impugned by the death of the court stenographer before he had transcribed more than a third of his private notes. The transcription and the enlargement were done, without Chessman's approval, by a relative of the prosecutor.

2. The description of the red light bandit, given before the arrest, did not entirely fit Chessman. 3. He was identified not in the line-up, but in handcuffs. 4. He had committed a wide variety of crimes, none of them involving attacks on women before this arrest. 5. He said he was innocent of the crimes for which he was sentenced to death.

After Chessman died in the death chamber, Governor Brown said he was sorry he had had no power to stay the execution and claimed he said this even though he was fully satisfied of Chessman's guilt. It was reported he then went for a lonely, sorrowing ride in the country. A detective who worked on Chessman's case and later married one of the victims attended the execution at San Quentin and said, when the death was at last accomplished, "I'm satisfied."

The end was reported with prodigal fullness. As I gluttonously read a dozen newspapers—a dozen newspapers all telling the same story of the gas pellets, the winks, the final lip-read goodbyes, the last struggles of the body—I remembered a hanging that had taken place in my youth. On the morning a Negro was to be hanged in the courthouse yard, other Negroes stayed at home from their work for fear of the way the wind might blow. That same morning a relation of mine went downtown to shop in a department store. The Negro who would ordinarily have been operating the elevator was at home, quietly waiting for the dangerous day to pass. My relation fell down the elevator shaft and suffered ghastly damage to her body and mind.

SEYMOUR KRIM

The Insanity Bit

I

UNTIL THIS TIME of complete blast-off in seemingly every department of human life, the idea of insanity was thought of as the most dreadful thing that could happen to a person. Little was actually known about it and the mind conjured up pictures of Bedlam, ninnies walking around in a stupor, a living death that lasted until the poor damned soul's body expired and peace tucked him or her away for eternal keeps. But in this era of monumental need to rethink and redefine almost every former presumption about existence—which has inspired a bombing way of looking at what once were considered the most unbudgeable rocks of reality—the locked door of insanity has been shaken loose and shall yet be hurled wide open. Until one day the prisoners of this definition will walk beside us sharing only the insane plight of mortality itself, which makes quiet madmen of us all.

Every American family has its "psychotic" cousin or uncle; every friend has wept, prayed, hoped (and finally slid into indifference) for another friend sweating it out in insulin- or electric-shock behind the gray walls (public institution) or beyond the clipped roses (private sanitarium). Although my brother, Herbert J. Krim, was institutionalized when I was barely in my 20's—and I cosigned the certificate for a prefrontal lobotomy which ended with his death by hemorrhage on the operating table at Rockland State Hospital—I still had the conventional ideas about insanity that are shared by all "responsible" readers of the New York *Times*. It is true that as a serious writer I had inherited a great tradition of complete independence and honesty to my actual experience, regardless of what I was supposed to feel; but this was sabotaged by my youth, my ignorance, and an inability to separate my own personal life from a responsibility to question the clichés of experience to their ultimate depth. Like most American writers, from would-be's to celebrities, I was intensely preoccupied by my acutely painful and highly exaggerated subjective image—the Jewish cross, looks, sex, masculinity, a swarm of fears and devices for concealment that were secondary to my decent abilities and serious obligations as a writer intent on telling the truth. In other words: I was too narcissistically and masturbatorially stuck on myself to appreciate the horrible waste of my brother Herbert's death; and with the snotty sense of superiority usually felt by the young American writer, I thought *I* would be forever immune to the judgments of a society which I loftily ignored, or nose-thumbed, without ever coming to grips with it on the actual mat of life. Like every creative type of my generation whom I met in my 20's, I was positive I was sanctified, protected by my "genius," my flair, my overwhelming ambition.

I was as wrong as you can be and still live to tell about it. In the summer of 1955, when I was 33, the thousand unacknowledged human (not literary) pressures in my being exploded. I ran barefooted in the streets, spat at members of my family, exposed myself, was almost bodily thrown out of the house of a Nobel Prize-winning author, and believed

God had ordained me to act out every conceivable human impulse without an ounce of hypocritical caution. I know today that my instinct was sound, but my reasoning was self-deceptive. It was not God who ordained me, but I who ordained God for my own understandable human purposes. I needed an excuse to force some sort of balance between my bulging inner life and my timid outer behavior, and I chose the greatest and most comforting symbol of them all. He was my lance and my shield as I tore through the New York streets acting out the bitter rot of a worldful of frustrations that my human nature could no longer lock up. I was finally cornered on the 14th floor of the St. Regis Hotel by two frightened friends and another brother; and with the aid of handcuffs seriously-humorously clipped on by a couple of bobbies I was led off to Bellevue, convinced all along that I was right. I tolerated those who took me away with the kindly condescension of a fake Jesus.

From Bellevue I was soon transferred to a private laughing academy in Westchester and given insulin-shock treatments. No deep attempt was made to diagnose my "case"—except the superficial and inaccurate judgment that I had "hallucinated." Factually, this was not true; I did not have visual images of people or objects which were not there; I merely believed, with the beautiful relief of absolute justice which the soul of man finds when life becomes unbearable, that God had given me the right and the duty to do everything openly that I had secretly fantasied for years. But this distinction was not gone into by my judges and indifferent captors. They did not have the time, the patience, or even the interest because work in a flip-factory is determined by mathematics: you must find a common denominator of categorization and treatment in order to handle the battalions of miscellaneous humanity that are marched past your desk with high trumpets blowing in their minds.

Like all the other patients, I was considered beyond reasoning with and was treated like a child; not brutally, but efficiently, firmly and patronizingly. In the eyes of this enclosed world I had relinquished my rights as an adult human being. The causes for my explosion were not even superficially examined, nor was the cheek-pinching house psychiatrist—with a fresh flower in the buttonhole of his fresh daily suit—truly equipped to cope with it even if he had tried, which he did not. Private sanitariums and state institutions, I realized much later, were isolation chambers rather than hospitals in the usual sense; mechanical "cures" such as the one I underwent in a setup of unchallenged authority, like the Army or a humanitarian prison, slowly brought 75 per cent of the inmates down to a more temporarily modest view of reality. Within nine or ten weeks I too came down, humbled, ashamed, willing to stand up before the class and repeat the middle-class credo of limited expressiveness and the meaning of a dollar in order to get my discharge.

In three months' time I was out, shaken, completely alone, living in a cheap Broadway hotel room (having been ashamed to go back to Greenwich Village) and going to a conventional Ph.D. psychologist (I had been to three medically-trained therapists in the preceding decade) as a sop to both my conscience and family. I had broken beyond the bounds of "reality"—a shorthand word which is used by the average psychiatrist for want of the more truthfully complex approach that must eventually accommodate our beings' increasing flights in higher altitudes—and come back to the position I was in before. But once again the causes that had flung me into my own sky continued to eat me up. Sexually unconfident, I went to whores, ate my meals alone, and forced myself to write a few pieces in that loneliest of places, a tiny blank hotel room in the middle of nowhere. For the first time in my life the incentive to live, the isolation and frustration of my existence, grew dim; while the psychologist smiled and smoked his pipe—and did the well-adjusted, tweedy, urbane act behind his tastefully battered desk as he ladled out platitudes—I was saving up the sleeping bombs, and when I had enough to do the trick I burned the letters I had received through the years from the several men and women I had loved, destroyed my journal of 15 years' standing, and one carefully chosen night went to a hotel in Newark, N. J.

My plan was to take the pills and slowly conk out in the full bathtub, ultimately drowning like Thomas Heggen; if one missed the other would work. I splurged on a beautiful deathroom in a modernistic hotel, one that included a bathroom with the biggest tub in the house. But it was too small to fit my long body. The idea of not being able to drown and of surviving the pills afterwards, perhaps to become a burden or an invalid, began to scar what seemed like a paradise of suicide. I went instead to a Polish bar in downtown Newark, vaguely seeking the eternal anodynes of snatch and booze while I mentally played with my fate.

I found the booze and saw a coarse, ignorant Polish girl do such a life-giving, saucy, raucous folk dance (on the small dance floor to the right of the bar) that I broke into loving sobs like prayers over my drink. The sun of life blazed from her into my grateful heart. I went back to the beautiful hotel room, poured the pills down the toilet, and went to sleep. The next morning I returned to Manhattan a chastened man, shaking my head at how close I had come to nonbeing.

When I told my tale to Mr. Pipe, my psychologist, he speedily hustled me off to a legitimate head-doctor who doped me until a private ambulance came. Very much in my right and one and only mind but too paralyzed by drugs to move, I was once again taken on the long ride—this time to another hedge-trimmed bin in Long Island. I was helpless to protest, mainly because of the shame and guilt I felt for even contemplating suicide. Obviously I was not crazy, mad, psychotic, out of my mind, schizophrenic, paranoiac. I was simply a tormented man-kid who had never steeled himself to face the facts of life—who didn't know what it meant to have principles and live by them come grief or joy—and who thought that human worth and true independence comes as easily as it does in the movies we were all emotionally faked on. As a sputtering fiction-writer and fairly active literary critic, I had had occasional peaks of maturity and illumination; but as a man I was self-deceptive, self-indulgent, crying inwardly for the pleasures of a college boy even while in my imagination I saw myself as another Ibsen or Dreiser. Ah, the extraordinary mismating of thoughts in the mind of the modern American literary romantic, as fantastic and truly unbelievable a stew of unrelated dreams as have ever been dreamt, believe me!

Once again I was on the human assembly-line: electric shock clubbed my good brain into needless unconsciousness (and I walked to my several executions like a brave little chappie instead of questioning them) and unquestioned Old Testament authority ruled our little club. Good-natured, but mostly cowlike and uneducated male orderlies carried out the orders from above; and apart from the mechanical treatment and the unimaginative grind of occupational therapy, each patient was left completely on his or her bewildered own, a sad and farcical sight when one considered the $125 per week that their frightened families were paying.

I saw now that nine-tenths of the people I was quartered with were not "insane" by any of the standards a normally intelligent person would use: the majority had lost confidence in their own ability to survive in the world outside, or their families were *afraid* of them and had palmed them off on "experts," but positively no serious effort was being made to equip them to become free and independent adults. This was their birthright—beyond country and society, indeed an almost religious obligation—but they were palliated with pills or jolted with shock, their often honest rage echoed back to them as a sign of their "illness." Some of them must have been "sick," you say. I answer: Who can not be conceived as such in a world so complex ("The truth is there is a truth on every side"—Richard Eberhart) that each group has its own method for judging manners, behavior, ideas, and finally the worth of human values? What was more important was that I, a person from a hip milieu and with a completely opposite set of values, could see their so-called sickness with the human sensibility that an immersion in literature and experience had given me—rather than as a clinical manifestation. When I later recognized the objective provinciality of many psychiatrists in precisely the humanistic areas that could cover the actions of the majority of the inmates without finding it "psychotic," I realized that the independent thinker and artist today must learn to be resolute toward a subtle, socially powerful god-father who often drips paternalism: namely, the newly-enthroned psychiatric minority that has elevated itself to a dangerous position of "authority" in the crucial issues of mind, personality, and sanity.

I now began to fight persistently—but still with shakiness—for my release; my life was my own: it did not belong to the clichés of the salesman-aggressive, well-barbered, Jewish-refugee (my brother, my enemy!) house psychiatrist or to my smiling, betweeded nonentity of a psychologist, who paid me diplomatically inscrutable visits like a Japanese ambassador. Even if I had been or if there were such a reality as a "raving maniac"—which, perhaps childishly, I implore the over-imaginative, zeitgeist-vulnerable reader to believe is an impossible conception today—I would and should have fought for my release. What the institution-spared layman does not realize is that a sensitive and multiple-reacting human being remains the same everywhere, including a sanitarium, and such an environment can duplicate the injustice or vulgarity which drove your person there in the first place. By this I mean that a mental hospital is not an asylum or a sanctuary in the old-fashioned sense: it is just a roped-off side-street of modern existence, rife with as many contradictions, half-truths and lousy architecture as life itself.

Both of the sanitariums I was in were comparable to Grossinger's, in that they took in only financially comfortable, conventionally middle-class, nonintellectual people. By every human standard my being there was life's sarcastic answer to whatever romantic ideas I had about justice. Since the age of 19 I had deliberately led an existence of experimentation, pursuit of truth, bohemianism, and noncommercialism: fate's punishment for my green naïveté was for me to recover my supposed mental health in this atmosphere of uncriticizable authority, air-conditioned by just the whiffs of truth that are perfumed and bland, and based on a pillar of middle-class propriety with the cut-throat reality of money underneath. Could I accept my former life, which had produced some good work, as a lie to myself—which the house-psychiatrist wanted me to do (in effect) in his one psychotherapeutic pass at me (he left me alone after this)? I could not and never would: not only for myself but for the great principles and accomplishments of others, both living and dead, which had been my guide throughout my adult life. I might fail—but why go on having an identity at all if in a crisis you will throw away not only your past years, but the moral achievements of rare souls who have shared in your emotional and intellectual experience and whose own contributions to existence are also at stake?

When I heard this second house-psychiatrist literally equate sanity with the current clichés of adjustment and describe Greenwich Village as a "psychotic community," I saw with sudden clarity that *insanity* and *psychosis* can no longer be respected as meaningful definitions—but are used by limited individuals in positions of social power to describe ways of behaving and thinking that are alien, threatening, and *obscure* to them. (A year later when I took a psychiatrist friend of mine to the San Remo, she told me with a straight face that it reminded her of the "admission ward in Bellevue," where she had interned. This was her analogy on the basis of accurate but limited experience, that increasing chasm which prevents intelligent people from understanding each other. I realized with a sense of almost incommunicable hopelessness that the gap between her and the well-known poet with whom I had had a beer at the Remo two weeks before was tremendous, and that between these two poles of intelligence the neutral person—who could see the logic of each—was being mashed up with doubt and conflict. The poet was at home, or at least the heat was off, there; while the psychiatrist felt alien and had made a contemptuous psycho-sociological generalization. There was little bond of shared values and therefore genuine communication between both of these intelligent and honest human beings, each of whom contributed to my life.)

To finish with my four months in the sanitarium: I argued and reasoned for the basic right to the insecurity of freedom, and finally a good friend did the dirty in-fighting of getting me out. Had I to do it over again, I believe I would now have the guts to threaten such an institution or psychologist with a lawsuit, ugly as such a procedure can be to a person already vulnerable with the hash-marks of one legally defined "psychotic episode" and the contemplation of the criminal act of suicide. But I had been—as so many of Jack Kerouac's subterraneans are when faced with the machinery of official society—milk and sawdust when, in such situations, you must be iron and stone in spite of your own frailty. It is not that the present-day authorities of mental life want to railroad anyone, as in your Grade C horror movie; it is merely that as one grows older it becomes clear that there are almost irremediable differences between people in the total outlook towards life.

Mine had hardened as a result of my experiences, and I realized it was better to die out in the world if need be than be deprived of the necessity to confront existence because of the cheap authority of a lock and key. The majority of people who stay in mental institutions for any length of time do not want to return to the uncertain conditions outside the walls: which in our time spells out to emotionally anarchic, multidimensional, brain-trying, anxiety-loaded, and—O hear me mortality, from the Year One!—ultimate and divine life.

II

I returned downtown—to the very Village that I heard the psychiatrist place deep in Freudian Hell, with that pious overextension of terminology which reveals a limited private morality behind the use of so-called scientific language—and tried to tenderly pick up the threads of my former social life. I saw that my closest and most brilliant friends did not really understand, or were afraid to understand, the contemporary insanity bit. Almost all of them had been soul-whirled by psychotherapy at some time, and each had the particularly contemporary fear of insanity which has become the psychological H-bomb of city life; in theory they may have granted that insanity was no longer the uniform horror it seems to the inexperienced imagination—like a spook in the night—but centuries of inherited fear, plus the daily crises of 1950's living, made them emotionally cautious about seeing my experience as merely an *extension* of their own.

One, a poet-philosopher whom I admire, clapped me on the back and said with some literary awe that I had "returned from the dead, like Lazarus." This struck me as greatly melodramatic, untruthful, and saddening because intellectuals and especially artists should be the very people to understand that insanity today is a matter of definition, not fact; that there can no longer be a fixed criterion, just as there is no longer a reality like that described by Allen Ginsberg in *Howl* (an exciting achievement), where he sees "the best minds of my generation destroyed by madness."

I believe this is lurid sentimentality. Ginsberg may have seen the most gifted people of his generation destroyed by an *interpretation* of madness, which is a much more real threat in a time of such infinite, moon-voyaging extension to experience that the validly felt act is often fearfully jailed in a windowless cell of definition by hard-pressed authorities, whose very moral axis is in danger of toppling. Madness today is a literary word; insanity is a dated legal conception as rigid as an Ibsen play; and "psychosis," the antiseptic modern word that sends chills down the ravines of my friends' minds, has become so weakened (despite its impressive white-jacketed look) by narrow-minded, square, and fast-slipping ideological preconceptions that it must be held at arm's length, like a dead rat, for any cool understanding. When this is done, I believe you will see that the word and the state of mind it tries to fix are subject to the gravest questioning; much of which centers around the amount of freedom either permitted to human expression or, more important, what it must take for itself to live in this time when such *unfamiliar* demands are made on the being. Norms crack when they can no longer fight back the content that spills over cookie-mold conceptions of "sane" behavior —and they must be elasticized to stretch around the new bundle of life.

Two weeks before I was back walking down 8th Street a gratefully free neurotic, I had been thought of in the minds of compassionate but uninformed friends as a fairly wild-eyed psychotic. The mere fact that I had been in a sanitarium had pulled a curtain of emotional blindness down over my friends' vision; and yet I was the same person I had been when I entered the happy-house. The unexamined fear of an "insanity" which no longer exists as a framed picture conventionalizes the very people who should view this now only *symbolic* word with clear, unafraid, and severely skeptical eyes. I had not been among "the dead"—unless killing time looking at "Gunsmoke" and Jackie Gleason on TV, playing bridge, and reading Tolstoy and Nathanael West is considered death. I had not been "destroyed by madness," Mr. Ginsberg!—in fact, the act of incarceration made me realize how significant (indeed indelible) individual freedom is, and thus helped brick-and-mortar my point of view rather than destroy it. When I was once again semi-knit into a way of life in my new Village home, I discovered that other writers and intellectuals whom I knew had also undergone the sanitarium or mental-hospital holiday, but had kept mum because of indecision as to how frankly one should confess such a stigma.

I understood their practical caution, but discovered

that they lived in a sewer-light of guilt, fear and throat-gagging anxiety, instead of openly and articulately coping with the monster of doubt. "Do you think I'm sane?" is the question I ultimately began to hear from these brilliant people (one scarred tribesman to another!) who had been intimidated into denying the worth of their most pregnant ideas, the very ones that create *new concrete standards of sanity or sense* in a time that has emotionally, if not yet officially, outlived the abstractions of the past. For myself—although uncertain as to how expressive I should be, even with the very intellectuals I had always considered my brothers in a completely free inquiry into every nook and cranny of life—the problem was suddenly answered when a gifted young writer told a charming hostess I had just met that I had been in "two insane asylums."

I was pierced and hurt, not because I actually considered my supposed nuttiness a yellow badge of dishonor, but because the writer in question had ducked out from under his own experience (which I instinctively knew included some of the crises which had launched me upon the streets like a human missile) and pretended such melodrama was foreign to him. I was appalled because I thought that of all people my fellow highbrow writers should be the first to understand and concede the universal nature of the blows that had felled me in the eyes of official society. But I was wrong. There are spikes on the truth which are so close to the slashed heart of contemporary mortality that men and women will lie and refuse acknowledgment, even when it is necessary to the survival of others; they forfeit their humanhood and final worth to life by doing this, but even in the small band of the avant-garde the pursuit of the truth is given up with that weak excuse: "a practical sense of reality."

After this turncoat put-down by a member of my own club, so to speak, there was no longer any issue for myself. I could not live with the squirming burden of secretiveness because my personal history had become public gossip in the small Village group I traveled with. After snake-bitten laughter at my own romantically cultivated simple-mindedness in thinking my fall would be taken with the hip sophistication I had truly expected, I was glad I had become a stooge or victim; because I basically knew that I had played a juicy part in a contemporary American morality play that is going to do standing-room nightly until its implications are understood. We live in what for the imaginative person are truly hallucinated times, because there is more life on every side—and the possibility of conceiving this surplus in a dizzying multitude of ways—than our inheritance and equipment enables us to deal with. My type and perhaps your type of person only *acted out* what other less passionate people feel, but do not express. A "break-down" such as mine can therefore be learned from:

The first thing one can see is that the isolating of a person saves his or her friends and family from being embarrassed (trivial as this seems, it is a nasty factor in institutionalization), perhaps hurt, and theoretically stops the "sick" person from doing something irreparable while in the grip of the furies. Seen this way, the enforced shackling of an individual seems sad but reasonable. But contemporary adults, however disturbed (often with justice!), are not children; there is doubt in my mind whether we have any right, other than blunt self-interest, to impose our so-called humanitarian wishes on another to the degree where we jail them in order to save them. I must illustrate this with my own case. When I was considered out of my mind during my original upward thrust into the sheer ecstasy of 100 per cent uninhibitedness, I was aware of the "daringness" of my every move; it represented at heart an existential *choice* rather than a mindless discharge. It could not be tolerated by society, and I was punished for it, but my "cure" was ultimately a chastisement, *not a medical healing process.* In my own exhibitionistic and self-dramatizing way, when I flipped, I was nevertheless instinctively rebelling against a fact which I think is objectively true in our society and time: and that is the lack of alignment between an immense inner world and an outer one which has not yet legalized, or officially recognized, the forms that can tolerate the flood of communication from the mind to the stage of action.

Traditionally, it was always taught that the artistic person could work out his or her intense private life by expressing it on the easel or typewriter. In faded theory this seems reasonable, but with the billionaire's wealth of potential human experience both fore, aft and sideways in the world today, it is abnormal not to want to participate more Elizabethanly in this overabundant life. The hunchbacked joy the artist once may have had in poring over the objects of his interest, and then putting the extract into his work, can no longer be honestly sufficient to the most human hearts today. There has arisen an overwhelming need for the highly imaginative spirit (based on the recognition that the mere mind of man can no longer lock up the volume of its experience) to forge a bridge so that the bursting galaxy of this inner world can be received in actual public life. But there is such a time-lag between our literally amazing subjective life—which has conceptions of a powerful altitude equal to the heaven-exploring freedom of privacy—and the mummery of outer behavior, that when the contemporary imaginator expresses his genuine thoughts in public he often feels that he has exposed himself beyond redemption. Room has not yet been made by those who dominate social power for the natural outward show of the acrobatic thinking that ceaselessly swings in the surrealistic minds of our most acute contemporaries. Put crudely but simply, a bookish notion of what constitutes "normality" in this supremely a-normal age drives the liveliest American sensibilities back into the dungeon of self—creating pressures which must maim the soul one way or another—rather than understanding that the great need today is for imagination to come gloriously out in the open and shrink the light-years that separate the mind from external life. (Trying to fill this need is, hands-down, one of the significant accomplishments of the beats—in my opinion—no matter what defensive moralists say; the raw junk that they have peddled occasionally under a Kotex flag of liberation is a different matter, which doesn't rightly fit in here.)

It was trying to close this distance between Me and Thou, between the mind and externality, that I was instinctively attempting when I cut loose with my natural suffocating self in 1955 upon the taboo grounds of outer life. I could stand unfulfilled desire no longer. Thus it is my conviction today that ideals of social behavior must squat down and broaden to the point where they can both absorb and see the necessity for "aberrations" that were once, squarely and Teddy Rooseveltianly, regarded as pathological. The imagination of living human beings, not dead gods, must be openly embodied if there is to be some rational connection between what people actually are and what they are permitted to show. But as with every significant change in meaning, such acts of expressiveness will cost blood before they will be tolerated and understood by psychiatrists, sociologists, the law, police, and all other instruments of social force. Ironically, it is the very "psychotics" in institutions who have unwittingly done the most to initiate a bigger and more imaginative conception of what constitutes *meaningful* behavior. By dealing with people imprisoned in this category, the most perceptive laymen and psychiatrists are beginning to see symbolic meanings where before they saw flat irrationality, because their approach was literal (as if anyone who had the imagination to go "mad" would be stuffy enough to act in prose!). It is then borne in upon them, out of common sense and humility, that a much more expanded conception of what is "sane" is a prerequisite to doing justice to the real emotional state of human beings today; not the abstract theorems of a clean Euclidian conception, but the real, harsh, multiple, often twisted, on-again, off-again mishmash of the so-called normal mind. One can say without pretense that the pioneering "psychotic" is the human poet of the future; and the most imaginative, least tradition-bound psychiatrists are now playing the role of

New Critics, learning to read closely the difficult and unexpected meanings of what formerly were thought of as obscure —in fact, off-limits—warpings of humanity.

III

In my own case I was brought face-to-face because of my trial by shock (both electric and the human aftermath) with a crucial reality which I had long dodged. It can be put approximately this way: A serious artist-type must in the present environment, as always—clichés have a way of becoming profundities when you have to live them!—literally fight for survival if he or she is going to embody the high traditions that originally made the hot pursuit of truth through art the greatest kick in their lives. But to follow this ideal today is tougher than perhaps it has ever been before; and there are specific reasons why. Foremost is the increasing loss of position for the poet (the artist incarnate) as "the unacknowledged legislator of the race" in a period when the terrifying bigness of society makes the average person resort to more immediate and practical oracles (psychiatrists, sociologists, chemists) than to the kind of imaginative truth that the artist can give. Secondly, the artist-type in our mass society is no longer "privileged" in any way, if indeed he ever was; by this I mean that the laws and shibboleths of the huge democratic tribe judge him as severely as they do the shoemaker next door. Whatever pampering the serious artist once received has become a laugh in our time, when everyone is hustling on approximately the same level for success, lovers, status, money, headlines, thrills, security—for everything.

The emergence of an emotionally mutinous democracy has upset the old categories and cast us all into the boiling sea of naked existence, without the props of class, or profession, or the certainty about one's worth as judged by the seemingly clear-cut hierarchies of the past. While, in my opinion, this should be sizzlingly beautiful to every true artist-type, because it is adventurous in the highest conceivable and most mortally dangerous sense, it is also full of the most sinking fears and doubts. For example: can the intelligent writer, painter or composer—the individual with a view of life all his own, which he believes to be true—be indifferent to the prevailing social climate and risk everything by sticking to a viewpoint which will bring him into conflict with the most *normal* (shared by the most people) human emotions in a mass society? (Tag him with the label of "insanity," estrangement from the tempting pie of regular-guy and regular-gal American experience, bring him the isolating fate of being misunderstood even by the "enlightened," and regarded as a personal challenge by others who have made an uneasy truce.)

This is a very serious problem and entails a bigger threat than in the past. Since the artist-type can no longer be realistically considered as being "outside" our definition of society or human nature—and must in this country above all others be seen within the circle of a mass-democratic humanity, for that is where his final strength probably lies—his defections will be judged by those in positions of social power as fluky aberrations *no different from anyone else's.* He will be judged and penalized by the same standards; and in a majority of cases, from what I have seen, his will and stamina are broken (or rationalized into loose harness) and his point of view changed. Frankly, for the artist-type in our environment there is no longer any solid ground whatever under his feet—anything solid he possesses must be won from air and shaped by fanatical resoluteness. For all is open to question today, is a gamble, and has none of the "official" security of the acknowledged professions or even any semblance of unity within his own field. It is for such reasons that the genuine artist-thinker is in such an unenviable and peculiar position in America right now. He is of society and yet, by instinct and inheritance, apart from it: therefore he has to clarify his position in his own mind to a menthol-sharp degree if he wants to survive with intactness, because, as I've tried to show, he will be crushed subtly or conclusively unless he separates his eternal role in society from the onrush of personal doubt that every human being worth the name lives with today.

I learned as a result of my far-out public exhibition, and the manhandling that followed, to distrust the definitions of crude social authority as they pertained to myself and my friends, who share a generally akin point of view and are all either professionals or semiprofessionals in the arts and intellectual life. We can not be skimmed off the top and bracketed as thinly as I had been diagnosed at Bellevue; and the psychiatrists who impatiently felt for the bumps within my head, while presumably competent at a human-machine level, are not as a group sensitive, informed or sympathetic enough with my purposes in life to be of help. In fact, in a basic way they must be my defining opposition in history (daily life) while my friends beyond time (the ideal)—if that doesn't read too pretentiously. It was a sharp revelation for me to learn this as a result of my on-your-hands-and-knees, boy! defeat with authority. As I confessed before, like so many confused young Americans puttering around in the arts, I had phonily pumped into my serious intentions the gassiest dreams of what the struggle for ideas truly is, of false and sentimentalized views of authority (both bowing before it and blowhard defiance), and in general acted more like a Hollywood caricature of a "genius" than a person with the ballbreaking desire to uphold the immortal flame of art in his smallish hand.

I found after I had been handcuffed, ambulanced, doped, needled, marched in formation and given a leather belt to make as if I were in my dotage rather than the prime of life, that I *had to* disagree basically and deliberately with the cowardly normal notion of what constitutes insanity because it is only by *the assertion of the individual spirit that we can change definitions of reality that are already insecure and losing their hold on the conceptual imagination.* In other words, if a majority of people agree that what was once confidently called insanity no longer exists in its traditional sense, cannot truthfully be a determining measurement in a time like this where each good person in the reaches of his mind is often an amateur lunatic by older slogans of "rationality," then the enslavement of the word and meaning is broken. Not only was I forced to this simple attitude because my human spirit refused the reduction of my total self to only one exaggerated aspect of it—namely the pathological label—I saw in both sanitariums no consistency in what was thought of as "sick."

In short, I could no longer afford to think of contemporary insanity as an exact objective phenomenon, like thunder or cancer, but rather as an interpretation of human thought and behavior conditioned by inherited prejudices, fear, questionable middle-class assumptions of the purpose of life, a policeman's narrow idea of freedom, and dollar-hard AMA notions of responsibility and *expediency* ("1. Apt and suitable to the end in view; as, an expedient solution; hence, advantageous. 2. Conducive to special advantage rather than to what is universally right."—Web. New Colleg. Dict.). No longer could I see any true authority or finality in a conception that could be too conveniently tailored to fit the situation. I knew then that anyone who dares the intellectual conventions of this local time must be prepared to have "psychotic" or any of its variants—paranoid, schizophrenic, even the mild psychopathic!—thrown at him. The pathological interpretation of human nature has become a style in our period (overemphasized by the junior science of psychiatry) and has come to mirror the fears, anxieties and values of those currently in positions of social authority more often than the person who is being gutted. Within the iron maiden of this fashion—which undeniably hurts, right down to the roots of the soul—the independent person and the artist-type have no choice but to trust implicitly what they see with their intellect and imagination; for when the climate changes, only the individual vision will stand secure upon its God-given legs of having had faith in actual experience.

I therefore believe that the fear and even the actual

living through of much that used to be called "insanity" is almost an emotional necessity for every truly feeling, reacting, totally human person in America at this time—*until* he or she passes through the soul-crippling (not healing) judgment of such language and comes out of the fire at the point where other words and hence different conceptions are created from the wounds. The psychiatric vocabulary and definitions, which once seemed such a liberating instrument for modern man, have unwittingly woven a tight and ironically strangling noose around the neck of the brain; contemporary men and women—especially intellectuals—tremblingly judge themselves and others in the black light of psychopathology and shrink human nature to the size of their own fears instead of giving it the liberty of their greatest dreams. But we can be grateful that the human soul is so constructed that it ultimately bursts concepts once held as true out of its terrible need to live and creates the world anew just in order to breathe in it. One final thought: should any readers see this article as an effort at self-justification they are right, as far as they go; but they should remember that it is only out of the self and its experience (even if I have failed here) that new light has ever been cast on the perpetual burden of making life ever more *possible* at its most crucial level.

MARY McCARTHY

America the Beautiful: The Humanist in the Bathtub

A VISITING EXISTENTIALIST wanted recently to be taken to dinner at a really American place. This proposal, natural enough in a tourist, disclosed a situation thoroughly unnatural. Unless the visiting lady's object was suffering, there was no way of satisfying her demand. Sukiyaki joints, chop suey joints, Italian table d'hôte places, French provincial restaurants with the menu written on a slate, Irish chophouses, and Jewish delicatessens came abundantly to mind, but these were not what the lady wanted. Schrafft's or the Automat would have answered, yet to take her there would have been to turn oneself into a tourist and to present America as a spectacle—a *New Yorker* cartoon or a savage drawing in the *New Masses*. It was the beginning of an evening of humiliations. The visitor was lively and eager; her mind lay open and orderly, like a notebook ready for impressions. It was not long, however, before she shut it up with a snap. We had no recommendations to make to her.

With movies, plays, current books, it was the same story as with the restaurants. *Open City, Les Enfants du Paradis,* Oscar Wilde, a reprint of Henry James were *paté de maison* to this lady who wanted the definitive flapjack. She did not believe us when we said that there were no good Hollywood movies, no good Broadway plays—only curios; she was merely confirmed in her impression that American intellectuals were "negative."

Yet the irritating thing was that we did not feel negative. We admired and liked our country; we preferred it to that imaginary America, land of the *peaux rouges* of Caldwell and Steinbeck, dumb paradise of violence and the detective story, which had excited the sensibilities of our visitor and of the up-to-date French literary world. But to found our preference, to locate it materially in some admirable object or institution, such as Chartres, say, or French café life, was for us, that night at any rate, an impossible undertaking. We heard ourselves saying that the real America was elsewhere, in the white frame houses and church spires of New England; yet we knew that we talked foolishly—we were not Granville Hicks and we looked ludicrous in his opinions. The Elevated, half a block away, interrupting us every time a train passed, gave us the lie on schedule, every eight minutes. But if the elm-shaded village green was a false or at least an insufficient address for the *genius loci* we honored, where then was it to be found? Surveyed from the vantage point of Europe, this large continent seemed suddenly deficient in objects of virtue. The Grand Canyon, Yellowstone Park, Jim Hill's mansion in St. Paul, Jefferson's Monticello, the blast furnaces of Pittsburgh, Mount Rainier, the yellow observatory at Amherst, the little-theater movement in Cleveland, Ohio, a Greek revival house glimpsed from a car window in a lost river-town in New Jersey—these things were too small for the size of the country. Each of them, when pointed to, diminished in interest with the lady's perspective of distance. There was no sight that in itself seemed to justify her crossing of the Atlantic.

If she was interested in "conditions," that was a different matter. There are conditions everywhere; it takes no special genius to produce them. Yet would it be an act of hospitality to invite a visitor to a lynching? Unfortunately, nearly all the "sights" in America fall under the head of conditions. Hollywood, Reno, the sharecroppers' homes in the South, the mining towns of Pennsylvania, Coney Island, the Chicago stockyards, Macy's, the Dodgers, Harlem, even Congress, the forum of our liberties, are spectacles rather than sights, to use the term in the colloquial sense of "Didn't he make a holy spectacle of himself?" An Englishman of almost any political opinion can show a visitor through the Houses of Parliament with a sense of pride or at least of indulgence toward his national foibles and traditions. The American, if he has a spark of national feeling, will be humiliated by the very prospect of a foreigner's visit to Congress—these, for the most part, illiterate hacks whose fancy vests are spotted with gravy, and whose speeches, hypocritical, unctuous, and slovenly, are spotted also with the gravy of political patronage, these persons are a reflection on the democratic process rather than of it; they expose it in its underwear. In European legislation, we are told, a great deal of shady business goes on in private, behind the scenes. In America, it is just the opposite, anything good, presumably, is accomplished *in camera,* in the committee rooms.

It is so with all our institutions. For the visiting European, a trip through the United States has, almost inevitably, the character of an exposé, and the American, on his side, is tempted by love of his country to lock the inquiring tourist in his hotel room and throw away the key. His contention that the visible and material America is not the real or the only one is more difficult to sustain than was the presumption of the "other" Germany behind the Nazi steel.

To some extent a citizen of any country will feel that the tourist's view of his homeland is a false one. The French will tell you that you have to go into their homes to see what the French people are really like. The intellectuals in the Left Bank cafés are not the real French intellectuals, etc., etc. In Italy, they complain that the tourist must not judge by the *ristorantes*; there one sees only black-market types. But in neither of these cases is the native really disturbed by the tourist's view of his country. If Versailles or Giotto's bell-tower in Florence do not tell the whole story, they are still not incongruous with it; you do not hear a Frenchman or an Italian object when these things are noticed by a visitor. With the American, the contradiction is more serious. He must, if he is to defend his country, repudiate its visible aspect almost entirely. He must say that its parade of phenomenology, its billboards, super-highways, even its skyscrapers, not only fail to represent the inner essence of his country but in fact contravene it. He may point, if he wishes, to certain beautiful objects, but here too he is in difficulties, for nearly everything that is beautiful and has not been produced by Nature belongs to the eighteenth century, to a past with which he has very little connection, and which his ancestors, in many or most cases, had no part in. Beacon Street and the Boston Common are very charming in the eighteenth-century manner, so are the sea captains' houses in the old Massachusetts ports, and the ruined plantations of Louisiana, but an American from Brooklyn or the Middle West or the Pacific Coast finds the style of life embodied in them as foreign as Europe; indeed, the first sensation of a Westerner, coming upon Beacon Hill and the gold dome of the State House, is to feel that at last he has traveled "abroad." The American, if he is to speak the highest truth about his country, must refrain from pointing at all. The virtue of American civilization is that it is unmaterialistic.

This statement may strike a critic as whimsical or perverse. Everybody knows, it will be said, that America has the most materialistic civilization in the world, that Americans care only about money, they have no time or talent for living; look at radio, look at advertising, look at life insurance, look at the tired businessman, at the Frigidaires and the Fords. In answer, the reader is invited first to look instead into his own heart and inquire whether he personally feels himself to be represented by these things, or whether he does not, on the contrary, feel them to be irrelevant to him, a necessary evil, part of the conditions of life. Other people, he will assume, care about them very much: the man down the street, the entire population of Detroit or Scarsdale, the back-country farmer, the urban poor or the rich. But he himself accepts these objects as imposed on him by a collective "otherness" of desire, an otherness he has not met directly but whose existence he infers from the number of automobiles, Frigidaires, or television sets he sees around him. Stepping into his new Buick convertible, he knows that he would gladly do without it, but imagines that to his neighbor, who is just backing *his* out of the driveway, this car is the motor of life. More often, however, the otherness is projected farther afield, onto a different class or social group, remote and alien. Thus the rich, who would like nothing better, they think, than for life to be a perpetual fishing trip with the trout grilled by a native guide, look patronizingly upon the whole apparatus of American civilization as a cheap Christmas present to the poor, and city people see the radio and the washing machine as the farmwife's solace.

It can be argued, of course, that the subjective view is prevaricating, possession of the Buick being nine-tenths of the social law. But who has ever met, outside of advertisements, a true parishioner of this church of Mammon? A man may take pride in a car, and a housewife in her new sink or wallpaper, but pleasure in new acquisitions is universal and eternal; an Italian man with a new gold tooth, a French bibliophile with a new edition, a woman with a new baby, a philosopher with a new thought, all these people are rejoicing in progress, in man's power to enlarge and improve. Before men showed off new cars, they showed off new horses; it is alleged against modern man that he as an individual craftsman did not make the car; but his grandfather did not make the horse either. What is imputed to Americans is something quite different, an abject dependence on material possessions, an image of happiness as packaged by the manufacturer, content in a can. This view of American life is strongly urged by advertising agencies. We know the "others," of course, because we meet them every week in full force in *The New Yorker* or the *Saturday Evening Post,* those brightly colored families of dedicated consumers, waiting in unison on the porch for the dealer to deliver the new car, gobbling the new cereal ("Gee, Mom, is it good for you too?"), lining up to bank their paychecks, or fearfully anticipating the industrial accident and the insurance check that will "compensate" for it. We meet them also, more troll-like underground, in the subway placards, in the ferociously complacent One-A-Day family, and we hear their courtiers sing to them on the radio of Ivory or Supersuds. The thing, however, that repels us in these advertisements is their naïve falsity to life. Who are these advertising men kidding, besides the European tourist? Between the tired, sad, gentle faces of the subway riders and the grinning Holy Families of the Ad-Mass, there exists no possibility of even a wishful identification. We take a vitamin pill with the hope of feeling (possibly) a little less tired, but the superstition of buoyant health emblazoned in the bright, ugly pictures has no more power to move us than the blood of St. Januarius.

Familiarity has perhaps bred contempt in us Americans: until you have had a washing machine, you cannot imagine how little difference it will make to you. Europeans still believe that money brings happiness, witness the bought journalist, the bought politician, the bought general, the whole venality of European literary life, inconceivable in this country of the dollar. It is true that America produces and consumes more cars, soap, and bathtubs than any other nation, but we live among these objects rather than by them. American build skyscrapers; Le Corbusier worships them.

Ehrenburg, our Soviet critic, fell in love with the Check-O-Mat in American railway stations, writing home paragraphs of song to this gadget—while deploring American materialism. When an American heiress wants to buy a man, she at once crosses the Atlantic. The only really materialistic people I have ever met have been Europeans.

The strongest argument for the unmaterialistic character of American life is the fact that we tolerate conditions that are, from a materialistic point of view, intolerable. What the foreigner finds most objectionable in American life is its lack of basic comfort. No nation with any sense of material well-being would endure the food we eat, the cramped apartments we live in, the noise, the traffic, the crowded subways and buses. American life, in large cities, at any rate, is a perpetual assault on the senses and the nerves; it is out of asceticism, out of unworldliness, precisely, that we bear it.

This republic was founded on an unworldly assumption, a denial of "the facts of life." It is manifestly untrue that all men are created equal; interpreted in worldly terms, this doctrine has resulted in a pseudo-equality, that is, in standardization, in an equality of things rather than of persons. The inalienable rights to life, liberty, and the pursuit of happiness appear, in practice, to have become the inalienable right to a bathtub, a flush toilet, and a can of Spam. Left-wing critics of America attribute this result to the intrusion of capitalism; right-wing critics see it as the logical dead end of democracy. Capitalism, certainly, now depends on mass production, which depends on large-scale distribution of uniform goods, till the consumer today is the victim of the manufacturer who launches on him a regiment of products for which he must make house-room in his soul. The buying impulse, in its original force and purity, was not nearly so crass, however, or so meanly acquisitive as many radical critics suppose. The purchase of a bathtub was the exercise of a spiritual right. The immigrant or the poor native American bought a bathtub, not because he wanted to take a bath, but because he wanted to be in a *position* to do so. This remains true in many fields today; possessions, when they are desired, are not wanted for their own sakes but as tokens of an ideal state of freedom, fraternity, and franchise. "Keeping up with the Joneses" is a vulgarization of Jefferson's concept, but it too is a declaration of the rights of man, and decidedly unfeasible and visionary. Where for a European, a fact is a fact, for us Americans, the real, if it is relevant at all, is simply symbolic appearance. We are a nation of twenty million bathrooms, with a humanist in every tub. One such humanist I used to hear of on Cape Cod had, on growing rich, installed two toilets side by side in his marble bathroom, on the model of the two-seater of his youth. He was a clear case of Americanism, hospitable, gregarious, and impractical, a theorist of perfection. Was his dream of the conquest of poverty a vulgar dream or a noble one, a material demand or a spiritual insistence? It is had to think of him as a happy man, and in this too he is characteristically American, for the parity of the radio, the movies, and the washing machine has made Americans sad, reminding them of another parity of which these things were to be but emblems.

The American does not enjoy his possessions because sensory enjoyment was not his object, and he lives sparely and thinly among them, in the monastic discipline of Scarsdale or the barracks of Stuyvesant Town. Only among certain groups where franchise, socially speaking, has not been achieved, do pleasure and material splendor constitute a life-object and an occupation. Among the outcasts—Jews, Negroes, Catholics, homosexuals—excluded from the communion of ascetics, the love of fabrics, gaudy show, and rich possessions still anchronistically flaunts itself. Once a norm has been reached, differing in the different classes, financial ambition itself seems to fade away. The self-made man finds, to his anger, his son uninterested in money; you have shirtsleeves to shirtsleeves in three generations. The great financial empires are a thing of the past. Some recent immigrants —movie magnates and gangsters particularly—retain their acquisitiveness, but how long is it since anyone in the general public has murmured, wonderingly, "as rich as Rockefeller"?

If the dream of American fraternity had ended simply in this, the value of humanistic and egalitarian strivings would be seriously called into question. Jefferson, the Adamses, Franklin, Madison, would be in the position of Dostoevsky's Grand Inquisitor, who, desiring to make the Kingdom of God incarnate on earth, inaugurated the kingdom of the devil. If the nature of matter is such that the earthly paradise, once realized, becomes always the paradise of the earthly, and a spiritual conquest of matter becomes an enslavement of spirit, then the atomic bomb is, as has been argued, the logical result of the Enlightenment, and the land of opportunity is, precisely, the land of death. This position, however, is a strictly materialist one, for it asserts the Fact of the bomb as the one tremendous truth: subjective attitudes are irrelevant; it does not matter what we think or feel; possession again in this case is nine-tenths of the law.

It must be admitted that there is a great similarity between the nation with its new bomb and the consumer with his new Buick. In both cases, there is a disinclination to use the product, stronger naturally in the case of the bomb, but somebody has manufactured the thing, and there seems to be no way *not* to use it, especially when everybody else will be doing so. Here again the argument of the "others" is invoked to justify our own procedures: if we had not invented the bomb, the Germans would have; the Soviet Union will have it in a year, etc., etc. This is keeping up with the Joneses indeed, our national propagandists playing the role of the advertising men in persuading us of the "others' " intentions.

It seems likely at this moment that we will find no way of not using the bomb, yet those who argue theoretically that this machine is the true expression of our society leave us, in practice, with no means of opposing it. We must differentiate ourselves from the bomb if we are to avoid using it, and in private thought we do, distinguishing the bomb sharply from our daily concerns and sentiments, feeling it as an otherness that waits outside to descend on us, an otherness already destructive of normal life, since it prevents us from planning or hoping by depriving us of a future. And this inner refusal of the bomb is also a legacy of our past; it is a denial of the given, of the power of circumstances to shape us in their mold. Unfortunately, the whole asceticism of our national character, our habit of living in but not through an environment, our alienation from objects, prepare us to endure the bomb but not to confront it.

Passivity and not aggressiveness is the dominant trait of the American character. The movies, the radio, the superhighway have softened us up for the atom bomb; we have lived with them without pleasure, feeling them as a coercion on our natures, a coercion seemingly from nowhere and expressing nobody's will. The new coercion finds us without the habit of protest; we are dissident but apart.

The very "negativeness," then, of American intellectuals is not a mark of their separation from our society, but a true expression of its separation from itself. We too are dissident but inactive. Intransigent on paper, in "real life" we conform; yet we do not feel ourselves to be dishonest, for to us the real life is rustling paper and the mental life is flesh. And even in our mental life we are critical and rather unproductive; we leave it to the "others," the best-sellers, to create.

The fluctuating character of American life must, in part, have been responsible for this dissociated condition. Many an immigrant arrived in this country with the most materialistic expectations, hoping, not to escape from a world in which a man was the sum of his circumstances, but to become a new sum of circumstances himself. But this hope was self-defeating; the very ease with which new circumstances were acquired left insufficient time for a man to live into them: all along a great avenue in Minneapolis the huge stone chateaux used to be dark at night, save for a single light in each kitchen, where the family still sat, Swedish-style, about the stove. The pressure of democratic thought, moreover, forced a rising man often, unexpectedly, to recognize that he was *not* his position: a speeding ticket from a village constable could lay him low. Like the agitated United Nations delegates who got summonses on the Merritt Parkway, he might find the shock traumatic: a belief had been destroyed. The effect of these combined difficulties turned the new American into a nomad, who camped out in his circumstances, as it were, and was never assimilated to them. And, for the native American, the great waves of internal migration had the same result. The homelessness of the American, migrant in geography and on the map of finance, is the whole subject of the American realists of our period. European readers see in these writers only violence and brutality. They miss not only the pathos but the nomadic virtues associated with it, generosity, hospitality, equity, directness, politeness, simplicity of relations—traits which, together with a certain gentle timidity (as of very *unpracticed* nomads), comprise the American character. Unobserved also is a peculiar nakedness, a look of being shorn of everything, that is very curiously American, corresponding to the spare wooden desolation of a frontier town and the bright thinness of the American light. The American character looks always as if it had just had a rather bad haircut, which gives it, in our eyes at any rate, a greater humanity than the European, which even among its beggars has an all too professional air.

The openness of the American situation creates the pity and the terror; status is not protection; life for the European is a career; for the American, it is a hazard. Slaves and women, said Aristotle, are not fit subjects for tragedy, but kings, rather, and noble men, men, that is, not defined by circumstance but outside it and seemingly impervious. In America we have, subjectively speaking, no slaves and no women; the efforts of *PM* and the Stalinized playwrights to introduce, like the first step to servitude, a national psychology of the "little man" have been, so far, unrewarding. The little man is one who is embedded in status; things can be done for and to him generically by a central directive; his happiness flows from statistics. This conception mistakes the national passivity for abjection. Americans will not eat this humble pie; we are still nature's noblemen. Yet no tragedy results, though the protagonist is everywhere; dissociation takes the place of conflict, and the drama is mute.

This humanity, this plain and heroic accessibility, was what we would have liked to point out to the visiting Existentialist as our national glory. Modesty perhaps forbade and a lack of concrete examples—how could we point to ourselves? Had we done so she would not have been interested. To a European, the humanity of an intellectual is of no particular moment; it is the barber pole that announces his profession and the hair oil dispensed inside. Europeans, moreover, have no curiosity about American intellectuals; we are insufficiently representative of the brute. Yet this anticipated and felt disparagement was not the whole cause of our reticence. We were silent for another reason: we were waiting to be discovered. Columbus, however, passed on, and this, very likely, was the true source of our humiliation. But this experience also was peculiarly American. We all expect to be found in the murk of otherness; it looks to us very easy since *we* know we are there. Time after time, the explorers have failed to see us. We have been patient, for the happy ending is our national belief. Now, however, that the future has been shut off from us, it is necessary for us to declare ourselves, at least for the record.

What it amounts to, in verity, is that we are the poor. This humanity we would claim for ourselves is the legacy, not only of the Enlightenment, but of the thousands and thousands of European peasants and poor townspeople who came here bringing their humanity and their sufferings with them. It is the absence of a stable upper class that is responsible for much of the vulgarity of the American scene. Should we blush before the visitor for this deficiency? The ugliness of American decoration, American entertainment, American literature—is not this the visible expression of the impoverishment of the European masses, a manifestation of all the backwardness, deprivation, and want that arrived here in boatloads from Europe? The immense popularity of American movies abroad demonstrates that Europe is the unfinished negative of which America is the proof. The European traveler, viewing with distaste a movie palacc or a Motorola, is only looking into the terrible concavity of his continent of hunger inverted startlingly into the convex. Our civilization, deformed as it is outwardly, is still an accomplishment; all this had to come to light.

America is indeed a revelation, though not quite the one that was planned. Given a clean slate, man, it was hoped, would write the future. Instead, he has written his past. This past, inscribed on billboards, ball parks, dance halls, is not seemly, yet its objectification is a kind of disburdenment. The past is at length outside. It does not disturb us as it does Europeans, for our relation with it is both more distant and more familiar. We cannot hate it, for to hate it would be to hate poverty, our eager ancestors, and ourselves.

It there were time, American civilization could be seen as a beginning, even a favorable one, for we have only to look around us to see what a lot of sensibility a little ease will accrue. The children surpass the fathers and Louis B. Mayer cannot be preserved intact in his descendants. . . . Unfortunately, as things seem now, posterity is not around the corner.

ARTHUR MILLER

The Bored and the Violent

IF MY own small experience is any guide, the main difficulty in approaching the problem of juvenile delinquency is that there is very little evidence about it and very many opinions as to how to deal with it. By evidence I do not mean the news stories telling of gang fights and teen-age murders—there are plenty of those. But it is unknown, for instance, what the actual effects are on the delinquent of prison sentences, psychotherapy, slum-clearance projects, settlement-house programs, tougher or more lenient police attitudes, the general employment situation, and so on. Statistics are few and not generally reliable. The narcotics problem alone is an almost closed mystery.

Not that statistical information in itself can solve anything, but it might at least outline the extent of the disease. I have it, for instance, from an old and deservedly respected official—it is his opinion anyway—that there is really no great increase in delinquent acts but a very great intensification of our awareness of them. He feels we are more nervous now about infractions of the social mores than our ancestors, and he likes to point out that Shakespeare, Boccaccio, and other writers never brought on stage a man of wealth or station without his bravos, who were simply his private police force, necessary to him when he ventured out of his house, especially at night. He would have us read *Great Expectations, Oliver Twist, Huckleberry Finn,* and other classics, not in a romantic mood but in the way we read about our own abandoned kids and their depredations. The difference lies mainly in the way we look at the same behavior.

The experts have only a little more to go on than we have. Like the surgeon whose hands are bloody a good part of the day, the social worker is likely to come to accept the permanent existence of the delinquency disease without the shock of the amateur who first encounters it.

A recent book on the subject, *All the Way Down,** reports the experience of a social worker—of sorts—who never got used to the experience, and does not accept its inevitability. It is an easy book to attack on superficial grounds because it has no evident sociological method, it rambles and jumps and shouts and curses. But it has a virtue, a very great and rare one, I think, in that it does convey the endless, leaden, mind-destroying boredom of the delinquent life. Its sex is without romance or sexuality, its violence is without release or gratification—exactly like the streets—movies and plays about delinquency notwithstanding.

Unlike most problems which sociology takes up, delinquency seems to be immune to the usual sociological analyses or cures. For instance, it appears in all technological societies, whether Latin or Anglo-Saxon or Russian or Japanese. It has a very slippery correlation with unemployment and the presence or absence of housing projects. It exists among the rich in Westchester and the poor in Brooklyn

*By Vincent Riccio and Bill Slocum. Simon and Schuster, $3.75.

and Chicago. It has spread quickly into the rural areas and the small towns. Now, according to Harrison Salisbury, it is the big problem in the Soviet Union. So that any single key to its causation is nowhere visible. If one wants to believe it to be essentially a symptom of unequal opportunity—and certainly this factor operates—one must wonder about the Russian problem, for the Soviet youngster can, in fact, go right up through the whole school system on his ability alone, as many of ours cannot. Yet the gangs are roaming the Russian streets, just as they do in our relatively permissive society.

So no one knows what "causes" delinquency. Having spent some months in the streets with boys of an American gang, I came away with certain impressions, all of which stemmed from a single, overwhelming conviction—that the problem underneath is boredom. And it is not strange, after all, that this should be so. It is the theme of so many of our novels, our plays, and especially our movies in the past twenty years, and is the hallmark of society as a whole. The outcry of Britain's so-called Angry Young Men was against precisely this seemingly universal sense of life's pointlessness, the absence of any apparent aim to it all. So many American books and articles attest to the same awareness here. The stereotype of the man coming home from work and staring dumbly at a television set is an expression of it, and the "New Wave" of movies in France and Italy propound the same fundamental theme. People no longer seem to know why they are alive; existence is simply a string of near-experiences marked off by periods of stupefying spiritual and psychological stasis, and the good life is basically an amused one.

Among the delinquents the same kind of mindlessness prevails, but without the style—or stylishness—which art in our time has attempted to give it. The boredom of the delinquent is remarkable mainly because it is so little compensated for, as it may be among the middle classes and the rich who can fly down to the Caribbean or to Europe, or refurnish the house, or have an affair, or at least go shopping. The delinquent is stuck with his boredom, stuck inside it, stuck to it, until for two or three minutes he "lives"; he goes on a raid around the corner and feels the thrill of risking his skin or his life as he smashes a bottle filled with gasoline on some other kid's head. In a sense, it is his trip to Miami. It makes his day. It is his shopping tour. It gives him something to talk about for a week. It is *life.* Standing around with nothing coming up is as close to dying as you can get. Unless one grasps the power of boredom, the threat of it to one's existence, it is impossible to "place" the delinquent as a member of the human race.

With boredom in the forefront, one may find some perspective in the mélange of views which are repeated endlessly about the delinquent. He is a rebel without a cause, or a victim of poverty, or a victim of undue privilege, or an unloved child, or an overloved child, or a child looking for a father, or a child trying to avenge himself on an uncaring society, or whatnot. But face to face with one of them, one finds these criteria useless, if only because no two delinquents are any more alike than other people are. They do share one mood, however. They are drowning in boredom. School bores them, preaching bores them, even television bores them. The word rebel is inexact for them because it must inevitably imply a purpose, an end.

Other people, of course, have known boredom. To get out of it, they go to the movies, or to a bar, or read a book, or go to sleep, or turn on TV or a girl, or make a resolution, or quit a job. Younger persons who are not delinquents may go to their room and weep, or write a poem, or call up a friend until they get tired talking. But note that each of these escapes can only work if the victim is sure somewhere in his mind, or reasonably hopeful, that by so doing he will overthrow his boredom and with luck may come out on the other side where something hopeful or interesting waits. But the delinquent has no such sense of an imminent improvement. Most of the kids in the Riccio and Slocum book have never known a single good day. How can they be expected to project one and restrain themselves in order to experience such joy once more?

The word rebel is wrong, too, in that it implies some sort of social criticism in the delinquent. But that would confuse him with the bourgeois Beatnik. The delinquent has only respect, even reverence, for certain allegedly bourgeois values. He implicitly believes that there are good girls and bad girls, for instance. Sex and marriage are two entirely separate things. He is, in my experience anyway, deeply patriotic. Which is simply to say that he respects those values he never experienced, like money and good girls and the Army and Navy. What he has experienced has left him with absolute contempt, or more accurately, an active indifference. Once he does experience decency—as he does sometimes in a wife—he reacts decently to it. For to this date the only known cure for delinquency is marriage.

The delinquent, far from being the rebel, is the conformist par excellence. Hs is actually incapable of doing anything alone, and a story may indicate how incapable he is. I went along with Riccio and the gang in his book to a YMCA camp outside New York City for an overnight outing. In the afternoon we started a baseball game, and everything proceeded normally until somebody hit a ball to the outfield. I turned to watch the play and saw ten or twelve kids running for the catch. It turned out that not one of them was willing to play the outfield by himself, insisting that the entire group hang around out there together. The reason was that a boy alone might drop a catch and would not be able to bear the humiliation. So they ran around out there in a drove all afternoon, creating a stampede every time a ball was hit.

They are frightened kids, and that is why they are so dangerous. But again, it will not do to say—it is simply not true—that they are therefore unrelated to the rest of the population's frame of mind. Like most of us, the delinquent is simply doing as he was taught. This is often said but rarely understood. Only recently a boy was about to be executed for murder in New York State. Only after he had been in jail for more than a year after sentencing did a campaign develop to persuade the Governor to commute his sentence to life imprisonment, for only then was it discovered that he had been deserted by his father in Puerto Rico, left behind when his mother went to New York, wandered about homeless throughout his childhood, and so on. The sentencing judge only learned his background a week or two before he was to be officially murdered. And then what shock, what pity! I have to ask why the simple facts of his deprivation were not brought out in court, if not before. I am afraid I know the answer. Like most people, it was probably beyond the judge's imagination that small children sometimes can be treated much worse than kittens or puppies in our cities.

It is only in theory that the solution seems purely physical—better housing, enlightened institutions for deserted kids, psychotherapy, and the rest. The visible surfaces of the problem are easy to survey—although we have hardly begun even to do that.

More difficult is the subterranean moral question which every kind of delinquency poses. Not long ago a gang was arrested in a middle-class section of Brooklyn, whose tack was to rob homes and sell the stuff to professional fences. Many of these boys were top students, and all of them were from good, middle-class backgrounds. Their parents were floored by the news of their secret depredations, and their common cry was that they had always given their sons plenty of money, that the boys were secure at home, that there was no conceivable reason for this kind of aberration. The boys were remorseful and evidently as bewildered as their parents.

Greenwich, Connecticut, is said to be the wealthiest community in the United States. A friend of mine who lives there let his sons throw a party for their friends. In the middle of the festivities a gang of boys arrived—their own acquaintances who attend the same high school. They tore the house apart, destroyed the furniture, pulled parts off the automobile and left them on the lawn, and split the skulls of two of the guests with beer cans.

Now if it is true that the slum delinquent does as he is taught, it must be true that the Greenwich delinquent does the same. But obviously the lines of force from example to imitation are subtler and less easily traced here. It is doubtful that the parents of this marauding gang rip up the furniture in the homes to which they have been invited. So that once again it is necessary to withhold one's cherished theories. Rich delinquency is delinquency but it is not the same as slum delinquency. But there is one clear common denominator, I think. They do not know how to live when alone. Most boys in Greenwich do not roam in gangs but a significant fraction in both places find that counterfeit sense of existence which the gang life provides.

Again, I think it necessary to raise and reject the idea of rebellion, if one means by that word a thrust of any sort. For perspective's sake it may be wise to remember another kind of youthful reaction to a failed society in a different era. In the thirties, for instance, we were also contemptuous of the given order. We had been brought up to believe that if you worked hard, saved your money, studied, kept your nose clean, you would end up made. We found ourselves in the Depression, when you could not get a job, when all the studying you might do would get you a chance, at best, to sell ties in Macy's. Our delinquency consisted in joining demonstrations of the unemployed, pouring onto campuses to scream against some injustice by college administrations, and adopting to one degree or another a Socialist ideology. This, in fact, was a more dangerous kind of delinquency than the gangs imply, for it was directed against the social structure of capitalism itself. But, curiously, it was at the same time immeasurably more constructive, for the radical youth of the thirties, contemptuous as he was of the social values he had rejected, was still bent upon instituting human values in their place. He was therefore a conserver, he believed in *some* society.

Gide wrote a story about a man who wanted to get on a train and shoot a passenger. Any train, any passenger. It would be a totally gratuitous act, an act devoid of any purpose whatever, an act of "freedom" from purpose. To kill an unknown man without even anger, without unrequited love, without love at all, with nothing in his heart but the sheerly physical contemplation of the gun barrel and the target. In doing this one would partake of Death's irreproachable identity and commit an act in revolt against meaning itself, just as Death is, in the last analysis, beyond analysis.

To think of contemporary delinquency in the vein of the thirties, as a rebellion toward something, is to add a value to it which it does not have. To give it even the dignity of cynicism run rampant is also overelaborate. For the essence is not the individual at all; it is the gang, the herd, and we should be able to understand its attractions ourselves. It is not the thrust toward individual expression but a flight from self in any defined form. Therefore, to see it simply as a protest against conformism is to stand it on its head; it is profoundly conformist but without the mottoes, the entablature of recognizable, "safe" conformism and its liturgy of religious, patriotic, socially conservative credos.

The Greenwich gang, therefore, is also doing as it was taught, just as the slum gang does, but more subtly. The Greenwich gang is conforming to the hidden inhumanity of conformism, to the herd quality in conformism; it is acting out the terror-fury that lies hidden under father's acceptable conformism. It is simply conformity sincere, conformity revealing its true content, which is hatred of others, a stunted wish for omnipotence, and the conformist's secret belief that nothing outside his skin is real or true. For which reason he must redouble his obeisance to institutions lest, if the act of obeisance be withheld, the whole external world will vanish, leaving him alone. And to be left alone when you do not sense any existence in yourself is the ultimate terror. But this loneliness is not the poet's, not the thinker's, not the loneliness that is filled with incommunicable feeling, insufficiently formed thought. It is nonexistence and must not be romanticized as it has been in movies and some of the wishful Beat literature. It is a withdrawal not from the world but from oneself. It is boredom, the subsidence of inner impulse, and it threatens true death unless it is overthrown.

All of which is said in order to indicate that delinquency is not the kind of "social problem" it is generally thought to be. That is, it transcends even as it includes the need for better housing, medical care, and the rest. It is our most notable and violent manifestation of social nihilism. In saying this, however, it is necessary to short-circuit any notion that it is an attempt by the youth to live "sincerely." The air of "sincerity" which so many writers have given the delinquent is not to be mistaken as his "purpose." This is romanticism and solves nothing except to sentimentalize brutality. The gang kid can be sincere; he can extend himself for a buddy and risk himself for others; but he is just as liable, if not more so than others, to desert his buddies in need and to treat his friends disloyally. Gang boys rarely go to visit a buddy in jail excepting in the movies. They forget about him. The cult of sincerity, of true human relations uncontaminated by money and the social rat race, is not the hallmark of the gang. The only moment of truth comes when the war starts. Then the brave show themselves, but few of these boys know how to fight alone, and hardly any without a knife or a gun. They are not to be equated with matadors or boxers or Hemingway heroes. They are dangerous pack hounds who will not even expose themselves singly in the outfield.

If, then, one begins to put together all the elements, this "social problem" takes on not merely its superficial welfare aspects but its philosophical depths, which I think are the controlling ones. It is not a problem of big cities alone but of rural areas too; not of capitalism alone but of socialism as well; not restricted to the physically deprived but shared by the affluent; not a racial problem alone or a problem of recent immigrants, or a purely American problem. I believe it is in its present form the product of technology destroying the very concept of man as a value in himself.

I hesitate to say what I think the cure might be, if only because I cannot prove it. But I have heard most of the solutions men have offered, and they are spiritless, they do not assume that the wrong is deep and terrible and general among us all. There is, in a word, a spirit gone. Perhaps two world wars, brutality immeasurable, have blown it off the earth; perhaps the very processes of technology have sucked it out of man's soul; but it is gone. Many men rarely relate to one another excepting as customer to seller, worker to boss, the affluent to the deprived and vice versa—in short, as factors to be somehow manipulated and not as intrinsically valuable persons.

Power was always in the world, to be sure, and its evils, but with us now it is strangely, surrealistically masked and distorted. Time was, for example, when the wealthy and the politically powerful flaunted themselves, used power openly as power, and were often cruel. But this openness had the advantage for man of clarity; it created a certain reality in the world, an environment that was defined, with hard but touchable barriers. Today power would have us believe—everywhere—that it is purely beneficent. The bank is not a place which makes more money with your deposits than it returns to you in the form of interest; it is not a sheer economic necessity, it is not a business at all. It is "Your Friendly Bank," a kind of welfare institution whose one prayer, day and night, is to serve your whims or needs. A school is no longer a place of mental discipline but a kind of day-care center, a social gathering where you go through a ritual of games and entertainments which insinuate knowledge and the crafts of the outside world. Business is not the practice of buying low and selling high, it is a species of public service. The good life itself is not the life of struggle for meaning, not the quest for union with the past, with God, with man that it traditionally was. The good life is the life of ceaseless entertainment, effortless joys, the air-conditioned, dust-free languor beyond the Mussulman's most supine freedom. Freedom is, after all, comfort; sexuality is a photograph. The enemy of it all is the real. The enemy is conflict. The enemy, in a word, is life.

My own view is that delinquency is related to this dreamworld from two opposing sides. There are the deprived who cannot take part in the dream; poverty bars them. There are the oversated who are caught in its indefiniteness, its unreality, its boring hum, and strike for the real now and then—they rob, they hurt, they kill. In flight from the nothingness of this comfort they have inherited, they butt against its rubber walls in order to feel a real pain, a genuine consequence. For the world in which comfort rules is a delusion, whether one is within it or deprived of it.

There are a few social theorists who look beyond poverty and wealth, beyond the time when men will orient themselves to the world as breadwinners, as accruers of money-power. They look to the triumph of technology, when at least in some countries the physical struggle to survive will no longer be the spine of existence. Then, they say, men will define themselves through varying "styles of life." With struggles solved, nature tamed and abundant, all that will be left to do will be the adornment of existence, a novel-shaped swimming pool, I take it, or an outburst of artistic work.

It is not impossible, I suppose. Certainly a lot of people are already living that way—when they are not at their psychiatrists'. But there is still a distance to go before life's style matters very much to most of humanity in comparison to next month's rent. I do not know how we ought to reach for the spirit again but it seems to me we must flounder without it. It is the spirit which does not accept injustice complacently and yet does not betray the poor with sentimentality. It is the spirit which seeks not to flee the tragedy which life must always be, but seeks to enter into it, thereby to be strengthened by the fullest awareness of its pain, its ultimate non sequitur. It is the spirit which does not mask but unmasks the true function of a thing, be it business, unionism, architecture, or love.

Riccio's and Slocum's book, with all its ugliness, its crudeness, its lack of polish and design, is good because it delivers up the real. It is only as hopeless as the situation is. Its implied solutions are good ones: reform of idiotic narcotics laws, a real attempt to put trained people at the service of bewildered, desperate families, job-training programs, medical care, reading clinics—all of it is necessary and none of it would so much as strain this economy. But none of it will matter, none of it will reach further than the spirit in which it is done. Not the spirit of fear with which so many face delinquency, nor the spirit of sentimentality which sees in it some virtue of rebellion against a false and lying society. The spirit has to be that of those people who know that delinquents are a living expression of our universal ignorance of what life ought to be, even of what it is, and of what it truly means to live. Bad pupils they surely are. But who from his own life, from his personal thought has come up with the good teaching, the way of life that is joy? This book shows how difficult it is to reach these boys; what the country has to decide is what it is going to say if these kids should decide to listen.

WARREN MILLER

Poor Columbus

WHEN I TRY to imagine Paradise, it always looks like Cuba. Winters in New York, when I cannot go to Havana, I dream about it and mourn, as if it were a lost child. It was the first foreign place I had ever gone to under my own power—Europe had been a gift of the U.S. Army, which thought of it as a punishment for being drafted.

That first time, Batista was still in power and the night boat from Miami (it doesn't run any more) sailed on a strange Atlantic, one I had never seen before. It was flat as a pond and painted in stripes of blue and green, no relation to the ocean of the same name to the north, which was greasy gray and had to be fought. And not only a different ocean; the boat carried a different time, its supercargo was the twenties and the hold was full of memories of the Great Age of cruises. Men wore white linen suits (I had not seen the like since childhood); the Cuban women entered from some lost world of abundance and joy; and the ship's purser, his polished black hair parted in the middle, sang through a megaphone as the ship's orchestra (three pieces) played "A Pretty Girl Is Like a Melody." I ordered a daiquiri (what else?) and expected Somerset Maugham to enter at any moment, splendid in white drill, at home in this floating saloon where the wood of the tables was soft with the tropic damp; or at the very least, a beautiful half-caste to sit down at my table and ask for protection. *Here, take this ruby. It is all I have.*

In the morning, the port of Havana: odor of oranges and coffee; and two old men in the scummy water, screaming like sea birds, barking like dogs, diving for coins. When they surfaced, they opened their mouths to show the coin shining on their tongues. This was early in 1957 and Castro and eleven men had been in the mountains for almost two months. In the city, every sign bearing Batista's name was gouged and stained with flung filth.

I went back for the second time in January 1959, with my wife. We arrived from the Yucatán a day after Castro had marched into Havana. Except for the prisoners awaiting trial, every man was a brother; there was never anywhere so full of hope and glory as Cuba then. For us, there was the tremendous excitement of just being there, the thrill of standing in the center of History. Walking down the Prado, one could say to oneself: I am being epochal, yes I am. ("Some day," I told my wife, "I'm going to bring you back here and show you where I was wounded.")

There were no policemen. Batista's cops very quickly got out of uniform and, some of them, into jail; and Castro had not had time yet to organize a force of his own. Boy Scouts directed traffic in Havana, sometimes aided by intrepid clerks on their lunch hour. For a week, the entire island, six million people, lived by the honor system. Burglary and theft virtually came to a halt that week, and no crime of violence was committed. (A few days later, when the executions of the Batista gang began, a U. S. senator accused the Cubans of going on a killing spree. The Cubans were rather surprised to hear it. It was their impression that it had been the Batistanos who had done the mass killings, and their recollection that the U.S. Senate had said nothing about *that.*)

We went to Varadero, where we found a half dozen Americans. Drawn to each other by a common language and nothing else, we sat on the beach and listened to the sound of gunfire from the town of Cárdenas across the bay, where executions were taking place. (Not even Wayne Morse, the northwest mountie, said they weren't guilty. It was just that he wanted them to receive American-style justice in American-style courts, because that's the best kind there is. They'd have been found guilty anyway, but Wayne would have felt better about it.)

One of the Americans was an energetic old man called Dad. He was from Chicago, a retired gangster with cropped gray hair and a diamond set into his eyetooth. He went over to Cárdenas one day to see an old friend face the firing squad.

We waited for Dad to return, the craps dealer and his wife who were waiting on the beach for Fidel to reopen the casinos, my wife and I, and a couple who had bought a house in Varadero. He had been a police chief in a Midwestern city and, having made his bundle and his connection, was now living the good life in the tropics. One room of his rambling Victorian house was filled to the rafters with IBM typewriters and business machines sent him by kind friends back home. He, to keep his hand in, sold them to the local businessmen at attractive prices. His name was Mike and he had the face of a heavyweight who had met with little success.

Late every afternoon we left the beach and went up to Mr. and Mrs. Mike's porch to have a drink and watch the sunset, nature lovers all. We were sitting there when Dad returned, weary traveler with a story to tell, and sat down on a wicker rocking chair. He took out a cigar, lit up, and stuck a toothpick into the other end. He had told me that in the good old days in Chicago he had run a flat-store with a partner who had tuberculosis and also smoked cigars. After finding himself, too many times, smoking the germ-charged cigars of his partner in the excitement of fleecing a big corn-and-pig man from Cedar Rapids, Dad began the practice of fixing a toothpick into the end of his cigar as a means of identifying it.

On the beach one morning—he had just bought breakfast at the Pullman Bar for every shoeshine boy in town—Dad told me about his first strike. He had been seventeen when he made it. With two friends he had robbed a blind man of $7,000. The whole neighborhood had known and talked about it for years, that the blind man, not trusting banks, kept all his savings in his room. Everyone had known about it, but only Dad had the vision and the get-up-and-go spirit.

They split their strike three ways and the other two boys lost their take at the race track the same day. Dad held on to his for *five* days: this marked him as a coming man, a boy who knew how to handle himself. Well, it is the old American story. Dad proved himself in the business world. He went into the car business, repainted them, filed off the numbers himself; bought saloons and fixed up back rooms for friendly games of chance; and in his declining years found himself the owner of apartment houses in Miami and Chi, sojourner in Varadero.

The man he had gone to Cárdenas to see killed that day was a former Batista policeman. He had been in the habit of leaving his victims strung up along the highway, their testicles in their mouths, as an object to others. He had only wanted to spare people pain. The court, unconcerned with true (i.e., American) justice, found him guilty.

His eyetooth dazzling in the setting sun, Dad said, "Guillermo took it good." Guillermo had faced his executioners and himself gave the command to fire. The bullets knocked him several feet into the air, Dad said, as if they had exploded inside him.

"That's the way it goes," Mike said, his voice heavy with philosophy.

"He had no complaint comin'," Dad said. "He had ten good years and then he lost his connection. Now the new crowd gets their chance at the pie." Dad was the Gibbon of Varadero; he stated his Law: "If you don't have no influence any more, it's time to cut out."

"That's the truth for sure," Mike said, his presence in Varadero the living proof of it.

A year and a half later, in July 1960, we went back to Havana. The immigration officer—he may have been nineteen—looked at our passports and asked my wife was she a relative of Glenn Miller? She was not. *Que lástima.* An older man, in his twenties and therefore more dignified, asked to see my return ticket. I did not have one. But the law requires that I have one. But I did not have one. He said, "Well. All right. So you do not have one." He stamped our landing card. We went ashore, thinking: Nothing has changed; it's the same old Cuba.

Everything had changed. The next morning, a Sunday, we sat on the terrace of the craps dealer's apartment and watched the truckloads of farm workers being brought in from the country for a great rally to be held in front of the capitol building. Truck after truck came down the Malecon carrying banners that read: "Without Quota, but Without Masters." On the radio we heard the speeches and the repeated chant: *"Cuba Sí, Yanqui No!"* American friends who were at the rally told us later that they had been embraced, and everyone said, "We don't mean you. We don't mean you."

They meant the American ruling class. Mills' *The Power Elite* is a widely read book in Cuba; we were told that Castro has read it. If Mills had been really wise, he would have called it *The Power Elite at the Lazy S Ranch;* then, perhaps, *our* President would have read it. Still, he was a very busy man and we cannot expect an ex-president of Columbia to read everything published by the faculty.

Our friend the craps dealer was packing his bags; the last casino had been taken out from under him. He was sad to be leaving Havana, sadder still at the thought of returning to Vegas. In the past year in Havana he had moved from hotel to hotel as each had been intervened by the government. Technically, intervention does not mean confiscation; it means that the government will run your business for you.

The Americans who owned the big hotels and ran the casinos were cutting their losses; smart businessmen (like the English in China), they do not trifle with reality, know it cannot be changed by turning their backs to it and facing some imagined Formosa. They invited intervention by not meeting the payroll for the hired hands—the Cuban hands, that is. The American dealers and croupiers were always paid, and in U.S. money. In the last days at every casino, expecting intervention at any moment and not wanting to be caught with their safes full, the dealers left the casinos every morning with thousands of dollars on them. This money they took to a certain place. No one counted it and there were no receipts. The syndicate does not worry about dishonest employees. Mr. Lansky—his employees always refer to him as *Mister* Lansky—runs a tight shop.

One of the dealers (a murder indictment in Georgia holds him in Cuba, unwilling vacationer for the rest of his life) complained that they did not let him have a gun any more. He did not mean the Cuban police; he meant his employers. He felt naked without it; he did not like to be alone in his hotel room without it; you never could tell. "The only time they let me have one is when I have to go out and make a collection from some player who hasn't paid his debts. And then I have to turn it in as soon as I get back."

This man had won a medal for valor in the Pacific and, as far as he was concerned, Castro's government was irrevocably tainted by the presence within it of an American who had been with the revolutionary army in the Sierra Maestra and who was now a captain in the Cuban army and had his own bodyguard. "Do you know," the Georgian asked me, "do you know that this man received a *dis*honorable discharge from the U.S. Army?"

I had not known.

"I see him around. I know him. He told me Trujillo has put a price of fifty thousand dollars on his head because he organized the attack down there." The Georgian smiled. "Why, I'd knock him in the head for five thousand dollars myself. No trouble separatin' him from that bodyguard of his. I don't worry myself about nigger soldiers, they don't know the difference between sic 'em and c'mere. Just go up to him in some bar and say, 'Listen, *amigo,* I got a lady upstairs who's *dy*in' to meet you; got the finest notch in the Caribbean and will pleasure you in all kinds of ways from here to Lauden, Oklahoma.' He'd come with me, don't you worry about that. He'd come with me and I'd knock him on the head. No sir, I don't worry about no burr-head bodyguard. If they ever come to Georgia I'll buy me a white mule and make them call it Mister. Can you im*ag*ine that—a *dis*honorable discharge!"

All the American dealers were leaving; there were only a handful left. Changing their U.S. bills for pesos three to one on the black market they had created, they lived well in their last months in Havana and hated the thought of going back to where a dollar was only a dollar. Besides, after a few years in Cuba their aesthetic had altered radically: American women now seemed to them painfully thin, downright anemic, altogether lacking in hip and thigh, and far too white. They all looked sickly.

The Georgian said, "I'm going to be the last white man left in Havana." He was not worried about money; the syndicate looks after its own and would always be able to find a use for him there or on some other island in the vicinity. But it was going to be lonesome; he knew it was going to be mean lonesome in ole Havana. And he didn't like the Cuban girls. They fall in love with you, that's the trouble with them; and as *soon* as they fall in love with you, they start talkin' about death. How they love you so much they're gonna kill themselves. How they can't live without you. An' like that. He didn't go for that death shit. As *soon* as they start talkin' that way, why he just throws them out. He had a Chinese girl was the most beautiful girl you ever seen, but she started in with that death talk and he up and threw her out.

The casinos have no windows. From the outside, a casino is like a huge bubble that the tropic heat has pushed out of the hotel's wall. Inside it is both dark and at the same time well lighted; light there has a hard, defined edge: what needs to be seen is illuminated and at the edge it is cut off sharp as pie crust. It is refrigerated inside; simple air-conditioning is not enough. The players now are Cubans; in spite of Havana's air of austerity, each casino takes in about 200,000 pesos a week. Two brothers wearing black suits are the best customers; undertakers, they know better than you and me that you can't take it with you. There are the old women who put aside, out of their income, a few hundred a week for gambling. But mostly they are men, untouched by the revolution's purifying force, whose source of income is unknown.

Late one night we sat on the terrace listening, over the short-wave radio, to the Democratic Convention. The dealer's wife brought out candles so that I could see to keep a tally of the voting. Over the roaring international air we heard the ovation for Stevenson; then (*que lástima*) the voting began. And then, the militia arrived: two teen-age boys with pistols and crucifixes. We had been reported; apparently, we were thought to be sending signals out to sea; the candles looked suspicious.

It took them only a moment to see we were up to nothing sinister; then, almost tearful with anger and incomprehension, one of them said, "*Why* did Eisenhower cut the sugar quota? *Why* are you forcing us into the arms of Russia? We are not Communists. We have always been so close to you. We are more American than the Puerto Ricans.

Why do you do such things to us?" After a while, as unsatisfied with our answers as we were, they left, taking with them their fragile hope that a new president in the U.S., one who was both Democrat and Catholic, might better understand Cuba.

(This was a month and a half before Secretary of State Herter stated clearly our policy toward Cuba at the OAS meeting in Costa Rica. That policy, in brief, is: If I can't have you, no one shall have you. Reading the New York *Times* account of this OAS session I was reminded of the statement, made about a year ago, by *Times*-man Herbert Mathews, who had interviewed Castro while he was still in the mountains. Mathews said no big news story in the past ten years had been so badly handled by the press as the story of Cuba's revolution. I do not recall that he excepted his own paper from this charge; although I recently heard an editor of the *National Review* declare that the *Times* was responsible for Castro's coming to power. At any rate, when Cuba's foreign minister, Roa, replied the next day to Herter's wounded-lover cry, the *Times* reported that Roa's delivery was so rapid it made translation difficult. Translation: I'm used to waiting for the press officer's mimeographed handout and this time I didn't get one. The *Times* was able to report only that Roa said Cuba had the right "to be the friend of its friends"; that "the most serious problem faced today by the Americas is not a hypothetical, extra-continental intervention, but the actual and present threat of aggression" by the U.S.; and that Cuba stood ready to negotiate "on a footing of equality . . . her grave differences with the government of the U.S." Mr. Herter replied [his delivery, apparently, was slow enough to be understood by the *Times* man] that any friend of Russia was no friend of his: and what was the matter with the friends *we* had chosen for Cuba? He put it this way: "I am confident that the foreign ministers here assembled will examine today's speech by the Cuban foreign minister . . . and reach the right conclusion." Further translation: All right, boys, let's get this resolution on the road. He also said that Roa's speech [which *we* didn't get to read] revealed a "basic and calculated antagonism to the U.S., which will render more difficult the constant efforts of my country to restore friendly relations with Cuba." Such efforts as . . . uh . . .)

After a week in Havana we went once again to Varadero. A deserted village in winter, now in summer Ferris wheels turned over what had always been empty lots; hotels I had never seen open, houses that had always been shuttered, throbbed with Cubans and music. That long, exquisite beach was now full of vacationers and vendors of sweets and roasted pork.

The pension where we had always stayed had been knocked down along with several other houses and hotels to make way for a park that would extend from one side of the town to the other, from the bay to the ocean, a distance of perhaps four city blocks. Curving walks were being built and, under them, eight thousand lockers for those who wanted to go to the beach but could not afford a hotel.

We went to a hotel we had always thought of as a place we could not afford: a small hotel with a patio thick with shade and a Good Eating sign that Duncan Hines had left to mark his passage. It had been run for twenty years by a woman famous in Varadero. She too had invited intervention by not paying the help for several months; she had been annoyed at the Castro government because it had taken from her the monthly pension granted by the Batista government. She had been receiving an allotment of $1,000 a month because she was the granddaughter of a former Vice-President of Cuba. In the lobby there were autographed photos of famous guests: Walter Pidgeon, the young Duke and Duchess of Alba on their honeymoon.

The dealer's wife had told us that in the old days this hotel had been restricted: no Jews, that is. It goes without saying that there had never been Negro guests; the old register, still in use, had a line to be filled in labeled *Raza;* and out of habit the Cubans were still writing in that space:

Blanco. While we were there most of the guests were Jewish, Havana businessmen and their families; the children wore T-shirts with the names of their schools in Hebrew letters. All had cousins in the Bronx but only one man was thinking of leaving Cuba. In Havana the young Zionists are loyal supporters of Castro, seeing in his land-reform program a kinship to Israel. Meanwhile, at Varadero, their parents rested and gossiped. "Mira, Esther, *in die letste voch . . .*" Señora Rosenberg told us that she and her husband were very worried about us. Because we went into the water so soon after lunch. We should wait at least three hours. She knew a man—and her husband confirmed this—who went into the water at Miramar Beach without waiting the full three hours. Heart attack. A man of forty. *"Fünftzig,"* her husband said. So we should be very careful, she said. We promised.

At the Cine Varadero there is a new double feature every night. We see Westerns starring George Montgomery, dramas about farm workers with Mamie Van Doren. We saw a Hollywood movie about the Maquis which proved, beyond doubt, that the French underground was a Communist organization whose only purpose was to aid Russia. I don't remember exactly how it happened, but atomic secrets fell into the hands of a Maquis unit; the leader was going to take them to Russia. Cornel Wilde would not permit this. He made an anti-Communist speech. The audience broke into heavy applause. It has to be understood that these are the same people who, a few days later, on July 26th, marched through the streets chanting, *"Patria o muerte"* and *"Cuba Sí, Yanqui No."* Communism is one thing (and 99 per cent of the Cubans do not like it); but it has nothing to do with *their* revolution. Communism in Cuba is a big issue in the *Journal-American,* but not for the Cubans.

In Cuba I had the feeling that Castro was moving too fast and making mistakes he could not afford; he has, for example, lost the support of a great section of the middle class. Now that I am home, reading our newspapers again,

I think that Castro is not moving fast enough. Nor does it matter how many mistakes he makes. He will not be destroyed by his actions, but by ours. Our government will destroy him, because we cannot permit him to live. Alive, he is too harsh and frequent a reminder of our economic depredation of Latin America. He tells us all those things we do not want to hear; he presents us with an image of ourself we want desperately to forget. Pirates, living easy on our spoils, practicing respectability, we do not want to remember the good old days (ah, those were the days) when we had only to claim a thing and it was ours.

And in spite of one's sympathy for the revolution, one's desire for it to succeed, we are still Americans one and all (aren't we?) and we throw down our newspaper and lament: *Why* must he say those things! He is paranoid. Why does he make it so difficult for us to love him? We want to dump democracy on his shores like so much surplus wheat. Why doesn't he let us?

I suppose we will have to be brave and face up to the simple answer: Cuba doesn't want our democracy, having no need for it now, needing so many other things first. For the first time, a few million Cubans are getting one good meal a day, and for the first time they can permit themselves to hope that it will continue. Perhaps, when their daily caloric intake is half of ours, they will be able to think about our kind of democracy. Meanwhile, they have fish to fry.

We wish the revolution well, people like us, but we also wish the whole sorry mess had never come about; it nags too much at us, conscience smarts, we would like to forget the whole damn thing and, like Rubén Darío in his poem to Columbus, say:

> Oh that it had pleased God and these untouched waters might never have reflected a white sail, and the astonished stars had never seen your ships reach shore . . .
> Poor Columbus, pray to God for the world you have discovered.

Of course, Darío was an old man when he wrote that, and

tired; denouncing the Panama Canal and T. R. had exhausted him.

But why are *we* so tired, you and I, reader? Is it because we have such a good thing going for us and don't want to be disturbed? I think it is, I think it is. We've made our strike: the shell game's going full tilt in the city, and the old badger game keeps us happy in the suburbs, and the profits keep rolling in. (Go way, kid—you botherin' me.) One dollar will get you ten. One dollar will get you ten.

WILLIAM SAROYAN

The Debt

I BEGAN a moment ago by implying there was something to say, something to be said, something to *have* said after half a century since the arrival of memory in my life, since the arrival therefore of myself into it. I have tried to say, I have meant to say, I have believed I might say, but I know I haven't said, and while it doesn't trouble me, or at any rate not violently, as it would have troubled me thirty-five years ago when I wanted to say everything in one swift inevitable book, it also doesn't please me, and I feel that I must try again.

We are here. We have been here for some time. Before reaching here we were not here for a long time, and after we leave here we shall be away from here for a long time.

What did we do?

Eat?

Yes, we ate.

Talk?

Yes, we talked.

Work?

Yes, we worked.

Anything else?

Yes, we did other things, too.

When I think of the writing of the good writers, I am appalled. They know how to write, they know how to make the saying of nothing seem like the saying of something, and now and then like the saying of everything, but my writing is like my drawing, like my piano-playing, like my walking, all in a straight line, and pretty much from nothing and nowhere to nothing and nowhere, and back again.

Well, don't just stand there, *say anything*.

Hello, folks.

Is that it?

Well, it's a start, perhaps.

Goodbye, folks.

Well, *that's* also a start, of sorts.

Now, if you had only been a general in the war, you could tell the folks about *that*.

Folks, I *wasn't* a general in the war, and I'll tell you about it.

Folks, it was a great responsibility not having twenty million men under my supervision, because if you want to know the truth I don't have any particular ability as a non-supervisor. Folks, I'm really a song-writer.

Gad, the weight of the books, the weight of the memoirs of generals.

I have so far mainly considered the earliest times, not especially intending to do so, but falling into it, as it were, perhaps because when the nature of your work is to remember, you tend to start at or near the beginning, and then to go back again and again, expecting most likely to find out a little more fully why you have become estranged, why you are one place and the world another, as the Armenian saying is. It means one of you is mistaken, the world or yourself. And so perhaps now it might be in order to begin at the other end, and to say the nothing that must be said about the actual now, the actual present, for me.

I live in Paris, where I have lived on and off for a year and a half. The on and off of it is that last year at this time I sailed from Genoa to Sydney, and from there flew to San Francisco, and from there took a train to New York, and from there sailed back to Paris.

From the last day of October last year to the first day of December I sailed from the old Mediterranean city to the capital of the littlest continent, the island continent, the continent of the marsupials, down under, as they say, the continent I call *Joey in the Pouch.* I was running away from the quicksand of gambling, the quicksand and lightning of myself, the quicksand, lightning, and snowstorm of my family, my people, my lineage, the unknown, the unknowable Saroyans.

The entire month of November I was at sea, with short stops here and there. On this very day last year, for instance, November 15th, I walked in Djakarta, Indonesia, but that was 1959 and this is 1960, and now I am in Paris, in this fifth-floor flat on Rue Taitbout, back of the Opera, a little past Trinity, a little before Notre Dame de Loret, one of my favorite buildings in Paris, with larger-than-life statues standing around at the top.

This is an ice-cold flat, and while there is a butane heater on rollers to light and to move around in here from place to place, and a small electric heater to plug in, I prefer the cold, but such matters are really none of my business at this time.

The first day in Sydney I found the only game in town, won the equivalent of $2000 in fifteen minutes, and then lost it all back in three hours, along with five or six hundred more.

And then, precisely three months ago, I took a ship from Le Havre to Leningrad, and from there I traveled all over Russia in Europe.

Again I was running away from the quicksand of gambling, but this time, unlike last time, I had run through almost all of the money I had in the world.

In Moscow I went out to the Hippodrome and bet the trotting races, trying to get the hang of what was going on from a program printed in Russian, and of course I wasn't able to get the hang of it. I made losing bets on four races and let it go at that.

Now, I came to Europe to earn the money I need by which to pay the Tax Collector in full, and get him off my back where he's been for fifteen years. It's not his fault he's there, it's my fault, but I don't like him there just the same. I would much rather he got on somebody else's back for a change, and I mean on the back of anybody who knows how to accumulate money, how to keep it, and how to get more.

I haven't been able to keep it so far, but now as the years go by and time grows short I must confess with something very nearly like profound embarrassment that I have finally decided I *must* earn money, I must pay the Tax Collector, and I must find out how to keep money.

Before I went to Australia I was in possession of $40,-000 which I had earned soon after reaching Paris, which I had put aside for the Tax Collector. I earned the money by doing what is known as hack writing, but I don't do hack writing, so I will have to call it something else, something more accurate. I wrote a play for a producer of movies. The play is a good play, although I was *hired* to write it. I took what we call an original idea for a story to the producer, and he liked it and asked me to write what is known as a treatment of it. I told him I didn't write treatments, I didn't know what they were. He told me to write a scenario, but I didn't know what a scenario was, either. I told him I knew what a play was and I would go to work for him and write a play, based on the original idea, and he could have somebody else put the play into any form he liked.

My wages were $60,000.

The worth of the play is not possible to guess, although it is probably far more than that. It is also prabably worth not much more than sixty cents.

The play was a hit in Vienna, and later in Berlin. In the German language, of course. I wrote a cabbage, that is. A cabbage is any writing that is done for money, and doesn't belong to the writer.

As a rule I try not to write cabbages, but I had had no choice.

Now, while $60,000 isn't a small sum, you must understand that to a maker of movies it is a *very* small sum, for he will pay thirty or forty times as much to others before his film is finished and his flacks make an heroic effort to ram it down the throats of the poor public.

In short, I should have been paid more, but as I was in Europe to make money, I had to put aside any notion of *not* being hired, of not earning something, of not being a hack. I worked like a desperate dog, and wrote a good play.

The writing was *my* writing, and the best I knew how to do. I don't know how to write two ways, one for money, and one for truth. I have got to believe I go for truth every time, even when I am hired and am writing for wages.

And I may say it is contrary to policy for me to *sell* a play. I am only willing to lease it, but this was different. If I didn't start making money and stashing it for the Tax Collector I might *never* get him off my back.

Later in 1959, for the same producer, I took some writing he owned, which was useless to him as it stood, and I transformed it into another play, and this time my wages were $20,000. Of its kind—a kind I don't like—this was a good play, too, but my connection with it was secondary, or less than that. The original idea of it was based upon a courtroom novel, which in turn had been adapted into a play, which in turn I had made over into a new play, hack work of the most unappealing order for me, but again I had had no choice.

As a matter of fact, my son and my daughter were with me in Paris at that time, in a big rented apartment, and I took the matter up with them. After three or four days of thinking about it, from every angle, my daughter, then thirteen, said, "It's a job, like any other job. Sometimes a writer has got to take a job, too, Papa. Do it."

And my son, then fifteen, said, "It's a lot of money from one point of view, and from another it's nothing. A lot of hard-working people, some of them movie-writers, don't make that much in a whole year, sometimes in two years, or even in three or four. Do it if it won't take up too much of your time. It certainly can't do you any harm."

I like to speak to members of my family about anything of that kind that's on my mind, and so I told them about it, and we thought about it for a number of days, and finally we all decided I would hire out again.

That made it $80,000 earned in 1959. It's probably a lot of money, but if there *is* a lot, I need a lot, and frequently I need a lot when there isn't a lot. I mean, I have obligations to meet, and I myself have got to live while I am hiring out and earning money, and everything costs more than it used to. I certainly didn't gamble away every penny of the $80,000 before I went to Russia three months ago. I drank some of it away, and I bought a raincoat.

The Time

THE YEAR 1959 started in Malibu, with the closing of a house on the beach, after six years.

The pain of packing the old manuscripts, books, and papers was great. The stuff was hauled off and put in storage, and I hauled off and left that place forever.

From the beginning I had thought of the place as

heaven, as perhaps it was, but even heaven will not do, cannot do, forever. It must be closed, and the back must be turned to it.

I went to New York, but it was not for me.

I went to Belgrade, but it was not for me.

I bought a Red Racer, and I raced. To Trieste, Venice, Milan, Geneva, Aix-en-Provence, Nice, San Remo, Monte Carlo, Cannes, and finally up to Paris, where I wrote a play for money, as I've said, rented an apartment on Avenue Victor Hugo, to which my kids flew from New York.

For three and a half months we were together, and then they were gone, and I was back in a hotel room. I drove the Red Racer to Spain and back, and then I took a ship from Genoa to Australia.

In the rented apartment on Avenue Victor Hugo I wrote a book called *Not Dying*. On the ship to Australia I wrote a book called *Joey in the Pouch*. In the apartment I also wrote a play called *Nobody in His Right Mind, or The Moscow Comedy*, and on the ship I also wrote a play called *Kangaroo and Boomerang*. And that was 1959.

From Malibu in 1958 I went around the world, taking with me the daily work of writing *Fifty Fifty*, started on the first day of my fiftieth year, September 1, 1957, finished on the last, August 31, 1958, as planned. A million words, give or take a couple of thousand. Too many, too long, and I wasn't interested in revising it, in finding out what I had, so it went into storage with the rest of my junk.

My kids came out to California from New York that summer, and mainly we had a lot of fun, but one thing happened that was no fun.

We drove up to San Francisco to spend a couple of weeks at my sister's home, and then we drove back to Malibu, by way of Fresno, and as we were driving around among the vineyards near Malaga my son asked me to stop, so we could pick some grapes. So we could *steal* some, if you like. I stopped, and ran out into the vineyard and began picking the grapes, only to notice that my son was just standing there looking at them. I told him to start picking, but he just went right on looking.

"I don't think they're ripe," he said.

"Even so," I said, "pick a couple of bunches."

I ran back to the car. He came back, taking his time, but he didn't have a single bunch of grapes with him.

This bothered me.

He had asked me to stop, and I had stopped, and then he hadn't done anything to make the stop worth anything.

I bawled him out about this, and about his boredom all during the drive, and then I bawled out my daughter, too. My sister said something, and I bawled her out, too, and then for an hour or more nobody spoke.

By that time I felt foolish, but at the same time I couldn't understand my son, so I asked if he had had a bowel movement in the morning.

He hadn't. And he'd had a headache all day.

I told him about myself when I had been his age. I had had nothing, but I had always been interested, fascinated even, by everything. On and on.

I knew it at the time, I know it now, and I suppose he knew it, too: I was being angry at his mother.

It was stupid, but I couldn't help it, that's all.

I stopped somewhere for an aspirin for him, but he said he believed a Coke would do him more good, so he had a Coke, as everybody did, but whatever had been going on went right on going on.

My past was kicking me around, and with it I was kicking my son around, and every now and then my daughter, a little, too.

I tried to get out of it, to get myself out of being so mad at their mother, and at them, too, but it didn't work, and so I blamed my son.

Why wasn't he livelier, more comic, more alert, so that I would be driven out of the madness?

He didn't know. All he knew, but didn't say, was that

he hated me, and I couldn't blame him, but I hated being hated.

I said that my trouble had been that I had loved them too much, had tried to do too much for them, had paid too much attention to every wish they had ever had, and of course they knew I meant their mother hadn't, which I believed to be true. From now on I would be different, I said. I would be like other fathers. I would give them orders. The other fathers were right, I was mistaken. I had looked upon them from the beginning as equals, or even superiors, and now I could see the folly of that.

I talked for hours and miles, and nobody replied, nobody dared, or cared, or needed to.

Now, I must point out that such talking is traditional in my family. It is invariably loud, intense, righteous, and critical of all others.

All families probably have their own procedure for the achievement of psychiatric therapy or the restoration of balance, and the better part of this procedure is based upon talk, although it frequently moves along to shouting and fighting.

Six or seven times during the long recitation I tried to get out of the whole thing by laughing at myself, by making known that I knew I was being a fool, by saying things I believed were both true and amusing, but nobody laughed.

It was a very hot day in July, and from the beginning it had been a bad day.

In the back of the old Cadillac my daughter sat beside my sister, and beside me sat my son, drawn away on the car seat, the old Saroyan scowl all over his face.

At last the car began to climb the hills of Pacific Palisades, and soon we would be home.

I was still going strong when suddenly my son said in a tone of voice that still hurts me, and has twice come to me in my sleep: "Papa, Papa, will you stop the car, please?"

I stopped the car, he leaped out, and in the very leap began to buckle and vomit, trying to hide behind a tree whose trunk was too narrow for hiding. The sound of his sickness sickened me. Once, twice, three times, four times, five times. Silence. His face was drained of color and covered with sweat.

Immediately after he had jumped out of the car my daughter jumped out, saying, "Aram, what's the matter? What's the matter, Aram?"

My sister said in Armenian, "You've made the poor boy sick. He isn't like you. He's like himself."

We got home, and I got him into the shower, and then into a robe, and at the table for some hot chocolate and toast and boiled eggs, and then I had them both go to bed, even though it was only beginning to be dark, and their old friends in the neighborhood were coming to the door to ask them out for games.

That's the thing that bothered me in 1958, and will go right on bothering me the rest of my life.

I only hope it isn't the last thing I remember.

He told me the next day that it hadn't been my hollering at him that had made him sick, it had been other things.

I thanked him, but I didn't believe him, because I couldn't.

And my sister had been right in saying that he wasn't like me, only she'll never know how like him I was, but never vomited, because if I had, I might not be able to stop.

And I was sorry he wasn't like me, in that, because it is better not to get sick, it is better to find out how not to, it is better to insist on it, even, until it's almost impossible to get that sick, because getting sick doesn't get it, doesn't do it, at all.

But he hurt me, he hurt me deeper even than the failure and death of friends, and I loved him more than ever, and despised myself for never having been able to get sick that way, and for having made him sick that way, making him vomit for me forty years ago.

I went home one night from the winter streets of Fresno, possessed. Something had taken possession of me, hushed me, estranged me, put me aside from myself, and I wanted to get rid of it. The house was dark and empty when I got there, and cold, and I didn't know what to do. In the dining room was a bench my mother had made by placing planks over two apple-boxes and putting a coarse woven covering over the planks: red and black checks made out of some kind of sacking, made in Bitlis by somebody in the family. I couldn't sit and I couldn't lie down, so I kneeled on this bench and then put my head down, as Moslems do in praying, and I began to rock back and forth slowly because by doing that the thing that had taken possession of me, the sickness, the uselessness, whatever it was, seemed to go away. I half-slept, I half-prayed, and I thought, "What *is* this, for God's sake? What's the matter? Why is my head like a damned rock?"

At last I heard somebody at the door and quickly sat in the corner of the room, on the bench. My mother turned on a light, came in, and looked at me. I got up and fetched sawdust from the barn, so she could get the fire going, and in that way she wasn't able to notice that I was possessed, I was sick, I was useless, my head was a rock. Nobody would know.

The big event of 1958 was my son's sickness, known.

In 1957 I went from Malibu to New York to pick them up at the beginning of summer vacation, and took them to Venice by boat, and from there by train to Trieste, Belgrade, and Athens. And from there by boat to Naples and Barcelona, where we spent a month because the Avenida Hotel gave us a pleasant suite, and the food there was so good.

We decided to find out about Barcelona. Best for my son were the bullfights, to which he sometimes went alone. Best for my daughter were the *sardanas,* the public dancing of the Catalans.

And best for me was the two of them together.

In 1956 it was trips to New York, and drives from Malibu to San Francisco, Las Vegas, and Tijuana.

And that's far enough back for all practical purposes in this reverse chronology.

WILLIAM STYRON

Mrs. Aadland's Little Girl, Beverly

It usually requires a certain arrogance to say of a new book that it is a masterpiece. For one thing, the risks are large; in his runaway enthusiasm, the person who is rash enough to proclaim a new book "great," "a staggering achievement," "a work of art of the highest order" (these are the phrases most commonly employed) is likely to be proved wrong, even long before time and posterity have had a chance to assay his judgment. Recall, for example, *By Love Possessed*. A masterpiece? The reviewers seemed to think so, yet now it seems apparent that it wasn't that at all—at least not proven; opposed to what was originally claimed for it, too many people have considered it an unfair struggle and a thickheaded bore. At certain rare moments, however, there will appear a work of such unusual and revealing luminosity of vision, of such striking originality, that its stature is almost indisputable; one feels that one may declare it a masterpiece without hesitation, or fear that the passing of time might in any way alter one's conviction. Such a book is *The Big Love,* a biography of Beverly Aadland by her mother, Mrs. Florence Aadland. To Mrs. Aadland and her collaborator, Tedd Thomey, we owe a debt of gratitude; both of them must feel a sense of pride and relief at having delivered themselves, after God alone knows how much labor, of a work of such wild comic genius.

I would like to make it plain, however, that—as in most high comic art—there is a sense of moral urgency in *The Big Love* which quite removes it from the specious and, more often than not, sensational claptrap we have become accustomed to in popular biography. Witness the first line of the book—a first line which is as direct and in its own way as reverberant as any first line since "Call me Ishmael."

"There's one thing I want to make clear right off," Mrs. Aadland begins, "my baby was a virgin the day she met Errol Flynn."

Continuing, she says: "Nothing makes me sicker than those dried-up old biddies who don't know the facts and spend all their time making snide remarks about my daughter Beverly, saying she was a bad girl before she met Errol. . . . I'm her mother and she told me everything. She never lied to me. Never."

Already it is obvious that we are in contact with a moral tone entirely different from, let us say, the lubricity of Errol Flynn's own biography, *My Wicked, Wicked Ways,* or the self-exploitation and narcissism so prevalent in those boring memoirs, which appear almost monthly, of yet another international lollipop. In striking this note of rectitude, Mrs. Aadland makes it clear that furthest from her desires is a wish to titillate, or in any way to make sensational an affair which, after all, ended in such tragedy and heartbreak for all concerned. Indeed, if it were not for the sense of decency and high principles which informs every page of *The Big Love,* we would not be in the presence of a comic masterwork at all, but only one more piece of topical trash, hardly distinguishable from the life of a Gabor sister.

The stunning blonde who was to become "Bev" to her mother and, at the age of fifteen, "Woodsie" (because of her resemblance to a wood nymph) to Errol Flynn, was conceived, so Flo Aadland tells us, in an apartment on Mariposa Avenue in Hollywood on December 7, 1941. The date, of course, was ominous, contributing much to further Flo's lasting suspicion that her own life, and now Bev's, was "preordained." Tragedy had dogged much of Flo's life. She possessed, for one thing, an artificial foot, the result of a traffic accident, and this misfortune—usually referred to as "the tragedy of my leg"—coupled with a previous miscarriage had made it seem to her that life had hardly been worth living until Bev came along. Bev—who was a precocious child, walking at ten months, singing "all the radio commercials" at a year—altered the complexion of Flo's life entirely. "She was such a different baby, different in intelligence as well as beauty. I wondered . . . if she had been given to me . . . to make up for the tragedy of my leg." Shortly after this her speculation was confirmed when, riding with little Bev on a Hermosa Beach bus, she met a female Rosicrucian "who had made a deep study of the inner ways of life."

Discussing Bev, the Rosicrucian told Flo: "This baby has an old soul. . . . She is very mature. . . . Were the babies you lost before both girls?"

" 'Yes,' I said.

"The Rosicrucian lady nodded and then held both of Beverly's hands tightly in her own. 'Twice before, this baby tried to be born. . . . She has always known she was to fill the emptiness that entered your life when you lost your leg. . . . And you must realize this also. . . . This child has been born for untold fame and fortune.' "

Bev's early life was the normal one for a Hollywood youngster. So gifted that she was able to sing, in immaculate pitch, a popular song called *Symphony* at seventeen months, she was also almost overwhelmingly beautiful, and at the age of three, impersonating Bette Davis, won the costume beauty contest at the Episcopal Sunday School (an Episcopal activity peculiarly Californian in flavor). Later she was chosen mascot for the Hermosa Beach Aquaplane Race Association, cut the ceremonial tape for a $200,000 aquarium, and, not yet six, played in her first movie, a Technicolor epic called *The Story of Nylon.* As young as Bev was, she already exerted upon men a stupefying enchantment. A Hollywood doctor—"a very learned man, an authority on Eastern religions who had lectured all over the world and written many books"—was the first to pronounce the somber warning. "He held her hands the way that Rosicrucian lady had done. . . . 'Mrs. Aadland,' he said seriously, 'wherever did you get this little girl?' . . . Then he sat down in his chair and did a very strange thing. He closed his eyes and passed his hand back and forth just above Beverly's bright blonde curls. 'I think I see sort of a halo on this girl,' he said." Shortly Flo hears the gloomy, admonitory words: " 'I think men will be terribly affected by this girl. . . . Be very careful with your daughter. . . . I think men are going to kill over this girl. I have the feeling in my heart that she has the scent of musk on her.' " Her religious training enables Flo to comprehend: "I knew what he meant [about musk]. It wasn't the first time I had run into that phrase. I had read it in the Bible."

When Flynn began seeing Bev—then aged fifteen, and dancing in the movie version of *Marjorie Morningstar*—Flo sensed no impropriety. Thrilled that her daughter should be dating such a famous man, "overwhelmed by the fact that my baby called this man Errol," she confesses that she nearly fainted dead away when first led into his presence. To be sure, she says: "I'd read about his trials for the statutory rape of those two teen-agers in 1942. And I'd seen the headlines in 1951 when he was charged with the rape of a fifteen-year-old French girl." As for Bev, however, ". . . I still didn't believe he would take advantage of her." Against this gullibility may be measured Flo's near-insane outrage, some months later, when, during the course of a plane ride to join Errol in New York, Bev reveals that not only was she no longer chaste, but that Errol—on their very first night together—had done what the cynical reader knew he had done all along: he had, indeed, ravished her, tearing her seventy-five-dollar bolero dress, muttering "Woodsie, Woodsie" over and over, and "growling in his throat." Flo's indignation, however, is short-lived; despite this traumatic event, Bev seems deeply in love with Errol and Errol with Bev. On sober second thought, in fact, the future looks pretty rosy for Flo. "While [Bev] talked, the love bloom was all over her—in her eyes, making her cheeks pink. 'Mama,' she said, 'can't you imagine what it's going to be like with Errol from now on? Can't you imagine the lovely clothes, the spending, the famous people we'll meet? . . . Mama . . . he's told me how good I am for him. He's told me that we're going to write the Arabian Nights all over again.' "

And so the incredible joy ride commences, and the sedulous Florence is rarely absent from the scene, or at least its periphery. There are drinking bouts, yachting trips, dances, and other social events, including a well-publicized nude swimming party at a country estate near New York which Flo, with characteristic delicacy, assures us was *not* an orgy. "Beverly later told me all about it. [The people] *weren't* riotously drunk or mad with passion. It was an unconventional but casual swim. Afterwards they got out, dressed, and enjoyed some pork chops and apple sauce together. Beverly helped serve the food and was complimented by the others on her clothes and manners." The East Coast holds Flo—L.A. born and bred—in its thrall; her description of the Connecticut countryside, "the homes with their unusual gabled roofs," has a quality both eerie and exotic, as if it were the Norwegian troll country. At one club function, a handsomely swank place, also in Connecticut, Bev has her first encounter with snow. ". . . We sat down at a table . . ." Flo says, and describes a boring situation. "I looked around for a movie magazine or something interesting to read, but could find only copies of *Time* and *Fortune*. . . . Pretty soon we noticed it was snowing outside. Without saying a word to me or anyone else, Beverly got up and went outside. It was the first time Bev had ever seen snow falling and, being a native Californian, she was thrilled. I watched her through the large picture window. . . . She held up her arms gracefully and whirled them through the air, touching the falling snowflakes. She never looked lovelier. Her cheeks were flushed to a healthy pink and she wore one of her nicest outfits, a gorgeous peach-colored cashmere sweater and matching skirt. . . . As the big white snowflakes come down thicker and thicker, she did a very crazy thing. She took off her shoes and began dancing and skipping around on the golf greens. . . . She looked like an absolutely mad fairy princess, whirling and cavorting, holding her arms out so beautifully. . . . When she came in, she said: 'Oh, Mother, it was so beautiful!' Her nose was red as a raspberry and when I touched it with my finger tip it felt like a cold puppy's nose."

The note of pathos here, fugitive but intensely real, as it is in all comic art of a high order, is the mysterious ingredient which pervades every page of *The Big Love* and compels the book, in a grotesque fashion which surpasses all aesthetic laws, to become a kind of authentic literary creation in spite of itself. It was along about the passage just quoted that I was persuaded that Tedd Thomey, Mrs. Aadland's ghost, was in reality Evelyn Waugh, come back after a long silence to have another crack at the bizarre creatures who inhabit the littoral of Southern California. In truth, however, from this point on the book more reasonably brings to mind Nathanael West's *The Day of the Locust,* if for no other reason than the fact that, as in that fine and funny book, in which horror and laughter are commingled like the beginning of a scream, the climax of *The Big Love* swiftly plunges toward nightmare and hallucination in a fashion which all but overwhelms the comedy. Errol Flynn dies of a heart attack in Vancouver, and Beverly goes to pieces. She becomes the unwilling object of the attentions of a young madman, who, one night in Hollywood, rapes her at pistol point, and then in her presence blows out his brains—a tragedy which, Flo concludes, like the multiple tragedy of Errol Flynn and Beverly and Florence Aadland, must have been "preordained." Flo is charged with five counts of contributing to the delinquency of a minor; Beverly, in turn, is remanded into the custody of a movie-colony divine, the Reverend Leonard Eilers, whose wife Frances, in an admirable spirit of Christian guardianship, is now chaperoning Bev during her appearances on the Midwest night-club circuit.

But at last the true comic spark returns, jewel-bright, in the ultimate scene of this terrifying, flabbergastingly vulgar, and, at times, inexplicably touching book. It takes place, appropriately enough, in the celebrated Forest Lawn Memorial Park, whither Flo, out on bail, and Bev and a friend have gone one morning at dawn to deposit flowers on Errol's grave, near a spot called the Garden of Everlasting Peace.

" 'My God,' I said to Bev. 'Can you imagine an unpeaceful man like the Swashbuckler in here?'

"We took the flowers from the car and placed them on the grave. . . . Then, although Errol's grave now had more flowers than any of the others, Beverly and our friend decided he deserved even more.

"So they went to the other graves and took only a few of the fresh flowers that had been left the day before. They took a bit of larkspur from one, a daisy from one and a lily from another. Then, frisking around like wood nymphs, the two of them leaped gracefully over Errol's grave, dropping the flowers at his head and feet.

"I watched them dance . . . for a few more moments and then I said to Beverly: 'You didn't kiss him yet, did you?'

" 'No, Mama,' she said.

"Then she knelt down very carefully and touched her lips to the grass near Errol's headstone.

" 'Mama!' she said suddenly.

" 'What's the matter?' I said.

" 'Mama!' she said. 'I just heard a big belly laugh down there!'

"After that we left. . . . As we drove away, we waved and called out gaily: 'Good-by, Errol!' "

It had been, Flo muses, "a tremendously swanky graveyard."

HARVEY SWADOS

The Pilot as Precursor

If you want to talk to a pilot today, you have to make an appointment. He does not frequent bars. He cannot drink anything alcoholic for twenty-four hours before he flies. He does not congregate at the union hall. He regards it not as a hangout but rather as a technical headquarters. And you cannot watch him at work, because nowadays it is easier to watch a surgeon performing a brain operation than it is to check in with a flight crew and follow them through a routine run, say, from Salt Lake City to New York.

The "typical" pilot, seen through the spyglass of a survey, is a white man of about thirty-seven, who owns his own home and has a wife and two children. He has had three years of college, belongs to a union (the Air Line Pilots Association), and earns about $14,000 a year.

Fourteen thousand dollars a year is a lot more than the ordinary union member makes. For pilots' salaries to average out to this figure, many of them have to earn up to $25,000 a year, and do. But high earnings are only one of the factors which mark the pilot as different not only from his AFL-CIO brothers, but also from the vast middle class, of which he considers himself to be a fairly representative member. These differences are really more suggestive than superficial similarities.

For one thing, pilots represent an elite group psychologically as well as physically. Drawn for the most part from the high-standard Air Force (45 per cent, with perhaps 35 per cent coming from the Navy and the Marines), they have to start all over again through a battery of examinations in order to qualify for the big new jets. Only one applicant in sixty makes the grade. The man who is cleared at last to fly these planes is not merely an A-1 physical specimen; he is, as Ed Mack Miller, who teaches him how to fly them at United Air Lines' Flight Training Center in Denver, puts it, "a very highly developed human being."

This human being, whose vision and reflexes and heart and blood pressure and nervous system must be such as to place him in the top 1 per cent of the population, can never rest on his good fortune at having once passed both government and private examinations, like the doctors and dentists who can coast after their state boards, or the professors who can vegetate after acquiring their Ph.D.'s. He is subject four times a year to a test of his flying skill and twice a year to a severe review of his physical condition. At any time he may be debarred forever from air line flying. This boils down to the fact that a pilot of sixty has to meet the health and proficiency standards of a pilot of thirty. Obviously, only a selected group of a selected group can stay on the job until sixty. His union itself figures the average rate of attrition to be about 3 per cent a year. Of a given group of one hundred copilots all twenty-five years old, only 10 per cent have a mathematical chance of flying until age fifty-five. Of the group, 89 per cent will have been separated before sixty years of age.

But there is something about these pilots that is even more special than their physical and psychological qualifications: They love their work. By and large it would seem (although it can hardly be proved) that fewer and fewer of us are happy with our work. When you come upon a group of men who are fanatically devoted to what they do for a livelihood, it is a remarkable phenomenon. There are so few pilots who have voluntarily quit the air lines that they can be called up by name by their fellow fliers, as eccentrics or misfits.

This is worth a little examination. Some years back we might have waved it away by writing off the pilots as perpetual adolescents who loved to court danger, who craved glamour, easy dough, and the thrill of thumbing their noses at death, like racing drivers or soldiers of fortune. But now that air line operations have become as routinized as railroads or buses, pilots can buy life insurance at the same rate as office workers. These healthy, responsible, cautious men are a good risk.

Then why? What is there about flying that continues to enthrall them? The answer has to be divided into three parts. First, what they are doing is necessary. Second, it can be performed only by a highly selected elite group. Third, it is fascinating.

In inverse order: Every pilot with whom you speak insists that he likes to fly because every flight involves a series of swift and important decisions. Even the most routine and presumably boring milk run must have a takeoff and a landing; the slightest shifting of wind can make either the takeoff or landing a singular and dramatic experience. The closest analogy might be to the riverboat or harbor pilot or to the master of an ocean liner, whose job may often be boring or exhausting but also has the potentiality at any moment of intense excitement and rapid decision-making. It is this potential of great demand on the individual's skill, ingenuity, and resourcefulness that is the source of the enormous pull of commercial flying for pilots, replacing the old charge that the daredevils used to get from contact flying in planes made by hand. This potential has not been at all diminished by the development of the jet airliners. Quite the contrary. The technical work in flying the new airplanes, despite (or perhaps because of) the fact that they are actually easier to fly than the old piston aircraft, is awesome to a layman. As Ed Miller explains it, the new pilot has to be "a computer with legs." Miller, who trains pilots in the simulators, and who is himself a successful writer as well as a pilot with twenty years' experience, details a dizzying series of computations and decisions that have to be made almost automatically, and with split-second precision, by the pilot of the jet as it is leaving the ground or returning to it.

The pilot takes a natural pride in the fact that not many men can qualify to fly a commercial jet. There are thousands of competent pilots in the military services, as well as civilian holders of various classifications of licenses, who would not be permitted near the flight deck of a DC-8 or a Boeing 707. Inevitably the fraternity remains closely knit—a fact of which the Air Line Pilots Association has taken intelligent advantage. The air line pilot has a highly developed sense of exclusivity as well as of command.

He knows too that what he is doing becomes increasingly important, increasingly essential, with every passing hour. If it was hair-raising fun to fly the mail thirty years ago, letters could always be delivered by rail if you were killed or went on strike. But all passenger travel today is practically dependent on the scheduled air lines; if all of the 15,000-odd air line pilots in the country were to walk out at once (a situation which is not practically possible) the country would be in the grip of a national emergency more immediate and far more irksome than that gradually brought on by a strike of half a million steel or auto workers.

The pilot is different from other Americans in some other ways that are even more interesting, perhaps because they are unexpected. He is more worldly and somewhat more sophisticated than the average citizen, particularly if he is flying an overseas route. He tends to read more newspapers and magazines than his neighbor, and by virtue of the fact that one day he is in Karachi and another in Bangkok and another in Berlin, he is more aware than are most Americans of the true size and shape of the world and of his native land's place in it. At its best, this concern can issue in the kind of constructive selfless action taken by Captain Charles C. Dent, who donated all of the $5500 bonus awarded him for a safe crash landing to the United States Committee for the United Nations to help promote its program.

If he is a more concerned American, the pilot is also a more stable one. It should hardly be surprising that his home breaks up so infrequently that most people in the industry find it hard to name offhand any pilot who has been recently divorced. (He is not *always* a model husband. One learns from ex-stewardesses that the "key game" flourishes as a weekend diversion among flying families in the upper Midwest. Although there is no corroboration of this gossip that in certain communities blasé pilots and their wives play switch, like other bored suburbanite couples, there are others to assure you that when one air line based its pilots and stewardesses in the same Honolulu hotel a few years ago, the shack-up incidence and the subsequent marriage breakup rate were so high that sexual segregation had to be instituted.)

In the main, though, the pilot does tend to participate more wholeheartedly than his neighbors in somewhat more respectable neighborhood activities, such as scout leadership and civic affairs, maybe because he has more free time at home than they do. Surely most surprising about this middle-class man so jealous of his position in the community is the extent of his active participation in a tough union, the Air Line Pilots Association. But of this, more later.

There are pilots who in their free time are insurance salesmen, aviation consultants, travel agents, ski instructors, novelists, sail-plane enthusiasts and fliers-for-fun, teachers, cattlemen, cow-punchers, farmers (from potatoes to oranges, depending on locale), dog fanciers, aircraft brokers, ministers, parachute jumpers, woodworkers and furniture makers, real estate brokers and property managers, executive recruiters, big-game hunters. At a guess only 5 per cent have income-producing sidelines, but many of them do become passionately interested in avocations which may possibly become full-time jobs in the event of grounding or retirement. Pilot after pilot will tell you that he goes into those sidelines not at all because he dislikes flying but because he has considerable free time and does not get the variety of satisfactions from his work or his relations with his employers that he comes to feel life ought to hold. One suspects that he is merely anticipating all of those Americans who will sooner or later be going on a four-day week, or a six-hour day, or both, and who, whether or not they like their work, will find themselves unable to spend their long lives simply staring at television or building barbecue pits.

The future pilot usually goes to college for several years and then, bored and restless, signs up for a four-year tour of duty and is sent, say, to Lackland Air Force Base. He discovers that not everyone can strap the bird to his back, not everyone can fly a hot jet. So he is proud when he earns his wings, but like most of us he chafes under rigid military discipline, and he turns to the civilian career possibilities of the commercial air lines.

Here, however, he is taught that while there are bold pilots and old pilots, there are no old bold pilots. So he becomes, if he was not to start out with, a technically minded and very careful man. In his mid-twenties, he learns to forget hot jockeying, and to value stability and the ability to avoid even involvement, if possible, in emergency situations.

He learns too that the very size and speed of the big jet has shrunk more than distances. It has also shrunk job possibilities for the men at the controls. Aside from the fact that it is a simpler plane to operate, it can take more people from one coast to the other in half the previous time. This means that the pilot who is supposed to fly eighty hours a month has to make more flights, and that as the air lines

turn to jets, pilots with less seniority are being laid off. Many of those who manage to hang on find that promotion has become very sluggish indeed; in an industry from which the romance has disappeared, some are coming to terms with the idea that a man can make a life's career out of being a copilot. (If he shrinks from the thought of what will happen in the coming decade when supersonic flight becomes a reality and the ocean is spanned in an hour and a half, he knows that his work-week will have to be shortened again and that only his union is currently doing any substantial research in the multiplicity of problems that will accompany the supersonic age.)

Nevertheless, as an American he is an optimist, even if a worried one. He is more aware than are most people that although flying is as popular in this country as reading, it is just as restricted to a special segment of the population. Three out of every four Americans have never flown with the air lines. Only 2 per cent of the peoples of the world have ever been off the ground. More of them are going to want to fly, and, as living standards rise, are going to be able to; and the pilot looks forward to flying them. Far more important is the potential in the air cargo business, which can only increase, with fantastic possibilities in store not merely for inventories and business in general, but for pilots. If we reach the point in this country where, with the development of modified jets and all-cargo planes, even 2 per cent of all cargo is shipped by air, there will have to be a threefold increase in aircraft personnel.

This is why the hopeful pilot believes that the employment slump brought about by the jet age is only temporary, and that great days lie ahead, probably in the latter part of the Sixties. If right now there is a surplus of pilots, despite the substantial attrition rate, he thinks that in a few years there will be a shortage, as the older men retire and the youngsters are not attracted to the industry in sufficient numbers from the military or from no-longer-star-struck high school boys. He is convinced that it is going to be

necessary to train pilots in the universities, perhaps under government subsidy, since, as the missile age develops, the services will simply not be giving flight training to many young men. He points to England and France, where the corporations themselves, while state-owned, already sponsor nonmilitary flight-training programs.

The pilot, who knows that it takes better than four crews to keep one airplane operating efficiently around the clock, sees the air lines—like the automobile manufacturers —merging and consolidating; and he is aware too that the top money is in the Big Four, where average first-pilot earnings in 1958 were better than eighteen thousand dollars. Since he loves to fly, he is stimulated far more than he is annoyed by new developments. There is nothing like novelty, challenging one's adaptability, to keep a job interesting. As one veteran pilot turned executive says, "Even the transition from the DC-3 to the DC-4 was comparable in complexity to that from piston to jet. Every technological advance is an added insurance that flying will continue to be fascinating."

Nevertheless, although he is almost unique in having a job that pays well, that is highly respectable, and that he loves, the pilot is going to be bucking in years to come—like his friends and neighbors in the ranch houses across the country—for more pay and shorter hours. Which brings us back to the intriguing question of his union.

Captain C. C. Spencer, who flies for Pan American in addition to having served as Regional Vice-President of the Air Line Pilots Association (in effect running the New York office of ALPA), estimates that there are some seven hundred pilots who are active on a day-to-day basis in the operation of the union. This is particularly remarkable when you consider, first, that these are solid homeowners, the majority of whom probably vote Republican (or at least did until General Eisenhower appointed their bane, General Elwood Quesada, as head of the Federal Aviation Agency) and have neither a family tradition nor a compelling per-

sonal interest in a militant labor movement; and second, that their union has but two salaried full-time officers, the President and the Executive Vice-President: all of the other officials are unpaid and fly for a living. The Local Executive Council of the ALPA, its basic unit of organization, varies in size, depending on the size of the air line it represents, from six hundred down to ten members. The councils pretty much run their own affairs. (There are fifty-two air lines in this country having separate union agreements, all separately administered.)

Naturally, you will find griping about the union, mostly apparently from the younger men who feel that they are being frozen out or ignored by their seniors who have their own cliques and their own political machine. The union's official response to this is not merely its constitution and its carefully democratic table of organization, or its well-advertised freedom from corruption and collusion, but also the practical evidence that each Master Executive Council generally has two new members serving on it during any given election period, and that there is always an active search for new-member participation in the rotating positions.

How are we to explain the fact that these individualists, who like to think of themselves as professional men, and who feel no particular bonds with the main body of the organized labor movement, participate so actively in the running of their union? The answer is not to be found by approaching this union as basically a trade or professional pressure group like the American Medical Association, primarily engaged in such monopolistic practices as locking up existing jobs, restricting entry into the field, and boosting income to astronomical heights. Other unions and associations behave like this and do not as a necessary consequence elicit from their membership the kind of voluntary effort so impressively in evidence at the ALPA.

In the union's handsome Midway Airport headquarters in Chicago, President Clarence H. Sayen, the forty-two-

year-old former Braniff pilot who has headed the union since the expulsion in 1951 and subsequent death (in 1953) of its first president and charter member, Dave Behncke, is voluble on this matter. The contrast between the two is almost too pat a lesson in recent American history. Behncke was a swashbuckler out of the Roaring Twenties, a barnstorming stunt man from the hazardous early days, with a hairline mustache and a flair for theatrics, but with no administrative ability or the faintest notion of the functions of a union in the second half of the twentieth century. Sayen is an academically oriented young man with a master's degree in economics, who has been a college instructor, is sensitive to the new political and social currents, and gives speeches—substantial ones, too—with titles like *The Cultural Impact of Jets,* to commerce and industry associations. Sayen has his own theories about the wide extent of member participation in ALPA and its implications for AFL-CIO organizing efforts, abysmally unsuccessful so far, among the millions of technical and white-collar people.

His union has been so successful in engaging not only the attendance but the freely given aid of its members (some 10 per cent of whom, by his reckoning, are actively engaged in union work at any particular time) that other unions, all much larger numerically than ALPA, have been coming to his office for advice and suggestions on matters of white-collar organization. Sayen is proud of this and attributes it by strong implication to several factors.

First would be the enormous concentration of union attention to problems of safety. About five hundred pilots, or enough to operate a medium-sized air line, are engaged in union safety projects on a part-time basis. The projects are both voluntary and nonprofit. Pilots involved in them are reimbursed only for lost flight time. A brief listing may give some idea of the well-nigh fanatical dedication with which the pilots concentrate on safety work: (1) Investigating crashes. (2) Flight evaluation. (3) Aircraft evaluation. This includes at-the-factory examination of designs, mockups,

etc. (The DC-6 and DC-8 have 112 design modifications made as a result of ALPA suggestions.) (4) Surveillance of airport facilities. (5) Air traffic control improvements. An ALPA group worked on airborne radar. (6) Physical standards. ALPA is a corporate member of the Aero Medical Association. (7) Special projects. One example: the centerline approach light system, enormously important for obscured landing conditions; one pilot has worked on this problem for over ten years.

This is where the second factor of member involvement enters the picture. The ALPA has apparently discovered, whether deliberately or through a series of fortuitous events, how to capture the interest of its membership, or at least of a substantial enough fraction so that it can rely upon their varied backgrounds for much of its own necessary work. Air line pilots are in all likelihood the most safety-conscious group of people in the United States; significantly, it is not their employers so much as their union which has channeled that consciousness into serious and productive achievement.

"Safety not only in the workplace but in the product as well is surely a proper prerogative of the union," Sayen says. "If the United Auto Workers were to insist on building safer cars, and to show how it could be done, not only would the public benefit, but the union would be drawing even more than it does now on the intelligence and ingenuity of its members."

The ALPA has been encouraging a number of pilots to go on to graduate school, secure in the knowledge that it can tap the brains and skills of these men when necessary. ALPA is able to set up committees of members who have degrees in law, physics, etc., and who can, as Sayen concedes, "offend the hell out of people with a more leisurely approach. They are aggressive because of what they know and want, and can experience a lot of frustration." It is his union, he feels, which is doing the job abrogated by management. "Really, we run a big management-training school."

The implication is that other unions might well do likewise. While all of the full-time ALPA staff, from legal counsel to public relations men, is professional, they co-ordinate their work with pilot committees. Pilots themselves, often with a background of study in economics or accounting, negotiate their own contracts side by side with the professional staffers. "The pilot's horizon," says Sayen with a sententiousness reminiscent of Walter Reuther (with whom he obviously has a good deal in common), "expands to total responsibility."

Maybe. Nonetheless it is true that one ALPA member has done a Ph.D. thesis on the control of air space, another a thesis on the 1950 reorganization of his union, a third, in psychology, on full-field vision (a problem allied to aviation). In each case, as well as those where pilots have been encouraged to study writing, commerce, business administration, the union has benefited from the pilot's avocation.

It is an avocation which may do more than aid the union: it may become a livelihood. Few people need a second string to the bow more than a pilot—only one out of ten air line pilots flies to age fifty. And while ALPA sponsors an excellent insurance program against grounding, it is a fact that most men are grounded—whether for a heart murmur, high blood pressure, failing vision, or whatever—not toward the close of their careers but at their very peak, during their thirties and forties. "If we can get our members through the male menopause," Sayen says wryly, "they're usually set until retirement."

Not only are pilots under the constant pressure of knowing that they may be grounded at any moment by one of the two physicals and four proficiency checks to which they are subject annually, but they are now compulsorily retired by government edict at age sixty—younger to my knowledge than almost any other trade or profession in the country.

I sat in the suburban Oak Park living room of a sixty-year-old pilot shortly after his involuntary retirement and listened (it was all the consolation I could give) while the grounded pilot returned again and again to his obsessive bewilderment at having been forced out by fiat.

"One minute I was entrusted with bringing that plane into Midway with eighty passengers, all those lives and millions of dollars' worth of property. The next minute it was past midnight and I was a menace. I was forbidden to do what I can do as well as any man living. Why?"

It is humiliating for a skilled man to be put to pasture at the peak of his performance, particularly when it is done arbitrarily and when he has demonstrated year after year his physical capability to perform like a thirty-year-old, and with an accumulation of incalculable experience and judgment simply unavailable to any thirty-year-old. But more than this, he is cut off from his livelihood just as he has gained the uppermost earning bracket of those top-seniority chief pilots in command of the new jets—and, at sixty, five years before his social security checks will start to arrive.

In the next two years about two hundred and fifty pilots will reach age sixty and compulsory retirement. Their trying situation is coming about not as a result of attempted economies by their employers, but by virtue of a nonreviewable administrative regulation presumably promulgated in the interests of aviation safety (a particularly bitter pill to men who have been seriously concerned with safety all of their working lives).

Indeed, the battles over retirement and flight inspectors between the union and the FAA, together with the maze of government regulations with which every working pilot must be intimately familiar (his union participated in the drafting of the legislation which set up the FAA), have been cited as contributing—along with the broadening effect of travel—to the pilot's high degree of sophistication. These struggles with the government over "technical" matters might, one would suppose, be taken as one more factor setting him apart from the general run of the population.

But here we may begin to draw the pilot back into the general community once again. We have been enumerating the peculiarities of his craft which tend to make the pilot special and to differentiate him sharply from the millions in the American labor force. But won't virtually every one of those peculiarities (with the possible exception of his extraordinary need for exceptional physical fitness) be increasingly true of Americans in general in the coming decades? Even that final element, the increasing tendency for resentments and consequent strikes and litigation to be located not so much between labor and management as between specialist and bureaucrat, is coming to be characteristic of the American scene, as more and more of us either work directly for the government or find our working lives and our working benefits (regardless of which party is in power) dependent upon decisions made by appointed officials of the federal government.

This holds true even in the seemingly smallest areas of the pilot's working life. Not long ago the FAA promulgated another regulation, forbidding pilots to leave the flight deck except for emergencies or bodily necessities. Aside from the fact that it struck the pilots as one more slap in the face, it served to put an end to company-encouraged fraternalization between flight officers and passengers. It emphasized the godlike remoteness of the pilots in their now inaccessible control room and threw the air lines' public relations burden on two of the most unstable occupational groups to be found anywhere—sales personnel and stewardesses.

If the pilot is increasingly isolated from the passengers whom he flies, isn't this too a condition of working life which he holds in common with all those who find themselves, thanks to rationalization, mechanization, and automation, more cut off than were their fathers from patients, customers, clients—in short, from human beings? Stewardesses, incidentally, tend to look upon the pilots of their planes either as tyrants who treat them like slaveys, or as distant but kindly figures, daddies away from home; their efforts to achieve autonomy, though, for the Air Lines Stewards and Stewardesses Association, have been frustrated not only by the brevity of their employment, but also by the ALPA, which insists that it knows what is best for these less-skilled sister-unionists, apparently because it fears being outvoted under conditions of equality.

If the pilot is increasingly isolated, too, from the other members of his craft, except for those few with whom he shares the flight deck, and those with whom he is associated in union committee work, this is a condition already true of many others, and one that can only be accentuated as work place and living place become more widely separated in decades to come. His friendships, like those of his fellow Americans, will be formed less as a consequence of shared work patterns; more likely they will come from community involvement, shared hobbies, or common social or political beliefs and behavior.

Today many pilots who have the seniority to bid on the best flights, the long-distance runs, instead pick the worst, the milk runs or the up-and-down runs, only because then they can remain based near their homes. But there are many who want it both ways, and hence commute by private plane or by sports car hundreds of miles to the airports. They would seem to be the vanguard of all those—yes, even coal miners—who will continue to flee the megalopolis, but will have to come back to it for their livelihoods, and will, when commutation flying has caught up with high-speed flying, be traveling fifty and a hundred miles to work within our own lifetimes.

The consequences of all this for ordinary living, from friendships to family relationships, are incalculable and perhaps best left to the trend spotters and the sociological columnists. But one thing is sure: the daredevil flyboy of recent memory has died. In his place we have a splendid physical specimen, true, but also a skilled technician, an active unionist, a community-minded hobbyist and a concerned parent who—whether you think of him as a paragon of the American virtues or as a square caricature of responsible respectability—is as close as you can get to a living exemplar of the American workingman of the future.

GORE VIDAL

Barry Goldwater: A Chat

JULIUS CAESAR stood before a statue of Alexander the Great and wept, for Alexander at twenty-nine had conquered the world and at thirty-two was dead, while Caesar, a late starter of thirty-three, had not yet subverted even his own state. Pascal, contemplating this poignant scene, remarked rather sourly that he could forgive Alexander for wanting to own the earth because of his extreme youth, but Caesar was old enough to have known better.

I suggest, with diffidence, that Pascal did not entirely understand the nature of the politician; and the inner mechanism of a Caesar is no different in kind from that of an Alfred M. Landon. The aim of each is power. One would achieve it through military conquest, the other through what it pleases us to call the democratic process. It is natural for men to want power. But to seek power actively takes a temperament baffling to both the simple and the wise. The simple cannot fathom how any man would dare presume to prevail, while the wise are amazed that any reasonable man would *want* the world, assuming he could get it.

Suspended then between simplicity and wisdom, self-delusion and hard practicality, is the operative politician. He is not at all like other men, though he must acquire as protective coloration the manners of his society, join in its rituals (Caesar, the atheist, was a solemn high priest and our own Calvin Coolidge wore an Indian war bonnet), exploit its prejudices and anticipate its hungers.

Like his predecessors, an American politician in the mid-twentieth century must conform to certain conventions. He must be gregarious (or seem to be), candid (but never give the game away), curious about people (otherwise, he would find his work unendurable). An American politician must not seem too brainy. He must put on no airs. He must smile often but at the same time appear serious. Most disagreeable of all, according to one ancient United States Senator, wise with victory, "is when you got to let some s.o.b. look you straight in the eye and think he's making a fool of you. Oh, that is gall and wormwood to the spirit!" Above all, a politician must not sound clever or wise or proud.

Finally, the politician must have that instinctive sense of occasion which is also the actor's art. To the right challenge he must have the right response. He is, in the purest sense, an opportunist. He must be an accurate barometer to the weather of his time. He must know the phases of the political moon and the hour of the tides. He must be ready at a moment's notice to seize that prize which is the game's reward, power. He must know in the marrow of his bones when it is right to make the large effort. For example, at the Democratic convention of 1956 the Vice-Presidential nomination was unexpectedly thrown open to the floor. The young Senator from Massachusetts went for the prize. The moment was wrong but the move was right. In a car on his way to the convention the day of the voting, John Kennedy was heard muttering grimly to himself, "Go, go, go!" When to go, when to stay; that is the art.

Even those who write knowledgeably about politics tend to make certain fundamental errors. They look for subtle motives where there are none. They believe there is a long-range plan of war when there is seldom anything more than quick last-minute deployments of troops before unscheduled battle. In a society like ours, politics is improvisation. To the artful dodger rather than the true believer goes the prize.

The junior Senator from Arizona, Barry Goldwater, is a politician of some grace and skill who at this moment is studying the political sky for omens, waiting for a sign in which to conquer. His moment may come in the Presidential election of 1964 or of 1968 or never. There is every evidence that he is, this year, a divided man, uncertain how to proceed. His sense of occasion is keen; his sense of history is practical. He knows perfectly well that his views are at variance with the majority views of his time. To do great deeds, to take the prize, he must, paradoxically, surrender many of those positions he has so firmly taken in his reaction to a society he neither likes nor, many feel, understands. Yet, again paradoxically, his entire celebrity is due to his appealingly cranky rejection of those positions the majority reveres. In short, he is loved for those very attitudes which a majority of the electorate does not accept.

Goldwater's success is phenomenal considering that he is only a second-term Senator with no significant legislation to his name. He comes from a politically unimportant state. By his own admission he is not a profound thinker. His success in Arizona was due not only to his charm and hard campaigning in a state usually Democratic but also to the popularity of his family, one of the oldest in the state, whose business, Goldwater's department stores, is to Arizona what Macy's is to New York.

It is a clue to Goldwater's recent success that he was primarily a salesman in the family business (his one creative contribution was the invention and promotion of men's shorts decorated with large red ants in the pants) and he considers his role at the moment as salesman for the conservative point of view, which is not necessarily the Republican view. But, spokesman for the majority of his party or not, bumper stickers with GOLDWATER IN '64 are beginning to appear around the country (as well as a few GOLDWATER IN 1864 stickers).

Goldwater's path to higher office is strewn with many hazards, not all of his own making. His father was Jewish (the family name originally was Goldwasser), yet he is an Episcopalian. Since he favors right-to-work laws and limitations on unions, organized labor is against him. Personally, he sees nothing wrong with Negro and white children together in the same schools. But he opposes permitting the Federal government to interfere with the rights of the Southern states to maintain segregation, even in the face of the Supreme Court's decision. Goldwater has about as much chance of getting the Negro vote, according to one Tennessee politician, as "a legless man in a pants-kicking contest." Reluctantly, Goldwater realizes that Social Security is here to stay—it is too late to take it away—but he does think the program should be voluntary and certainly not enlarged to include medical care for the aged or anything else. He favors breaking off diplomatic relations with the Russians; he wants to present them wherever possible with a take-it-or-leave-it, peace-or-war attitude which many thoughtful conservatives who approve his domestic program find disquietingly like brinkmanship. In his own party he is blocked not only by the attractive and liberal Nelson Rockefeller but by that moderate near-winner Richard Nixon.

As if all these difficulties, inherent and assumed, were not enough, he is now seriously endangered by his admirers. Like most radicals of Right or Left, he is attractive to every sort of extremist. His most compromising support comes from the mysterious John Birch Society, whose beleaguered "Founder" (a title last used by the creator of Hollywood's

Forest Lawn Cemetery), Robert Welch, is firmly convinced, among other odd notions, that forty million Americans are Communists, including such unexpected conspirators as Milton and Dwight D. Eisenhower. Stubbornly, Goldwater has refused to repudiate the Birch Society, a stand which has led one Republican leader to say, "That's the end of Barry."

Yet, despite great handicaps, Goldwater is perhaps the country's most popular politician, after Kennedy. He gets enormous crowds wherever he goes. They are enthusiastic and—hopeful sign—they include many young people. He has caught on as a personality even if his policies have not. It is common to hear, "O.K., so a lot of his ideas are cockeyed, but at least he tells you where he stands. He isn't afraid to speak up, the way the others are." That many of Goldwater's ideas are in a state of flux and that many of his positions are quite as obscure as those of any other politician does not penetrate. Once a man's "image," good or ill, is set in the public's mind, he can contradict his legend every day and still be noted for his consistency.

Yet Goldwater *is* something new on the scene. He is perhaps the first American politician who, though spokesman for an unpopular minority, finds himself personally popular for reasons irrelevant to his politics. People like him as they like Arthur Godfrey or Jack Paar, forgiving the autocracy of the one and the tantrums of the other in precisely the same way they forgive Goldwater when he speaks against the $1.25 minimum wage, union activities or the Supreme Court's power to integrate schools. So what? He's a nice guy, and nice guys are not dangerous. He is also sincere, a vague quality far more admired by the lonely crowd than competence or intelligence.

Barry Goldwater's office is on the fourth floor of the old Senate Office Building. The corridors are marble with high ceilings and enormous doors which tend to dwarf not only visitors but Senators. There is an air of quiet megalomania which is beguiling in its nakedness.

Behind the great mahogany door with its sign MR.

GOLDWATER, ARIZONA is the outer office: wooden paneling, a view through large windows of the Capitol grounds. I was greeted by the Senator's secretary, Mrs. Coerver. She is small, amiable, gray, with that somewhat fixed smile politicians and their aides develop. (One smile is a vote gained, maybe. One frown is a vote lost, definitely.) "The Senator will see you in just a moment." She beamed.

I approached this meeting with curiosity. For one thing, since his book, *The Conscience of a Conservative,* Goldwater's fundamentalist ideas about the Constitution and society had undergone changes. When the Presidential virus attacks the system there is a tendency for the patient in his fever to move from the Right or the Left to the Center where the curative votes are, where John Kennedy now is. Other observers of Goldwater had also detected a perceptible shift to the Center. Further shifts would depend entirely on whether the patient took a turn for the White House. I wanted, simply, to take his temperature as of that day, for like all illnesses the Presidential virus has its own peculiar ebb and flow. At night in the company of good friends the fever blazes. In a cold dawn on the way to an airport to speak in some far-off town the virus is at its lowest point: To hell with it! thinks the patient, almost cured.

Also, I wanted to get an impression of character. I have often thought and written that if the United States were ever to have a Caesar, a true subverter of the state, (1) he would attract to himself all the true believers, the extremists, the hot-eyed custodians of the Truth; (2) he would oversimplify some difficult but vital issue, putting himself on the side of the majority, as Huey Long did when he proclaimed every man a king and proposed to divvy up the wealth; (3) he would not in the least resemble the folk idea of a dictator. He would not be an hysteric like Hitler. Rather, he would be just plain folks, Will Rogers or Arthur Godfrey, a regular guy, warm and sincere, and while he was amusing us on television the Storm Troopers would gather in the streets.

Now I have put the case extremely only because in recent months there has been an unusual rash of extremist groups like the John Birch Society, reminding us that there is a totalitarian potential in this country just as there is in every country. Fortunately, barring military or economic disaster, none of these groups is apt to come to much without a leader who could appeal personally and irrelevantly to a majority because of his personal magnetism. It seemed to me that Goldwater was perhaps such a man: (1) He has already attracted many extremists, and he has not denied them; (2) he oversimplifies a great many issues (getting "tough" with the Russians is fine and getting rid of the income tax is fine, too, but toughness costs money; where will it come from?); (3) he is exactly the sort of charming man whom no one would suspect of Caesarism, least of all himself.

Barry Goldwater entered Mrs. Coerver's office in his shirtsleeves and said, "Come on in." At the door to his own office he turned to a departing interviewer and said, finishing some earlier thought: "You know, of all the untrue things they write, the wildest one is how I'm a millionaire. I've been called that now so many times I'm beginning to feel like I ought to live like one." Chuckling at his own hyperbole (he is a millionaire; he does live like one), he led me into his office. The large desk was catercornered so that the light from the windows was in the visitor's face. Beside the desk was a bookcase containing, among other works, a leather-bound set of the speeches of Barry Goldwater. On the mantel of the fireplace was a bust of Lincoln. In the far corner of the room stood three flags. One of them was the Senator's own flag: he is a brigadier general in the Air Force Reserve. On the walls were photographs of the Arizona landscape, as beautiful and empty as a country of the moon.

We sat and looked at each other a moment. At fifty-two, he is lean and obviously in fine condition. The hair is gray. The eyes are alert, dark and small; the face tanned from a recent trip home. The nose is pleasantly crooked.

The nostrils are odd, visible only when he tilts his head back, like the small neatly round punctures in a child's rubber mask. The mouth is wide and thin-lipped, the jaw square. The smile is attractive but when his face is in repose there is an unexpected hardness, even harshness. Neither of us, I noticed, was very good at looking straight at the other. Simultaneously, each looked away. I looked out the window. Goldwater examined his brigadier general's flag (for those who believe the old saw that an honest man must have a direct gaze, I refer them to a contemporary's report that the shiftiest-eyed man he had ever met was Thomas Jefferson).

I began compassionately: "You must get awfully tired of being interviewed." He smiled. "It's repetitive, but . . ." His voice trailed off. It is a good voice for politics, light but earnest, with a slight rural accent of the sort made familiar by television Westerns.

I had debated whether to bring a tape recorder. I knew that Goldwater had a small wristwatch recorder which he used gleefully to disconcert others as well as to protect himself from misquotation. I decided to take notes instead. On a small pad of paper I had written a few topics. First, the John Birch Society. Recently Goldwater had said that "a great many fine people" were members, including "Republicans, liberal Democrats, conservatives," and he thought it would cause considerable political embarrassment if they were attacked en masse. He had also implied that besides the two known Birchers in Congress, Representatives Edgar Hiestand and John Rousselot, both Republicans of California, there were others. In one interview, however, he suggested that Robert Welch resign. Later he denied he had said this. I asked him how well he knew Welch. He frowned thoughtfully.

"Well, I've known Bob Welch five, maybe six years. But I didn't really get to him until that summit business, you know, when we all tried to keep Eisenhower from meeting Khrushchev. Welch and I worked together then. Of course all that stuff of his about Eisenhower being a Communist and so on was silly. Fact, I told him when he gave me that book of his [*The Politician*] to read, I said. 'Unless you can prove every one of those statements about people being Communists is true, you better go destroy every single copy of that book.' "

"Do you think Welch should resign as head of the society?"

The answer was quick: "I do. Just the other day I sent somebody over to the Library of Congress to get me the bylaws of the Birch Society, and I was disturbed about this dictatorial thing, how he personally can chuck people out any time he pleases. I didn't like it."

"What did you mean when you said there were liberal Democrats in the Birch Society?"

"Because there are. There're all kinds of people in that group. I know. I've met 'em and a nicer-looking bunch you never saw. That thirty- to forty-five-year-old group you want in politics. They're thoughtful people and they're concerned. But don't get the idea they're all conservatives because they're fighting Communism. A lot of people are fighting Communism who aren't conservative." I had the impression he wanted it made clear that his own conservative position was one thing and the fight against Communism was another thing. Most conservatives regard the two as synonymous. Goldwater does ordinarily, but this day I felt he was preparing a possible escape hatch.

I asked him if he knew of any members of Congress who belonged to the society, other than the two Californians. He paused. Then he said, "No." It was a slow, thoughtful "no," hard to interpret. Then: "You know, I don't really know that much about those people."

I asked him if he approved of their methods, as outlined in Welch's *Blue Book*. "Never read it. I don't know." It seemed to me strange that he would read the bylaws and *The Politician* yet not read the *Blue Book,* which contains not only the bylaws but a ten-point program on how to expose and discourage "Communists."

I mentioned some of Welch's gambits: infiltrating

school boards and library boards, getting "mean and dirty" with known liberals, encouraging students to spy on teachers.

Goldwater interrupted. No, he didn't like that, of course. "In fact, I've always been in favor of teaching Communism in schools. Show the kids what we're up against. Naturally I'd want a good course in American history to balance it. After all, the only way you're going to beat Communism is with a better idea, like Nero and the Christians . . . you know? He couldn't stamp 'em out, because there was that idea they had. Well, that's what we've got to have."

Goldwater had been against Federal aid to education. First, he is not convinced any aid is needed. Second, he feels that to give money to the states is an invasion of states' rights. Recently he testified before a House Education subcommittee in the interests of a bill of his own which he said would solve the whole problem. He proposed giving property owners a rebate on their Federal income tax up to one hundred dollars, the amount to represent what the property owner had paid in local school taxes. Even Goldwaters admirers found this solution baffling. His exchange with Representative John Brademas in committee had a good deal of unconscious humor in it.

Brademas asked Goldwater why he had proposed a bill to answer a problem which he did not believe existed. Soon both men were lost in a maze of: "I said 'if.' Well, if there is a problem, which I don't believe, then here's the answer. . . . All right, but if there is *not* a problem, then why propose . . .?"

In the course of his testimony, Goldwater unexpectedly came out for minimum academic standards to be set by the Federal government for the entire country. Brademas pointed out the contradiction: to set such standards and requirements would mean government intervention of the most extreme sort. Goldwater saw no contradiction: the government's minimum standards would not be compulsory; they would be "guide lines." He felt, too, that although

Federal aid to education was unconstitutional, *if* there was to be such aid parochial and private schools should be included.

I teased Goldwater about his exchange with Brademas. He laughed. He then repeated his position: There was no problem, and it was growing less. He quoted statistics. . . . Neither of us listened. I had touched a familiar button. He was responding as he had many times before.

I was amused during the Nixon–Kennedy debates by those who were astonished at the wide range of knowledge displayed by the two men, at their mastery of detail. Actually, neither was asked a question he had not already answered on an average of a dozen times a day for months. After such rehearsal any politician can discuss a number of subjects with what seems encyclopedic detail. It is a trick of the trade but a dangerous one, for answering the same questions over and over interferes with thought. Goldwater finished his statistics and waited for me to press the next button.

Not wanting to get him on a familiar track, I thought quickly, a little desperately. I wanted a general subject. The idea of the Presidency occurred to me. What would *he* do if he were President? Goldwater had once said to a journalist that, all in all, he preferred the Senate to the White House because as a Senator he could speak his mind, "where if you're President you can't. You got to be cautious and watch what you say." When the journalist asked Goldwater what he had been saying as a Senator that he would not feel free to say as President, he had looked baffled and finally said, "Well, damned if I know."

On the word "President" I noticed a faint flush of the fever. His eyes glittered. He sat back in his chair. "If I was President," he began with a new weight and authority, "I'd move slowly, cautiously at first. You'd have to feel your pathway. Not that my ideas are new ideas. No, they're old, old ideas."

Then he talked of government farm supports. In the

campaign, he had demanded "prompt and final termination of all subsidy." But he has changed. He would still eliminate supports, but gradually. I mentioned that only about half of the nation's farmers are needed to grow most of our food. Without supports a lot of people would be thrown on the labor market—in addition to the five million already unemployed. This, I suggested, was a real crisis. He agreed. They would have to be absorbed gradually. But how? Well, management and labor would get together (*without* the government) and set up a joint program to retrain and reallocate displaced people, "Not just farmers either, anybody who's been displaced by mechanization, and so on," and to sponsor "basic research for new gadgets—you know, for a lot of things like that we need."

Could labor and management be relied upon to do the job without some urging from the government? He thought they could. "Of course back in the 1920's management was pretty stupid, but I think they've come of age now, lot of fine new people at the top. The day of those self-made men, the founders, all that's over. In fact, labor's at the same place today management was in the 1920's. All those labor leaders, they're the same type of self-made man ran big business in the old days."

I asked him about his quarrel with Reuther. ("I would rather have Jimmy Hoffa stealing my money than Walter Reuther stealing my freedom.") He shook his head. "It's not personal. I just don't believe labor should be in politics." I was about to ask him what he thought of management in politics (the N.A.M., the Chamber of Commerce) when we were interrupted. A visiting lawyer was outside. He would like to shake the Senator's hand. He was ushered in.

The lawyer was a pleasant-looking, somewhat tense young man who was in Washington for the American Bar Association's antitrust conference. Goldwater came around from behind his desk. He smiled warmly. They shook hands. The young lawyer said in a voice shaking with emotion, "I just wanted you to know, Senator, there are a lot of people over in that Justice Department who better get off their fud and realize we've got some states that can do the job." Goldwater was sympathetic. I turned away, embarrassed. Two conservatives had met and I felt their intensity, their oneness. They spoke in their own shorthand and they knew the enemy.

I made notes while they talked. I wondered idly if I should ask Goldwater what he liked to eat and whether or not he wore pajamas and if he liked movies. I have always enjoyed reading those interviews which are made up of an incredible amount of minutiae; like coral islands they rise bit by bit out of the sea of personality, formed of dead facts. Absently, with what I hoped was the eye of a naturalist-novelist, I began to record the objects on his desk: a large transparent plastic duck mysteriously containing a small metal elephant, all mounted rather disagreeably on a penholder. Next to the duck was a clipping from a Hartford newspaper whose editorial began, *Well, What About Goldwater?* On the wall behind the desk hung a number of small photographs. There was one of Nixon, smiling, with a long inscription which I was too far away to read. There was a similar photograph of Eisenhower, also smiling, also inscribed. Why are politicians so happy when on view? "Always smiling," I wrote neatly on the pad. Then the young lawyer shook hands again. Goldwater smiled. I smiled. The photographs smiled. Only the young lawyer did not smile. He knew the Republic was in danger. He left. Goldwater and I put our smiles away and resumed the interview.

I had been told that the one question which made him uncharacteristically edgy was: Who wrote his book, *The Conscience of a Conservative?* I asked it. He frowned. "That's what wrote it," he said, somewhat irrelevantly. He ran his hand across the row of leather-bound books. "My speeches. The book's nothing but a selection from speeches, from a lot of things I've been saying for years. After all, I've written four books, a lot of magazine articles, my column."

I had been told that among his literary ghosts were

Steve Shadegg and L. Brent Bozell. I started to ask him about them but decided not to. It was cruel. It was pointless. We live in an age of ghosts: singers whose high notes are ghosted by others; writers whose works are created by editors; actors whose performances are made out of film by directors. Why should one harry politicians for not writing their own books and speeches? Few have the time or the talent. In any case the work published must necessarily reflect the views of its "author."

I was ready to drop the subject, but Goldwater was not. He told me he was planning another book. He was going on a cruise with his wife in the fall. While traveling, he would write the first draft. Then he would go over it carefully for "improvement in expression. Then after that I'll submit it to an author . . . I mean publisher." I suspect that Goldwater knows even less about Freud than I do, which is little, but we both know a Freudian slip when we hear one. The dark eyes darted anxiously in my direction. Had I caught the slip? I had.

He talked about conservatism. "Bunch of us got together after the convention and we all agreed we'd never heard such conservative speeches get so much applause, and then they go and accept that platform which 95 per cent of them were against." He sighed. "I don't know. What's wrong with the word 'conservative' anyway? Must be something." He said he had been impressed by the British Conservatives' comeback in 1951. They had got out and sold the party to the young people. This was his own plan. He would sell conservatism wherever he could, preferably to the young and uncommitted. "Of course the Conservative Party in England is about like the New Deal was here."

I asked him his impression of Kennedy. "Well, I guess I know him about as well as anybody around here. I like him. Of course we disagree on a lot of things. He thinks the government should do a lot more for people than I do." He mused about the campaign. He had advised against Nixon's television debates with Kennedy. "Funny, when my sister saw the first one, she said, 'Why, that Kennedy isn't so young!' And I knew then and there that was it. Of course, on sheer debating points Nixon took Kennedy every time. Anybody who knows about these things could see that. Especially on Quemoy and Matsu. Boy, if *I* had been debating Kennedy, I sure would have jazzed him all over the lot —Berlin, Laos, everything!"

I commented that Nixon had been a victim of his own legend. He had been pictured by both admirers and enemies as a rough infighter, a merciless debater, a ruthless killer, yet in the campaign and in the television debates it was quite clear that of the two, Kennedy was by far the tougher fighter. Goldwater nodded. "I warned Nixon about that a long time ago when the real mistake was made, 'way back there in California in that Senate election. You see, Nixon was sold by these people on putting himself over as a real gut fighter. They figured it would do him good against Helen Gahagan Douglas. So they built him up tough and mean, when of course he wasn't, when all he ever did was just tell the truth about that woman. The whole thing about him being so mean was nothing but publicity. So I told him: 'You wait and see, when you get to running for President and you start getting rough, the way you *got* to, they'll jump on you and say it's the old Nixon.' And they did. And then he'd pussyfoot." Goldwater shook his head sadly.

We talked about medical care for the aged to be paid through Social Security. The Senator was against it. He said that at the Arizona hospital of which he was a director, only one elderly person had been unable to pay. He had also seen a poll from western Florida where the elderly people had voted firmly against Federal aid. I suggested that those who could afford to retire to Arizona and Florida might be comfortably off. He said no, their average income was about $300 a month. Anyway, people ought to look after themselves either through their own foresight or through help from their families. Failing that, indigence should be handled the way it has always been: at the local level, by charities and so on.

I suggested that with taxes as high as they are, and longer life expectancies, there would be more rather than fewer programs for state and Federal aid in the coming years. He agreed. That was why he felt the whole tax structure had to be overhauled. And though he no longer favors repealing the graduated income tax, as he suggested in his book, he did feel that taxes on business should be reduced and greater allowance made for depreciation. "I told Jack Kennedy: you could be President for life if you'd just lift some of those taxes so that businessmen—and I know hundreds of 'em—would have some incentive to get new machinery, to overhaul their plants, to *really* start producing."

Publicly, no American politician can admit that we have anything to learn from the experiments of any other society. The ritual dialogue between office seeker and electorate is one of mutual congratulation, and to suggest that perfection has another home is treasonable. But privately our more conscientious legislators do ponder other countries' penal reforms, medical programs, educational methods. From his book and speeches I suspected Goldwater had done little or no homework. He was firmly against socialized medicine, but he seemed to know nothing about how it worked in Scandinavia, West Germany, England.

Goldwater was honest. No, he didn't know much about European socialism. "But I did meet this Norwegian doctor, matter of fact her name was Goldwater, which is how she happened to get in touch with me. She said the thing *seemed* to work all right, but that being assured of a certain income every month from the government kept her from feeling any real urge to study harder—you know, keep up at her profession. There was no incentive." I asked him if he thought that the desire to be good was entirely economic in origin. He said of course it was. I then asked him to explain how it was that two people as different as ourselves worked hard, though in neither case was money the spur. He was startled. Then he murmured vaguely and slipped away from the subject.

I asked him what he felt about some of his more oddball admirers. Goldwater became suddenly cautious. The quick, easy responses were replaced by a slow, careful measuring of words. He knew, he said, of some 250 organizations either conservative or anti-Communist. He admitted it was often difficult to figure out who was what. "Every invitation I get to speak, I have to check it for this and check it for that, make absolutely sure they're O.K. You never know what you may be getting into. Some are first-rate, like this fellow in New Orleans, Ken Courtney. He publishes a magazine down there. He's quite a guy." He asked on the phone for the magazine's name. I mentioned the Young Americans for Freedom, an organization founded by those who had been involved in the Youth for Goldwater movement at the Chicago convention. He approved of them highly, especially of "What's his name—Gaddy? Caddy, that's right. Nice kid, a real savvy guy with a lot on the ball."

Mrs. Coerver entered. "The magazine's called *Independent American,* and his name is Kent, not Ken, Courtney." She left.

More than once, Goldwater has complained that though the Republican Party's leaders are conservative they invariably choose liberal or moderate candidates to run for President on the false (to him) premise that a true conservative could never win. I asked him, Why not start a third party?

Goldwater sat up briskly. "If I thought it would work, I might. But I don't know . . . third parties never get off the ground in this country. There was Teddy Roosevelt, and there was . . ." He shook his head. "No, I don't see it. For one thing, conservatism is pretty divided. Suppose I started a party. Then somebody would come along and say, 'Well, look here, you're not *my* kind of conservative,' and then he'd go off and start *his* party and you'd end up like France. That's the trouble with the conservatives. They've got this all-or-nothing attitude." He sighed. "Why, I got booed in New York when I said if it was between Rockefeller and Harriman I'd be for Rockefeller. I tried to explain how at least Rockefeller was a Republican and you got your foot in the door. . . . No. A political party can only start around a strong individual." He looked past me at the bust on the mantelpiece; his jaw had set. "Like Lincoln. The people were there looking for a party, looking for this strong individual. And there he was and that's how the Republican Party started. A strong individual."

The next question was obvious. Was Goldwater that "strong individual"? Could he lead his people out of the wilderness? Were there enough of them to allow him to recreate that dream of Eden which conservatives evoke whenever they recall the bright simple days of our old agrarian Republic? But I let it go. Neither of us knew the answer. He had his hopes, and that was enough.

I rose to go. He walked me to the door. We exchanged impieties, each about his own political party, then said good-by.

"Ignorant but shrewd" was the verdict of one colleague of Goldwater's. "He's read very little. He has no knowledge of economics. He's completely outside the world of ideas. Even his passion for the Constitution is based upon a misunderstanding of its nature." I am not sure I would agree that Goldwater's ignorance of ideas is necessarily relevant to his ability or his capacity for growth.

I was impressed by his charm, which, even for a politician, is considerable. More than that, in his simplifying of great issues Goldwater has a real appeal for a nation which is not at all certain about its future either as a society or as a world power. Up and down the land there are storm warnings. Many look nervously for shelter, and Goldwater, in the name of old-time virtue and ruggedness and self-reliance, offers them refuge beneath the venerable great roof of the Constitution. True or not, his simplifications are enormously appealing and, who knows, in a time of crisis he might seize the prize.

But I make no predictions. I would only recommend to Goldwater Cicero's warning to a fellow political adventurer, in a falling year of the Roman Republic: "I am sure you understand the political situation into which you have . . . no, not stumbled, but stepped; for it was by deliberate choice and by no accident that you flung your tribunate into the very crisis of things; and I doubt not that you reflect how potent in politics is opportunity, how shifting the phases, how incalculable the issues of events, how easily swayed are men's predilections, what pitfalls there are and what insincerity in life."

Notes on Contributors

Nelson Algren was born in Detroit, Michigan, in 1909. He is the author of *Who Lost an American?, Chicago: City on the Make, A Walk on the Wild Side, The Man with the Golden Arm* which was the winner of the National Book Award for Fiction in 1949, *The Neon Wilderness* and *Never Come Morning*. In addition to these books, Mr. Algren's stories have appeared in the O. Henry Memorial Award volumes and in *Best American Short Stories*. He has contributed to such magazines as the *Atlantic Monthly, Kenyon Review,* and *Contact*.

James Baldwin was born in New York City. He is the author of the controversial novel, *Another Country,* and two earlier novels, *Giovanni's Room* and *Go Tell It on the Mountain*. Mr. Baldwin is also the author of *The Fire Next Time,* which is already regarded as a classic statement of Negro-White relations, and two books of essays, *Nobody Knows My Name* and *Notes of A Native Son*. Mr. Baldwin is the winner of a number of literary fellowships and awards—a Eugene F. Saxton Memorial Trust Award, a Rosenwald Fellowship, a Guggenheim Fellowship, a *Partisan Review* Fellowship, and a Ford Foundation Grant-in-Aid. His stories and essays have appeared in *The New Yorker, The New York Times Magazine, The New York Times Book Review, Partisan Review,*

Commentary, The Reporter, The New Leader, Atlantic, Harper's Magazine, Esquire and many other magazines both here and abroad.

Saul Bellow was born in Quebec but moved to Chicago at the age of nine. He is the author of *Dangling Man, The Victim, The Adventures of Augie March* which was awarded the National Book Award for fiction, *Seize the Day* and *Henderson the Rain King*. He has appeared in such magazines as *The New York Times Book Review, The New Republic, The New Leader, Partisan Review, Harper's Bazaar, The New Yorker* and many literary quarterlies. Mr. Bellow is now at work on another novel and a play.

Herbert Blau is the co-founder and co-director of The Actor's Workshop of San Francisco. He has written many articles about the theater and is the author of *The Impossible Theater: A Manifesto.* He is also a playwright. Mr. Blau was born in Brooklyn, but now resides in San Francisco. As a director, he was in charge of the American premiere of Brecht's *Mother Courage,* Arden's *Sergeant Musgrave's Dance* and the production of *Waiting for Godot* that represented American regional theater at the Brussels World's Fair. Mr. Blau has also directed the production of his own play, *A Gift of Fury.*

George P. Elliott was born in Indiana. He is married and the father of a daughter and is now teaching at St. Mary's College in California. He is the author of two novels, *Parktilden Village* and *David Knudsen*; a book of short stories, *Among the Dangs;* a long narrative poem, *Fever and Chills;* and a forthcoming collection of essays.

Herbert Gold, editor of and contributor to FIRST PERSON SINGULAR, is the author of six novels, the most recent of which is *Salt.* Among his other novels are *The Man Who Was Not With It* and *Therefore Be Bold.* He is also the author of a collection of essays, *The Age of Happy Problems,* and over forty short stories fourteen of which appeared in *Love and Like.* Mr. Gold has received many literary prizes including Guggenheim and Hudson Review Fellowships, an award from the National Institute of Arts and Letters, an O. Henry Prize and a Ford Foundation Theatre Fellowship to work at the San Francisco Actor's Workshop. Recently, he was one of the Judges for the National Book Award in Fiction and for two years has been one of the American delegates to the Formentor Prize conference. Mr. Gold has taught at Cornell University, the State University of Iowa, Wayne University, Brandeis University and the University of California at Berkeley.

Paul Goodman was born in New York City in 1911. He is a graduate of City College in New York and received his Ph. D. in humanities from the University of Chicago. Mr. Goodman has taught at the University of Chicago, New York University and Black Mountain College and is a fellow of and teacher at the New York and Cleveland institutes for Gestalt Therapy. His work has appeared in such magazines as *Commentary, Politics, Kenyon Review, Resistance, Liberation, Partisan Review.* Mr. Goodman's fiction includes *The Facts of Life, The Break-Up of Our Camp, Parents' Day* and *The Empire City*. His non-fiction books are *Kafka's Prayer, The Structure of Literature, Art and Social Nature, Growing Up Absurd, Utopian Essays and Practical Proposals, Drawing the Line* and *The Community of Scholars.* He is co-author of *Communitas* and *Gestalt Therapy*. Mr. Goodman is married and the father of two children.

Elizabeth Hardwick is a native of Kentucky who has lived in Manhattan for many years. She is the author of two novels, *The Ghostly Lover* and *The Simple Truth,* and of short stories which have appeared in *The New Yorker, Partisan Review,* and elsewhere and have been widely anthologized. Miss Hardwick's most recent book is a collection of essays, *A View of My Own.* She is the wife of the poet Robert Lowell.

Seymour Krim is the author of *Views of a Nearsighted Cannoneer* from which his essay in this book was taken. He is the editor of two anthologies, *Manhattan* and *The Beats,* and has written literary criticism, short stories, and essays. At present, Mr. Krim is Editorial Director for *Nugget* Magazine.

Mary McCarthy is the author of *The Company She Keeps, The Oasis, Cast A Cold Eye, The Groves of Academe, A Charmed Life, Sights and Spectacles, Memories of a Catholic Girlhood, The Stones of Florence, Venice Observed* and *On the Contrary*. Her articles have appeared in many magazines, among them *The New Yorker, Harper's Magazine, The Reporter, Commentary, Partisan Review* and *Encounter.*

Arthur Miller was born in New York City in 1915. He is the author of two novels, *Focus* and *The Misfits* which was later made into a motion picture. As a playwright, he is known as the author of *All My Sons, Death of A Salesman, The Crucible* and *View from the Bridge. View from the Bridge* was awarded the New York Drama Critics Circle Award and the Pulitzer Prize in Drama. Mr. Miller has received the Hopwood Award for playwriting, the Theater Guild National Award, the New York Drama Critics Circle Award in 1947 and 1949, the Antoinette Perry Award and the Gold Medal for Drama of the National Institute of Arts and Letters. He has appeared in such magazines as *Harper's* and *Esquire.*

Warren Miller was born in Pennsylvania and educated in Iowa. He is the author of three novels, *The Way We Live Now, The Cool World* and *Flush Times,* and a book of non-fiction, *90 Miles From Home.* A dramatization of *The Cool World* was produced on Broadway several seasons ago. Mr. Miller received a Grant from the National Institute of Arts and Letters in 1960.

William Saroyan was born in Fresno, California, and first appeared on the literary scene during the mid-thirties. He is the author of many short stories, plays and novels. In 1940, Mr. Saroyan was awarded the Pulitzer Prize for his play *The Time of Your Life,* which he declined to accept. His best-known novel, *The Human Comedy,* has been made into a highly successful motion picture. Among his other works are *The Daring Young Man on the Flying Trapeze* and two works scheduled for publication in 1963, a novel, *Boys and Girls Together,* and a book of non-fiction, *Not Dying.*

William Styron was born in Newport News, Virginia. He is the author of three novels, *Lie Down in Darkness, The Long March* and *Set This House on Fire.* For his first novel, Mr. Styron was awarded the Prix de Rome of the American Academy of Arts and Letters. He now lives in Roxbury, Connecticut, with his wife and three children.

Harvey Swados was born in Buffalo, New York, and graduated from the University of Michigan. He is the author of two novels, *Out Went the Candle* and *False Coin,* two collections of stories, *Nights in the Gardens of Brooklyn* and *On the Line,* and a book of essays, *A Radical's America.* Mr. Swados' stories have appeared in half a dozen *Best American Short Story* anthologies and in magazines such as *Esquire, New World Writing* and *Discovery.* His essays have been published in *New Republic, Saturday Review, Dissent* and *Partisan Review.* Mr. Swados has been awarded a Hudson Review Fellowship, a Sidney Hillman Award and a Guggenheim Fellowship. He has taught at the State University of Iowa, New York University, San Francisco State College and Sarah Lawrence College.

Gore Vidal published his first novel, *Williwaw,* at the age of 19. He is the author of many other novels, *In a Yellow Wood, The City and the Pillar, The Season of Comfort, A Search for the King, Dark Green, Bright Red, The Judgment of Paris* and *Messiah;* a collection of stories, *A Thirsty Evil;* and a book of essays, *Rocking the Boat.* A playwright as well, two of Mr. Vidal's plays have been produced on Broadway, *Visit to a Small Planet* and *The Best Man.* As a literary and political critic, he appears in *The Reporter, Esquire* and *The Nation.*